CW01668796

Descartes

PHILOSOPHERS IN CONTEXT

General Editor: Professor Stephan Körner, Professor of Philosophy, Yale University.

This series provides authoritative and genuinely critical studies of the major philosophers—in the context of their own time and of ours. Each book, which has been specially commissioned, is devoted to an individual philosopher.

The series seeks to establish why the philosopher concerned was important in his/her own time—both in philosophical and in wider cultural terms. Each volume offers a systematic exposition and critical assessment of the main philosophical arguments of each philosopher, an assessment of the particular philosopher's living influence, and full guidance on further reading.

LOCKE
R.S Woolhouse

PLATO
Christopher Rowe

LEIBNIZ
Stuart Brown

RUSSELL
C.W. Kilmister

PHILOSOPHERS · IN · CONTEXT

DESCARTES

Marjorie Grene

Professor Emeritus of Philosophy
University of California, Davis

HARVESTER PRESS 1970 1985 FIFTEEN FORWARD-LOOKING YEARS

THE HARVESTER PRESS

First published in Great Britain in 1985 by
THE HARVESTER PRESS LIMITED
Publisher: John Spiers
16 Ship Street, Brighton, Sussex

© Marjorie Grene, 1985

British Library Cataloguing in Publication Data

Grene, Marjorie
Descartes.——(Philosophers in context; 5)
1. Descartes, Rene
I. Title II. Series
194 B1875

ISBN 0–7108–0571–3

Typeset in 11/12 point Times by Witwell Ltd, Liverpool
Printed in Great Britain by Chanctonbury Press Ltd.

All rights reserved

THE HARVESTER PRESS PUBLISHING GROUP
The Harvester Press Publishing Group comprises Harvester Press Limited (chiefly publishing literature, fiction, philosophy, psychology, and science and trade books), Harvester Press Microform Publications Limited (publishing in microform unpublished archives, scarce printed sources, and indexes to these collections) and Wheatsheaf Books Limited (a wholly independent company chiefly publishing in economics, international politics, sociology and related social sciences), whose books are distributed by The Harvester Press Limited and its agencies throughout the world.

To my grandchildren,
Sophia, Hannah, Jessica, and Clement,
and in memory of Daniel

Contents

Preface

Parts of this book have been presented as papers at a number of colleges and universities; I am grateful to all those institutions and to the audiences whose members offered me welcome advice and criticism. An earlier version of Chapter 1 was given at the University of Chicago, where Alan Donagan was my commentator (and Ed Curley arrived in time to correct some of my more egregious errors), and at the New Jersey Regional where Margaret Wilson was the commentator. The same version appears in the *Independent Journal of Philosophy*, 1985; I acknowledge gratefully their permission to use it here. No other parts of the book have been published elsewhere. Part of Chapter 3 was presented at the Pacific Division of the American Philosophical Association in March 1983, and another part at the *Donaganfest* at Illinois State University in the autumn of the same year. On the former occasion, Janet Broughton and Alan Donagan were my commentators. I am grateful not only to these colleagues, but to numerous others. When I was teaching a Descartes seminar at Douglass College (Rutgers University) in 1979, the comments of Peter Klein and Robert Matthews were especially useful. I was stimulated to the composition of Chapter 8 by a month's teaching at the University of Waterloo in Spring 1981, and thank my colleagues there, and Rolf George in particular, for that opportunity. Parts of the MS have been read by Roger Ariew, Richard Burian, Willis Doney, Lynn Joy, David Lachterman, and Jean-Paul Pittion, and I am most grateful for their encouragement and criticism. For all its faults, the book has been much improved by their assistance. Also, although I have acknowledged this recurrently throughout the following chapters, I should perhaps express here my indebtedness to the French tradition of Cartesian scholarship; it is pervasive.

The works and correspondence of Descartes are quoted (in

my translation) from the revised edition, C. Adam and P. Tannery, *Oeuvres de Descartes*, Vrin, Paris, 1964–75, abbreviated as *AT*. Gassendi's *Disquisitio Metaphysica*, edited with French translation by Bernard Rochot (Vrin, Paris, 1962), is referred to as *DM*. I am most grateful to Oxford University Press for allowing me to quote the Kenny version of a number of Descartes's letters; these are reprinted from *Descartes: Philosophical Letters*, translated and edited by Anthony Kenny (1970) by permission of Oxford University Press (Oxford University Press, 1970, published in paperback by Basil Blackwell and the University of Minnesota Press). All other translations are my own. Kenny's translation, where quoted, is designated in the text as *K*. Other works are referred to in brackets by author and year, and a list of all works cited is given at the end of the book.

Several typists at various institutions have suffered my dreadful typescripts. The final draft has been prepared by Sara McGuire; I am most grateful for her exemplary care and accuracy.

Marjorie Grene
Clash, Rathdrum, Co. Wicklow, Ireland
August 1984

Permanent
Res?

PART ONE

Descartes and the Dilemma of Modern Philosophy

1 *Idea and Judgment in the Third Meditation: An Approach to the Reading of Cartesian Texts*

1

In his *Descartes*, Bernard Williams distinguishes between the history of ideas and the history of philosophy (Williams, 1978, p.9). The former, he suggests, tries primarily to represent the past as in fact it was; the latter, while recognising historical differences in conceptions and interests between past and present, tries to produce a rational reconstruction that puts the problems of the philosopher studied into the perspective of our contemporary discussions. The distinction is a reasonable one. Historical studies, in philosophy, rightly fall flat if they simply retail the beliefs or arguments of A or B in the years——to——; we want on the one hand to put our questions into historical context and on the other to illuminate history, to comprehend and criticise the arguments of dead philosophers in the light of what seem to us live issues here and now. Yet much that has been written recently, especially on Descartes and especially in English, it seems to me, is so narrowly confined to the terms of late twentieth-century debate that the real Descartes is simply left aside altogether. And, since we are products of our past, that means that we miss not only Descartes in his own terms, but ourselves, too. In the narrowness of our own perspective we miss not only our historical target but the reflective awareness of our own beliefs that should be the aim of philosophy.

To put my claim somewhat more modestly, the chief Anglo-American tradition of Cartesian scholarship often appears to assimilate Descartes's arguments so thoroughly to the context of twentieth-century controversies, particularly with respect to scepticism, that it misses, on the one hand, subtleties in Descartes's own thought and, on the other, the bearing of the seventeenth-century problematic on (what ought to be) our own philosophical concerns. In contrast, this essay may be taken as a suggestion that we pay closer attention to the French, as distinct from the Anglo-American, or specifically analytic, tradition in Cartesian scholarship. That is not, of course, to deny the insights to be gained, for example, by a study of texts like those of Frankfurt (1970), Curley (1978) or Wilson (1978) or of the Kenny–Gewirth debate on the circle (see bibliography in Hooker, 1978, pp.202–4).[1] Nevertheless, there seems to be a temptation in much of this literature to be distracted by the delights of analytical debate from a more judicious historical perspective and hence (as I believe) from more adequate philosophical reflection.

2

To illustrate my thesis, I shall take a very small example from a familiar text, discuss one interpretation of it and then, in conclusion, put it briefly into the context, first of the work as a whole and then of the basic metaphysical and methodological issues at stake in that work and in our present thinking. The passage I am especially concerned with occurs near the beginning of the Third Meditation, *AT*, vii, pp.36–40, especially pp.36–8, the passage in which Descartes sorts out his thoughts, and I shall refer back also to the Second Meditation, *AT*, vii, pp.30–2, the conclusion of the wax argument, as well as ahead to Meditation Four.

We all 'know' these passages, one would suppose; but in studying Gueroult's commentary on the *Meditations*, (Gueroult, 1968)—a work which I had too long neglected—I have been persuaded that I had always misread the first-mentioned, and perhaps also the second, passage, taking Descartes too much in the terms of the Humean–Kantian tradition through which we are likely to approach him and not sufficiently in terms of what even I 'knew' to be his own conception of his method: a conception that, thanks to Gueroult, I now believe I understand much better than I had done previously.

3

The basic question at issue in the light of *AT*, vii, pp.36–40 is that of the place of judgment in the Cartesian quest for certainty. 'Judgment' renders Descartes's usage; twentieth-century philosophers are likely to speak of propositions, sentences, statements, depending on their preferences; but let's stick to 'judgment', thinking back to Aristotle's *On Interpretation* as well as forward to Kant and considering *a* judgment to be the product of the mind's bringing two terms together into an assertion or denial, like 'S is P', or 'No A φ's'. Judgments so understood are traditionally taken to be the locus of truth or falsity, so in the search for truth it is these we usually take as our units. Is it true that planets move in elliptic orbits or that the blood circulates or that men are descended from ape-like ancestors? If, as everyone agrees, it was Descartes who initiated the modern bent for epistemology, it should have been the legitimation of such assertions—of judgments that bring concepts together into assertable form—that concerned him. And of course in the Fourth Meditation, as we all know, Descartes gave us a recipe for sticking to the truth that recognised judgment as the power of assertion: keep your will within the bounds of your understanding, he warned; don't make a judgment, as you are free to do, unless you *know*. And his emphasis there on the act of judgment seems to confirm the notion that it is the resulting *judgments*, clearly and distinctly understood, that will be true.

Yet this comforting thought rests on at least two misapprehensions. First—the lesser one—it should be evident that in what I have just been saying, I have been confusing a judgment—an Aristotelian *kataphasis* or *apophasis* or a Kantian *Urteil*—with the act of *judging*, or 'making judgments', as Descartes puts it in the Fourth Meditation. If we are to understand Descartes's argument, we must keep this distinction in mind: for both in the Fourth Meditation and in the Second (in the hats and cloaks passage) it is *the mental act of judging* he is concerned with rather than judg*ments* as surrogate for logicians' propositions or linguists' sentences.

Second—the major error—when we take judgments as the sole locus of truth, we overlook altogether the nature of Cartesian method. Descartes's method was, indeed, as Locke, misunderstanding it almost altogether, yet rightly called it, a 'new way of ideas'. It was a way of ideas, and it was new. The unit of knowledge, and especially of the path to knowledge—the path of analysis—is what its discoverer earlier called an *intuition* and later a *clear and distinct idea:* as he defined an intuition in the *Rules*, the grasp of a pure and attentive mind, so plain that no doubt is left concerning that which is understood. The method of hyperbolical doubt exercised in Meditation One has the aim of sweeping out of the philosopher's way whatever does not fulfill this demand for total clarity. The first intuition arrived at in the course of the process of meditation is the *cogito*, the second is the idea of God. These can, it's true, be turned into judgments. 'I am, I exist'—this is true whenever I pronounce it. Or 'God exists.' And, indeed, our 'ideas' will be so transformed in the storehouse of Cartesian science (Beyssade, 1979). But there is a further peculiarity in the 'judgment' involved in this particular context. Insofar as both these ideas—of the *cogito* and of God—are translatable into judgments, they are, it should be noted, judgments of existence, not ordinary predications: *I* exist', 'God exists' not 'I as thinking thing am immaterial' or 'God is omnipotent' or the like. This oddity should put us on our guard, and remind us what Descartes is after: not judgments like those of Aristotle or Kant, but a series of entirely reliable mental acts that carry me by their very nature to trust the veridicality of their contents. Not that Descartes cannot elsewhere be concerned with other, more 'ordinary' judgments, but at this juncture, in so far as judgments can be invoked, it is these odd existential ones that are involved.

In this respect, moreover, as Gueroult emphasises, there is an important difference between the first and second intuitions of the *Meditations*. Granted that the *cogito*, because of its self-referential character, is safe from the Evil Demon: I exist in this moment, even as doubter, since my thought of my thinking is directed solely to, and identical with, itself. No Demon, however powerful, can come between my thought and itself. And this certainty, Gueroult argues further, is not psychological but scientific: it *is* the *aliquid firmum et mansurum* Descartes has been searching for, from which to build his universal science. Yet at this stage this certainty, though necessary and unshakable and a secure cornerstone of all our knowledge, is still *subjective*. I know as yet nothing of my substantial nature, let alone of the existence of bodies, or of the union of my mind with this particular piece of bodily machinery. Only my firm attention, in due course, to my innate idea of God, omnipotent and veridical, can take me from the sphere of consciousness to an external reality, or even to the stable reality of my existence as intellect—and to the truths first of arithmetic and geometry, then of physics, that my intellect contains. But at the opening of Meditation Three, where our passage occurs, that step has not yet been taken. All I have so far is consciousness, intellectual consciousness. From within it I must find a way to truths more stable and more wide-ranging. Let us see how Descartes proceeds at this juncture, and especially what role the reference to judgment plays.

4

We have had the usual review of the steps of our meditation to date: the sequence of doubts culminating in the Deceiver, with the *cogito* as shining exception. But the context has changed: the clarity and self-containment of the *cogito* suggests a general trust in my clear and distinct ideas. Yet a deceiving God could invalidate even those most luminous insights of arithmetic and geometry.[2] So I can go no further until I consider whether there is a God and if so whether He could be a deceiver, 'for while I am ignorant of this', says Descartes, 'I don't see how I can ever be entirely certain of anything else'. True, the reason for doubt at that stage had been 'pretty thin and so to speak metaphysical', but since so much depends on it, Descartes suggests, he must ask the double question about God 'as soon as the occasion arises'. What we are looking at here is the interval between the statement '*hac enim re ignorata...*' and the occasion provided on *AT*, vii, p.40 in the passage beginning: 'But another way occurs to me...', with which the first proof of God opens.

About the position at this point, two remarks are in order. First, the thesis that all other certainty depends on God's existence and on his veracity is to be taken as seriously as possible. As Gueroult's analysis makes plain, the movement of the *Meditations* is to God and from God. His veracity (Three to Five) and His goodness (Six) are the foundations of all science and all practice. Not that Descartes was a religious man in the sense, for example, of his followers in Port Royal or of their philosophical Father St Augustine. But he unquestioningly accepted the innate idea of an infinite all-good all-powerful Deity. His vision of science—which comes first—and of life, which follows (a little lamely) after, depends intellectually on that idea and on one other, which we shall meet in due course. Those who have seen in Descartes's theism a mere ruse to fool the theologians have been reading, not Descartes, but some claimant of their own invention (Caton, 1973). 'While ignorant of this matter, I don't seem to be able to be really certain of anything at all.' That's what Descartes says, and that's what he means. Indeed, it took the hyperbolical doubt of Meditation One not just to doubt arithmetic and geometry, but to doubt God himself, and that is the most 'metaphysical' point in the progression of doubt precisely because the reality called in doubt is in truth so patently and overwhelmingly evident.

Second remark: if that is so, why doesn't Descartes proceed to prove God's existence and veracity here and now? What has to happen before 'the occasion offers'? Two things in one: first, as we shall see in a moment, Descartes must classify his thoughts so as to find his way properly among them: in terms of the *Regulae*, he must perform an enumeration or induction (*AT*, x, p.388). But in the course of that enumeration—and this is the insight of Gueroult that I find so illuminating for the whole structure of the *Meditations* as well as for the interpretation of this passage in particular—in the course of that enumeration, he must once more (as he has recurrently been doing from the start) call in question and effectively put aside the prejudices of common sense and of scholastic tradition about the path to truth. He must question both judgment as the initiator or vehicle of truth and sense as the legitimator of judgment in order to clear a way for *ideas* as the vehicle of truth and *clarity and distinctness* as its criterion. To schematise the contrast:

	vehicle of truth	*criterion of truth*
common sense and schools	judgment	sensory origin (since sensations appear involuntary and are thought to resemble their objects)
Descartes	ideas	clarity and distinctness

Granted, the new way of ideas has already begun with the *cogito*; but a new way is hard to undertake. Think of dieting or jogging or giving up smoking or anything else you do to change your life-style. It takes discipline and repeated effort. Hence the technique of meditation. We have to find means over and over to keep ourselves from relapsing into the bad old ways. And here it is a question, further, of preparing for the step that will give us the ultimate metaphysical support, the abiding foundation, for all future progress in science and in life. Sense-based judgments must be thoroughly undermined and ideas of pure intellect firmly ensconced in their place.

Of course all the moves of the *Meditations* so far have been helping to accomplish this fundamental shift; but the way Descartes takes here is a particularly cunning one. As Gueroult's analysis shows (Gueroult, 1968,I, pp.159–71), he produces three successive enumerations, of which the first follows his own view of the nature of consciousness, while the second and third give his opponents rope to hang themselves—and allow him, while seeming still to go along with their kind of classification, to embark (in yet a fourth enumeration) on the 'other way' that will lead him in fact to a position diametrically opposed to theirs. Let us look carefully at these three steps.

5

The first classification of the content of consciousness is introduced in the original by the statement: 'order seems to demand that I first distribute my thoughts into certain classes, and inquire in which of them truth or falsity properly resides' (*AT*, vii, pp.36–7). This clear reference to Descartes's concept of the order of discovery is expanded in the French to read:

> And in order that I may have occasion to examine this [sc. the question of God's existence and veracity] without interrupting the order of meditating that I had set myself, which is to pass by degrees from the notions that I shall find as the first in my mind to those that I may find afterward, I must here divide all my thoughts into certain classes, and consider in which of these classes there is properly truth or error' (*AT*, ix,1, p.29).

The expansion shows clearly that Descartes sees in his own method a need to go *via* enumeration from the *cogito* to God. This is not a concession to his opponents, but the step demanded by his own conception of inquiry. He has, so far, *one* clear and distinct idea, that of himself as *res cogitans* whenever he is thinking. He has his thoughts and the thought of his thinking. But there are many thoughts, and since his aim is to find the way to truth, he must sort those thoughts out properly in order to find that class in which truth or falsity lies. So this division will be the one he needs in order to locate those clear and distinct perceptions that can be trusted to be true. What division is this? First, there are 'as it were, images of things, as when I conceive of a man, a chimaera, the sky, an angel or God'. These alone, Descartes avers, are properly ideas. And then there are: volitions, affections, judgments, which are not as such representative of anything. To mental content *they add something else*, like willing, fearing, affirming. They are what I do (or suffer), but on their own they cannot take me beyond myself to the truth of things. Only ideas, being representative *of* men, chimaeras, angels, or God, do that. Or so it seems at this point.[3]

But then comes a second enumeration which oddly crosses the first. Ideas in themselves, it appears, can never be strictly false, for 'whether I imagine a goat or a chimaera, it is true that I imagine it '. No error here. Nor is falsity to be feared in my volitions or affections: what I will I will, what I feel I feel. 'Only judgments remain in which it is to be feared that I err' (*AT*, vii, p.37). Surely it could as well be said that what I judge I judge. Indeed, that is what the previous enumeration suggested: volitions, affections and judgments, being all non-representative, are irrelevant to truth or, in another way, trivially true. They are what they are, and in that sense 'true', even though, making no claim to reach beyond themselves to reality, they do not carry the thrust to truth that belongs, in terms of the first enumeration, uniquely to ideas. But the trouble is that it is through judgment (rash judgment, as we are to discover in Meditation Four) that I stretch my ideas from their own undoubted existence as modes of mental life and take them to be copies of things outside: that is where I run into error. So now instead of

ideas, representative, so possible locus of truth

versus

volitions, affections, judgments: non-representative, so irrelevant in the search for truth,

we have

ideas, volitions, affections: true in themselves

versus

judgments: susceptible of error because claiming to go beyond the field of consciousness.

This is tricky. Because we are seeking truth, we started by asking where among the classes of thoughts 'truth or error is properly to be found'. First we found a claim to truth in the sense of representation, of a reaching from mind to reality, only in the sphere of ideas. The other three classes seem all irrelevant to the inquiry after truth—they just *are*, but don't take us anywhere. But then it seems that the risk of error, what we want to avoid, resides neither in ideas, volitions or affections but only in judgments—and specifically in judgments of likeness between ideas and things. But if that is where error resides, why not also non-error, i.e. truth? So do we concentrate on judgments because 'truth or error' are to be found there, or avoid them because only they will lead us astray?

It is the latter path, it seems clear, that Gueroult is endorsing as the proper Cartesian order. Only after he has investigated the objective value, i.e. the 'truth' of ideas, can Descartes proceed to investigate, in the Fourth Meditation, the means of securing reliability in judgments. The move here is less obvious than the turn against sense, but equally important, it seems to me, in the 'order of reasons'. This is a claim, however, to which many Cartesian scholars are resistant. Margaret Wilson, for example, in commenting on my argument, has stressed Descartes's concept of material falsity (*AT*, vii, p.43) and has suggested that ideas might, by analogy, possess a kind of 'material truth', even though truth belongs *sensu stricto* to judgments only. It appears to me, however, that the 'material falsity', passage, which is incidental to the introduction of the 'objective reality' argument, is intended to silence the common-sense-scholastic opponents (whose views, as Gueroult shows, had been taken into account in the earlier enumerations) rather than to state a definite Cartesian 'theory of material falsity'. Besides, there is no hint anywhere of a doctrine of material truth: on the contrary, both in the preface and in the Replies to the Fourth Objections, it is ideas taken materially that are said to have no connection with truth or falsity, though taken formally, as representative, they do! (*See* chapter 7 below.) Granted, strictly (or 'formally', in some sense of that well-worked term), as Arnauld will point out, truth resides in judgment. That will be the message of the Fourth Meditation, *after* our trust in clear and distinct ideas to lead to the truth has been vindicated. But ideas, through their objective reality, must lead the way.

This reading is confirmed by a striking passage in Descartes's letter responding to a summary of the Fifth Objections in the French translation of 1647. The Objections have remarked: 'My thought is not the rule of the truth of things' (*AT*, ix,1, p.207). This expression is ambiguous, says Descartes; but, 'in the sense in which the words should be understood here, I say that the thought of each person, that is, the perception or knowledge that he has of a thing'—in other words, his grasp of it, prejudgmentally, in clear and distinct ideation—'must be for him *the rule of the truth of that thing* [my italics], that is to say, that all the judgments he makes about it, must be in conformity to that perception in order to be good' (*AT*, vii, p.208). 'Perception', equals *knowledge*, has put us in contact with reality, 'the truth of things' (a phrase even Gassendi's friends have indulged in) *before* we venture to make judgments about what we know.[4] And this is of course 'perception' as apprehension in general, not *sense* perception.

Nevertheless, in reading Descartes, it is the road through judgment, rather than objective reality, that most of us have been inclined to follow. Good old Descartes, we say, he got off onto that stuff about ideas, but at bottom he must have recognised that only judgments can be true or false, so it's really judgments he is inquiring about. Ideas in themselves, like Humean sense impressions to come, just *are* the material of experience: no error there, but no truth either. It is precisely the assertion in judgments of correspondence between our sensations and the outside world that constitutes the heart of knowledge, and so of truth (but cf. e.g. Kenny, 1968, esp. pp.117–119). However, is that really what Descartes has said? No. The hasty reliance on judgment and particularly on sense-based judgment is just what he is rejecting. 'Only in judgment can I err,' he says—and the avoidance of error is what his whole effort is about. Admittedly, the subjective truth of ideas as modes of mind will not get me far. Alone with my thoughts I cannot build science. But Descartes will have to find—as he presently does—'another way' to get to things outside. The way of judgment, unfounded in clear and distinct intellection, is the wrong way, the way of 'scholasticism' and common sense, which must be shown up for the *ignis fatui* it is. As Gueroult puts it,

> the legitimacy of judgment, that is to say, the determination of its truth, cannot be founded except on the previous determination of the objective value of the ideas. Precisely, in this Third Meditation, it is a question of examining, not the truth or falsity of judgments, but the truth or, more precisely, the objective value of ideas (Gueroult, 1968,I, p.165).

The next (third) enumeration, and the investigation to which Descartes subjects it, confirm this interpretation. Although it may seem, at least for the moment, that judgments have been singled out as the class to be investigated, Descartes now returns to ideas, but classifies them according to their source. Some he has in the past taken to be adventitious, some factitious and some innate. His present question then appears to be: what ideas are adventitious? But *via* judgment, which may mislead, there is no way to find this out. A sign that he is here going, in a way, along with tradition rather than following his own path, is the way he puts his question and the answer he eventually gets. He seems to be looking for an adventitious idea, for something he can tell comes from outside himself. The innate ideas he lists here: what a thing is, what truth is, what a thought is, are conceptual, and so exist within, not beyond, his conscious life. And factitious ideas, hippogryphs and sirens, certainly won't help. But what is in fact the idea that rescues him from the isolation of the *cogito* and how has be acquired it? What saves him is the idea of God, which is innate.[5] Thus it is not an adventitious idea that he first discovers outside himself, and *a fortiori* it is not the existential judgments traditionally supposed, at least in Descartes's interpretation of the tradition, to lead us to the external world that are to be relied on to transcend the subjective truth so far established.

Descartes's rejection of the way of judgment as the primary path to truth becomes clear especially through the criticism to which he now subjects the claims of 'traditional' judgments of external existence. First, the way he takes these claims is peculiar. Once more, it is existential judgments, or perhaps meta-judgments of a sort, with which he is here concerned, certainly not ordinary predications of an Aristotelian kind. Not, again, that Descartes would not recognise other forms of judgment, but it seems odd, and oddly characteristic, that in this context he confines himself to judgments about whether the objects of his ideas exist. In an Aristotelian classroom, this wouldn't get him far. Thus in the case of the sun, for instance, he is not examining two judgments about the sun: 'the sun is small', 'the sun is large'. What he says is, rather, I have two ideas, one of a small object, derived from sense, the other of a huge object, derived from the reasonings of astronomy, and I ask in each case whether the thing is like my idea of it (*AT,* vii, p.29). In each case, further, I would 'naturally' be inclined to say, this idea bears some relation to some outside source. But clearly the common-sense idea of the sun, and the corresponding judgment 'this idea resembles its object', are not reliable. That insight in turn leads to the conclusion of this section: that it is not from *certain judgment* but only *from some blind impulse* that I have been led to judge that things like my ideas exist. Thus even when he tries to talk about judgment as the locus of truth, Descartes keeps reverting to ideas, and restricts judgments (in this context) to those that somehow compare ideas with their objects.

6

More generally, Descartes is here contrasting the obscurity of what I seem to be 'taught by nature' with the clarity of natural light. Judgment let loose from the control of clear and distinct ideas, and so especially judgment based on sense, is matched with the former. The 'other way', through the objective reality of ideas, will rely on the latter. The former, in contrast, resembles those impulses that often lead me astray in the choice of good. By analogy, this 'method' of reaching beyond my consciousness to things outside clearly will not do. I should beware in intellectual as in moral life of the merely instinctual (*AT*, vii, p.32). And by the same token, the present enumeration, into innate, factitious and adventitious ideas, does not of itself afford a criterion to lead me out of my thoughts to something real other than myself as momentary thinker. 'Another way' is needed—yet another enumeration, one, as it turns out, that sorts my ideas in terms of their degree of objective reality. *Here* is the way to God, to something beyond me, to reliance on the force of my clear and distinct ideas, first, essentially, for the distinction of mind and body, and then for physics—the existence of material things. Only putting firmly aside the primary or immediate relevance of judgment permits my success in this endeavour.

This interpretation, moreover, makes much more sense of what Descartes says of the teachings of nature *versus* natural light than do most readings. Aristotelian, or pseudo-Aristotelian, epistemology rested on a refinement of common sense: here we are, among sensible things; by exercising judgment on sensory contents we can arrive at principles of knowledge. No, says Descartes, we must look within. The dicta of natural light are what we find by the light of mind alone, cut off from the snares of everyday thought. Common sense can be reinstated in Meditation Six, once God's veridicality (and goodness) and the distinction in essence between thinking and extended substance have been firmly established. Indeed, in these terms even the famous circle becomes much less vexing. Natural light *can* tell us from within consciousness by what principles we may reason, before God's existence, guaranteed through the objective reality of our idea of Him, has in turn given firm and stable legitimation to our claims to know things beyond ourselves. Thus the rejection of 'nature's' teachings in Meditations Two and Three and their acceptance in Six, as well as Descartes's cavalier way with Arnauld in replying to the allegation of the circle, becomes much more intelligible (*AT*, vii, pp.245–6). As he saw it, there honestly was no circle. The elimination of impulsive claims and sense-founded judgments leaves the field free for the insights of natural light that we discover within our own consciousness. Only God's existence as non-deceiver, however, can guarantee that our clear and distinct ideas be true in the full sense of that term. All those principles about causality, ideas and so on are perfectly permissible within consciousness. Only through God's guarantee, however, do they yield metaphysical truths about a substantial world.

7

It may be objected, of course, that there are other passages in the *Meditations* where judgment seems important for the attainment of truth, not only for its explicit expression and preservation in scientific knowledge. I am thinking both of Meditation Four and of the piece-of-wax passage in Meditation Two. The former presents no difficulty, however. Descartes will there warn us not to 'pass judgment' unless we have carefully restrained our will within the bounds of understanding: in other words, only a clear and distinct idea, guaranteed by God's truthfulness, can in turn license the act of assertion in which judgment consists (*AT*, vii, 56,59). The bad habit of running about making judgments, especially under the lead of the senses, can now be curbed. Clear and distinct ideas come first and judgment is held in check by their guiding light.

As to the Second Meditation, the passage I mentioned there (*AT*, vii, pp.30–2), like the one in Three that we have been examining, seems at first sight to support the claim that judgment is central for the apprehension of the real. For clearly it is the correct judging what wax is that is there defended against the illusion that I 'know' this particular by imagination or sense. Thus we have for example: 'Nor would I rightly *judge* what wax is unless I thought it admitted more forms of extension than I could possibly imagine' (*AT*, vii, p.31). And it is the same with the 'men' passage: 'I see hats and cloaks, but *judge* that there are men' (*AT*, vii, p.32). Thinking in advance of Berkeley's *New Theory of Vision*, we are inclined to put great stress on the role of judgment in perception and on Descartes's perspicacity in seeing this. But surely the point of the examination of the piece of wax is to turn me away from my previous reliance on sense to admission of the priority of mind. Even what I seem to see, smell, touch, I grasp by a pure act of mind. What's more, even though that act may mistake its object—'although there may be error in my judgement'—yet 'I cannot perceive without a human mind': *non possum tamen sine humana mente percipere* (*AT*, vii, 32). There is a kind of progression of priority here: from sense to judgment as holding prior authority; from judgment, fallible as it is, to the mind that must be in order that judgment may be possible. Not judgment for itself, but the priority of the conceptual to the sensible, of mind to body, is what is at issue. If we recognise, with Gueroult, the importance to Descartes of training himself—and his reader—to overcome the traditional emphasis on sense as the primary source of information about things, we see easily that the act of judging here does duty for the mental as against sense, which seems to the untrained, pre-Cartesian thinker the reporter of circumstances out there in the external world. And by this emphasis we save ourselves the embarrassment of turning Descartes into a proto-empiricist, pointing to the role of judgment in sense-perception as against sensation.

8

Let us then take seriously Gueroult's interpretation of the opening paragraphs of Meditation Three and take seriously in consequence Descartes's confidence in his 'other way' to seek for knowledge beyond his own thoughts: the way, not of judgment, but of ideas, not of sense, which is confused, but of the examination from within of these ideas for their clarity and distinctness and in particular for the degree of their objective reality. What does this interpretation show us about the structure of the *Meditations* as a whole, and, finally, about the relation of our thought to Descartes's?

With respect to the former question, three conclusions follow. First, as I have already suggested, it is imperative that one accept Meditation Three and in particular the first proof of God, with its stress on degrees of objective reality, as the summit of the argument—as indeed Descartes himself presents it. Again, the movement of the work is to God and from God. Even the first clear and distinct idea that initiates Descartes's way to science cannot claim objectivity. The *cogito* establishes itself as the momentary self-validation of any intellectual act; it establishes the field of subjectivity. But Cartesian science must build up objective knowledge of all the human mind can know, and recognise with equal objectivity the limits at which knowledge ceases. Only the veracity of God and—as we shall see shortly—his goodness can start us firmly on this road.

Second, Gueroult interprets the *Meditations* as a diptych, proceeding through all possible sources of error, with the *cogito* as exception, to God as guarantor, and from there through all possible truths, with sensory illusion as exception (Gueroult, 1968, II, pp.272–92). True, one is more likely to think of a series of doubts ending with the *Deus Deceptor* and then the *cogito* as turning point; after that each item, beginning with God, is reinstated in inverse order. That is certainly, for example, the way Sartre takes it: the *cogito* is the only starting point for philosophy; and the Other, demonaic, takes the place of God as second intuition (Grene, 1983, ch.5). And, of course, the *Meditations* is one of those texts so rich as to admit of many mutually compatible renderings. But Gueroult's interpretation seems to me especially convincing, partly because of the light it sheds on passages like the one we have been looking at, and also because of the view it gives of the symmetry of the whole work. Taking Meditations Three and Four as giving us God's guarantee of clear and distinct ideas, we have first, in Meditation One, the chain of doubt, especially of judgments seemingly validated by sense, and in Six the reinstatement of the sensible world, with an explanation of—or better, an apology for—the inevitable errors we run into in it. Meditations Two and Five are also balanced in giving us, in Two, mind's self-awareness and the distinction from body, in Five a more securely grounded insight into the essence of body as extended, as against mind as thinking.

With Two on the one side and Five on the other, thirdly, we have now a clear presentation—first within the sphere of consciousness and then objectively grounded—of the second major principle on which the Cartesian edifice is built: the real distinction between mind as thinking and body as extended. It is the existence of these two as substance that God's veracity guarantees. The essence of mind and the essence of body, however, and their difference from one another, are already luminously clear. God's veracity allows us to affirm what is already evident to the unclouded intellect. On the other hand—and this is a point that so far as I know only Gueroult brings out clearly—the *union* of mind and body is, intrinsically, *un*intelligible (Gueroult, 1968, II, p.155). Not even God's veracity, but only his goodness, can guarantee our trust in it. God as non-deceiver guarantees our clear and distinct ideas; we have a clear and distinct idea of the separation of mind and body. In the light of that distinction, however, how can we understand what Descartes also asserts to be the case: that the mind is housed within the body, not as a pilot in a ship but much more intimately? Here it is God's goodness we trust to 'explain'—or rather to comfort us—in the face of an unintelligible fact. An often quoted remark of Descartes's to the Princess Elizabeth, (to which I shall return in the next chapter), confirms the importance of this paradoxical duality. He writes:

> 'It does not seem to me that the human mind is capable of conceiving quite distinctly and at the same time both the distinction between mind and body and their union; because to do so, it is necessary to conceive them as a single thing, and at the same time to conceive them as two things, which is self-contradictory (*AT*, iii, p.693).[6]

9

Finally, this general view of the *Meditations* is not only convincing; it shows us with exemplary clarity just where we differ—or ought to differ—from the Cartesian view, and just how thoroughly we must renounce our Cartesian heritage if we want to philosophise, in our own way and our own day, to any effect at all. Quite apart from Gueroult's interpretation, the alternative with respect to God is of course entirely plain. One can either comment with Hobbes on Meditation Three: there is no idea of God; the argument fails—or, as Descartes of course replied, one can say: there is that idea, the argument stands. The confrontation is simple: either we recognise that there is an all-good-all-powerful infinite Deity and all thought and being are grounded in Him, or we find in our consciousness no such imprint and we are astray in a world not grounded in His power. That does not mean a meaningless world, but it does mean a radically contingent one. The alternative looks rather different, but just as radical, in Four. When it comes to the problem of error, either we begin with God, who is both all-good and all-powerful, and explain error (and evil) away, or with Hume and Epicurus we begin with an imperfect world and find that, given error and evil, the concept of such a traditional Deity is self-contradictory. *Credo quia absurdum* or *non credo*. Any reading of the *Meditations* should make these choices clear. What Gueroult's interpretation provides, however, is a further alternative with respect to which, it seems to me, we need to stand in what looks like direct opposition to the Cartesian argument.

For Descartes, the separation of mind as intellect and body as extension is luminously clear; the way of ideas as distinct from the way of judgment demands precisely that kind of self-reliant intellect, cut off entirely from the unthinking physical world. The embodiment of mind, on the other hand, is for Descartes a muddle which only God's infinite goodness can excuse. This is opposition to common sense with a vengeance! There is, I submit, no such event as an experience of mind without some bodily resonance—'bodily', of course, not in the sense of *res extensa* (which is a fiction anyhow; even Descartes added forces to his physics, though it was only Newton who made them work)[7]—but in the sense of a live, breathing, organic body. J.W. Cook has argued in his excellent paper 'Human beings' that Descartes had no conception of body (Cook, 1969, pp.149–51). That is true. What he suspends in Meditation One and reinstates in Six is a dim surrogate for body: mere shapes and sizes, not growth and digestion and fatigue, comfort and discomfort—everything that the lived body at once is and means. Certainly I know the difference between solving a puzzle and being three feet square or between hoping and being circular, but so do I know the difference between being purple and being bored or between running and dissolving—and so on and so on. There are all sorts of distinguishable targets of my thought, as of my perception or imagination. But there is no one such distinction that specially separates my own awareness of myself as thinker from awareness of other things. Above all, my own awareness of myself is not a special, pure inner something set against the world. To be aware of myself is always and essentially to become sentient of my bodily existence, located here and now in this both biological and social place (Merleau-

Ponty, 1944, *passim*). That ambiguous yet pervasive thinking-through-my-lived-body is the datum with which, as a philosopher, I have to begin. It is the notion of separate mind that is *un*intelligible. It is not even a fact that needs explanation or apology. One can explain, historically, why Descartes the mathematician should have found it so clear. But there is no philosophical excuse for it whatsoever. It is distressing to acknowledge how much contemporary philosophising is still based on this illusory Cartesian certainty. Most philosophers have abandoned the traditional God as guarantor of knowledge, yet they retain the notion of the 'real distinction' to which only God's veracity could give metaphysical or even solid epistemological support and fail to recognise the richer bodily being of mental life that marks, not an abstract and outworn vision of the world, but the texture of experience as we live it both before philosophy begins and after the collapse of the Cartesian enterprise. Witness the fact that when mind, like God, fails them, they fall back on an abstract Cartesian *res extensa* as the alternative reality. This is an old story: that is, the story of Descartes's neglect of the category of life, and of the dead end at which twentieth-century philosophy has consequently arrived. I shall return in the epilogue to a suggestion—yet another suggestion, and not a new one either—of a possible way out of this impasse. What I wanted to do here was to show, at the start of our reading, how a historically illuminating reading of the *Meditations could* help us to understand both Descartes's own enterprise and our relation to it.

Notes

1. L.J. Beck's analysis of the *Meditations* (Beck, 1965) is, indeed, heavily grounded in (then) recent French scholarship. Although referred to, often peripherally, in later English-language works, it has scarcely been central in recent debate. I regret to have to confess that I did not consult it until this MS had been all but completed.
2. For the restriction of the Demon's power to undermining claims to external (or bodily) existence, *see* Richard Kennington (1971, pp.441–6). Only God could undermine the certainty of mathematics. It has been pointed out by Robert Matthews (oral communication) that the early

passages of Meditation Three introduce a further distinction: there is the Demon, 'some God' (*aliquis Deus*; *AT*, vii, p.36) and God. Exactly what range of doubts is inducible by each of these is a question beyond the scope of this inquiry.

3. 'Representation', of course, is not synonymous with 'copy'.
4. *See also* N. Maull, 'Cartesian optics and the geometrisation of nature', in S. Gaukroger *ed.* (1980) pp.23–40, esp. pp.32–3. And compare Descartes's statement to Mersenne, March 1642 (*AT*, iii, pp.544–5).
5. In what sense for Descartes all ideas are innate I dare not venture to suggest. *See* for example *AT*, iii, pp.414 ff., where it is suggested that all ideas not involving affirmation or negation are innate.
6. For a very different use of this passage, *see* Richardson (1982).
7. *See* Gueroult (1980), Gabbey (1980), Hatfield (1979).

2 *Cartesian Passions: The Ultimate Incoherence*

1

In his later correspondence about the passions, Descartes explains that he cannot really treat of this subject matter properly until he has completed his little treatise on animals, which he has not yet done. At the same time, when he does talk about animals on these occasions, 'passion' language creeps into his discourse about those alleged automata, in a way in which, in earlier pronouncements about beasts, it had not done. Such encroachment reflects, I believe, a fundamental incoherence in the Cartesian teaching about emotion, whether animal (if any) or human, and this incoherence in its turn lies at the heart of the notorious difficulty of making intelligible the detailed interaction of *substantia cogitans* and *substantia extensa*. Complicating this already complicated problem, however, there is the question of the relation of action and passion within the mind itself, apart from its relation, whether of action or passion, to its body. This question, further, bears on that of the relation of will and intellect in finite minds. In order to try to exhibit clearly (and distinctly!), therefore, the incoherence in the doctrine of the passions *sensu stricto*, that is of the 'movements' of the soul 'resulting' from its substantial connection with a body, I shall look separately at some texts, bearing first on the concepts of action and passion in general, then, second, on the question of action and passion in the soul itself, and only then, third, on the 'passions' inherent in the union of mind and body, comparing at this juncture Descartes's statements about the embodied life of human beings with his statements about animal behaviour. It is in connection with the third part of my exposition that the thesis stated above will be developed: the thesis, that is, of the fundamental incoherence of Descartes's theory of the passions. I shall put it forward in two contexts, first, as a commentary on Descartes's letter to the Princess Elizabeth of 28 June 1643, and second, as a thesis about Descartes's intellectual development: from a rigorous automatism with respect to animal (and human) bodies and a rigorous intellectualism (or voluntarism?) about the mind, to a more confused position about both, in which, despite himself, the fundamental untenability of his dualism emerges.

2

Article 1 of part 1 of *The Passions* reads: 'What is passion with respect to one subject, is always action in some other subject' (*AT*, xi, p.327). Thus Descartes appears to be taking action and passion as completely general concepts. Although the statement itself is unambiguous, and although the argument by which Article 2 is justified (*AT*, xi, p.328) is made to depend directly upon Article 1, one may nevertheless find some difficulty in interpreting the text of this first article both (a) in itself and (b) in the context of Cartesian doctrine as commonly interpreted.

(a) In the explanatory paragraph, Descartes, accusing the ancients of having totally misinterpreted this subject-matter, declares: 'I am therefore obliged to write here as if I were treating of a matter that no one before me had ever touched' (*AT*, xi, p.327). So far, so good. This attitude matches well the boast of Picot's preface (*AT* xi, p.x), in turn quoting Descartes's declaration that the Peripatetic philosophy had never solved a single philosophical problem. But then Descartes continues in a fashion that seems, at first sight at least, to credit his predecessors with the very view he is himself in process of asserting. 'And to begin,' he goes on, 'I consider that all that is done or happens for the first time [*de nouveau*] is generally called by the Philosophers a passion with respect to the subject to which it happens and an action with respect to the subject that makes it happen' (*AT*, xi, p.328). It follows then, that 'although agent and patient are often very different, Action and Passion nevertheless continue to be always one and the same thing, which has two names, because of the two different subjects to which one can relate it' (*AT*, xi, p.328). Isn't that just what Descartes himself is asserting? So what was wrong with the Philosophers' view? The paragraph is very condensed, but I think one can interpret it as follows.

In the Peripatetic tradition, Action and Passion are categories, so they are allegedly two kinds of entities, two varieties of accidental being. Now Descartes objects strongly, in general, to the elevation of such qualities to entitative status. As in other cases, here, too, philosophers have hypostatised events incident on change—whether on local motion or on the sequence of thoughts, the only kinds of change Descartes is able to acknowledge—and have failed to see that what is action for one subject is always passion for another and vice versa. So they have taken as real things, actions and passions, what are really just names for relations: the activity of one thing relative to the passivity of another. This is comparatively easy to show for physical events, for which Descartes consistently attempts to give a purely mechanical interpretation. The clapper strikes the hour (action) when the bell is pulled by the rope (passion). Like the muddled classification of 'motions', the muddled list of traditional categories, including action and passion, is quite unnecessary. In the case of the passions of the soul, of course, as they will be defined in the present treatise, there are indeed two very different kinds of subject concerned: the passion of one kind of substance (soul) is the action of the other kind of substance (body), and so, as Descartes will proceed to argue to Article 2, in this particular case we need to understand the functions of the soul as distinct from those of body, if we are to understand (actions and) passions of this particular kind.

Yet, strictly speaking, we could with equal propriety call the effects of the mind on the body not only (as we do call them) actions of the mind, but passions of the body. In his letter to Mesland of 2 May 1643, in fact (as we shall see), Descartes does speak of passions of bodies analogous to those of minds (*AT*, iv, pp.110 ff.). Usually, however, when he speaks of 'passions belonging to body' (e.g., letter to Regius, *AT*, iii, p.373), he is referring to pure motions of the body-machine, which are carried on independently of thought, not to the 'sufferings' of the body relative to the control or action of the mind. And in his express statement about the usage 'passions of the soul' he does appear to recognise the oddity of this terminology, at least. How it bears on the basic unity of his doctrine remains to be seen. For the moment, however, we need to take him at his word (implicit as well as explicit): first, the categoric distinction between action and passion was mistaken; one thing's actions are another thing's passions, that's all there is to it. So, far from being unique kinds of entity, 'action' and 'passion' are relational concepts, universally applicable. In the present context, Descartes will be examining the passions of one entity—soul—relative to the actions of another—body. The limitation of ordinary usage in speaking of 'the passions' should not blind us to the generality of the concepts involved (cf. *AT*, iv, pp.304 ff.).

(b) The above interpretation of Article 1, though clear in itself, I think, suggests a further difficulty that needs to be faced, at least briefly, at this stage. In the main interpretive tradition, and justifiably in the light of Meditation Two, it seems to me, one is inclined to take it that Cartesian mind is somehow fundamentally active and matter, that is, divisible, spread-out substance, passive. We know there *are* passions of the soul, but they turn up in a rather dreary postscript to Descartes's published work and are in themselves an embarrassment to his pure dualistic doctrine. So Sartre in rendering passions as 'magical' actions, the pseudo-actions of bad faith, seems at his most Cartesian. Perhaps the very adjectives, *cogitans*, *extensa*, have misled us: mind is think*ing*, body extend*ed*, subject, indefinitely, to division. But if we *are* misled, if we take action as principally mental and being acted on as principally bodily, surely it is the rhetoric, if not the logic, of the Second Meditation, and indeed the Fourth, that has persuaded us. Let him deceive me how he will, I am, I exist, as often as I pronounce these words. It is the self-containment of my *action* that guarantees my being, while the existence of body in its otherness can be guaranteed only by an omnipotent non-deceiving God, Himself infinite mind and so again agency. Besides, when I ask myself what I used to opine myself to be, I find I must banish all givens, everything that has been offered to me, so to speak, external to my thinking, and that seems to mean: I must banish all passivities. What first and essentially I am is my action: though there be no external world to *cause* my feeling, I feel (*sentio*); though there is nothing there to see, I seemingly see—and so on. It is mind as action that is primary. At the start of his methodological enterprise, moreover, in the *Rules*, Descartes had projected a sequence of intuitions and deductions (= inductions = enumerations), where each unit is somehow both a content and an action, a *conceptus*, a grasping of pure and attentive mind etc. And the very ambiguity of the term 'idea' seems to reflect this active aspect of Cartesian intentionality. Ideas are operations of the mind, in their very nature projected towards a content (Kenny, 1968, pp. 103 ff, cf. *AT*, vii, p.102). We do appear to have in thinking *versus* extended things an anticipation of the ultimate dichotomy of Sartrean for-itself and in-itself.

Now looking in a more pedagogical than scholarly perspective ahead to Kantian will and empiricist ideas—even short of the Sartrean debacle—that perspective is a tempting one. And if it were correct, it would stop us short of taking action and passion in the Cartesian ontology as neutrally general. But a number of texts, especially outside the *Meditations*, fail to support this view, so we must at least note in passing the counter-evidence: evidence for the application of the concepts action and passion to the mind itself, not for the moment insofar as the mind suffers an interaction with the body, but in its pure cogitative life. Only a full treatment of the relation between intellect and will in Cartesian mind would suffice to exhaust this question, and I shall certainly not attempt such a treatment here. But let us just look at some passages that describe the passions of pure mind, before we go on to consider our crucial subject-matter: the passions of the soul that arise in interaction with the body.

3

There are plenty of passages that support an 'activist' view of Cartesian thought. Among them we might want to mention a statement to Princess Elizabeth, according to which even imagination (usually considered relatively passive in relation to motions in the brain) is described as properly speaking an activity; if not only reason, clear and distinct conception, volition, judgment are actions, but even imagination, every mode of thought would seem to be an act (*AT*, iv, p.311).

What we have to weigh against all such pronouncements, however, are the straightforward statements about the passivity of mind. The clearest texts are two in the letters. First there is the letter of May 1641 to Regius, where Descartes declares:

> Finally, where you say 'willing and understanding differ only as different ways of acting in regard to different objects' I would prefer 'they differ only as the activity and passivity of one and the same substance.' For strictly, understanding is the passivity of the mind and willing is its activity, but because we cannot will anything without understanding what we will, and we scarcely ever understand something without at the same time willing something, we do not easily distinguish in this matter passivity from activity (*AT*, iii, p.372; *K*, pp.102–3).

Then there is the letter to Mesland already referred to:

> I regard the difference between the soul and its ideas as the same as that between a piece of wax and the various shapes it can take; just as it is not an activity but a passivity in the wax, to take various shapes, so, it seems to me, it is a passivity in the soul to receive one or other idea and only its volitions are activities. It receives its ideas partly from objects in contact with the senses, partly from impressions in the brain, and partly from precedent dispositions in the soul and motions of the will. Similarly, a piece of wax owes its shape partly to the pressure of other bodies, partly to its own earlier shape or other qualities such as heaviness or softness, and partly also to its own movement, when, having been pushed it has in itself the power to continue moving (*AT*, iv, pp.113-14, *K*, p.148).

In terms of Cartesian physics this is an accurate statement; but in terms of the passivity of mind it is quite definite—and we even have passions of the wax! This corresponds exactly to Part 1, Article 1 of the *Passions*. Article 17, on the functions of the soul, is just as unambiguous:

> After having thus considered all the functions that belong to the body alone, it is easy to recognise that there is nothing left in us that we should attribute to our soul, except our thoughts, which are chiefly of two kinds: to wit, some are the actions of the soul, the others are its passions. Those that I call actions, are all our volitions, since we find by experience [*experimentons*] that they come directly from our soul, and seem to depend on it alone. As, on the contrary, one can in general designate as its passions all the sorts of perceptions or items of knowledge that are found in us, since often it is not our soul that makes them such as they are, and because it always receives them from the things that are represented by them. (*AT*, xi, p.342.)

'Things that are represented', of course, include not only bodies but intellectual 'objects', like common notions or the truths of mathematics, or spiritual objects, like angels or God. This statement accords well with the pronouncements to Regius and to Mesland. We might also add a passage in a letter of March or

April 1648, probably to the Marquis of Newcastle, where, in replying to his correspondent's worries about intuitive knowledge, Descartes remarks:

> Intuitive knowledge is an illumination of the mind, by which it sees in the light of God whatever it pleases Him to show it by a direct impress of the divine clarity on our understanding, which in this is not considered as an agent but simply as a receiver of the rays of infinity (*AT*, v, p.136; *K*, p.229).

In view of the context, however, and of the missing context, that is, the letter to which Descartes is replying, this is perhaps not to be taken so very seriously as a gloss, say, on the *intuitus* of the much earlier *Rules* or the 'clear and distinct ideas' of the *Meditations* and *Principles*. Descartes's correspondent seems to have been raising questions of faith rather than of reason.

Be that as it may, we do have to take it, on balance, that mind in itself can indeed be passive. Part 1, Article 19, moreover, which sorts out perceptions caused by the soul from those caused by bodies, accounts at least, if not very satisfactorily, for the tendency to call all modifications of the soul 'actions' even when they are not volitions:

> Our perceptions are of two sorts, some have the soul for cause, others the body. Those which have the soul for cause are the perceptions of our volitions, and of all the imaginations or other thoughts that depend on them. For it is certain that we would not know how to will anything that we did not perceive at the same time that we will it. And as indeed with respect to our soul, it is an action to will something, one can say that it is also a passion in it (the soul) to perceive that it wills. However, because this perception and this will are in fact only one thing, the designation is always made in terms of what is nobler; and so we do not habitually call it a passion, but only an action (*AT*, xi, p.343).

Against this in turn we might set a remark, probably to Arnauld, in the letter of 29 July 1648. To a question about implications of Descartes's doctrine of thought as the essence of substance, Descartes replies:

> I tried to remove the ambiguity of the word 'thought' in articles 63 and 64 of the first part of the *Principles*. Just as extension, which constitutes the nature of body, differs greatly from the various shapes or modes of extension which it may assume; so thought, or a thinking nature, which I think constitutes the essence of the human mind, is far different from any particular way of thinking. It depends on the mind itself whether it

> produces this or that particular act of thinking; just as it depends on a flame as an efficient cause, whether it turns to this side or that, but not that it is an extended substance (*AT*, v, p.221, *K* pp.234–5).

Here it appears at first sight that mind is act—'the mind itself produces. . .', but so does it 'depend on a flame' 'what it does'! Indeed, action and passion here, it seems, simply do duty for cause and effect, whether in extended or cogitative things (or, as we shall have to try to understand, between the two). On the whole, then, I conclude, we should probably try to consider 'action' and 'passion', taken in the spirit of *Passions One* and the letters to Regius and Mesland, as general concepts, applying equally to mental and corporeal events, and indeed as synonymous with cause and effect. It is then a peculiar case of causality between two different kinds of finite substance that form the context for the study of the passions. Indeed, Descartes remarks to Princess Elizabeth, it is only through the effect of mind on body and of body on mind that their union is known (*AT*, iii p.665). That was just the kind of interaction, too, of course, that Descartes's critics so often worried about; yet, he insists, at least this is a case of cause and effect at a single ontological level, between substances, not, like the alleged operations of Aristotelian heaviness, for instance, an alleged effect of a quality—a mode, therefore—on a substance. That would be much more mysterious: almost like—inconceivably—a supposed action of a finite being on the Infinite! Any finite substance can be agent or patient to any other—what matter if one be spread out and divisible and the other non-located, essentially thought?

4

So we come at last to the *raison d'être* of this chapter: Descartes's treatment of the passions (*sensu stricto*) in connection with his doctrine of the body-machine of animals and men. As I said at the start, I shall not attempt to comment in detail on Descartes's account of the passions, but rather on what seem to me to be issues of principle. My thesis, again, is that it is in the context of this problem that the fundamental incoherence of Descartes's doctrine of the real distinction becomes apparent. And again, I shall argue for this first as a commentary on Descartes's letter to Princess Elizabeth on 28 June 1643, and secondly as a thesis about Descartes's intellectual development, which may reflect also on the interpretation of the passages noted above (pp.24–7).

In his letter of 28 June 1643, Descartes admits that we cannot understand 'very distinctly' at one and the same time the real distinction of mind and body and their substantial union. Now in the order of reasons, which is primary in the understanding both of Descartes's method and his doctrine, the real distinction antedates by several steps the awareness of substantial union: the real distinction, that is to say, as applied to the essence and existence of mind and their difference from body, whose existence is not yet known and whose essence has not yet been explicitly considered as a theme in its own right. First, in the *cogito*, I know myself indubitably as thinking being. Then, second, knowing God, and trusting in His veracity, I affirm, thirdly, my knowledge of the essence of material things, and only then, fourth, relying on his goodness, my knowledge of the existence of such material things as extended entities, in accordance with the clear and distinct knowledge of the geometer.

A parenthetical remark may be inserted here. Note that only two existences, my mind's and God's, can be acknowledged in reliance on His veracity rather than His good will. Admittedly, indeed, none of God's attributes are separable; yet it does make a difference in our conceptual priorities, and therefore in the ranking of *our* certainties, that mind, finite and infinite, is known, in epistemological order, before even the limited mathematical existence of bodies. Although as we look back on the history of Cartesianism, man as mind-in-machine may seem to us close to man = machine as the clear issue of dualism, in Cartesian methodology the idealist issue demands a shorter epistemological, and ontological, step. But that is by the way. Let me return to the Cartesian order of certainties, in particular with respect to finite things.

We had, first, the *cogito*, then, protected by God's existence and especially by His veracity, the essence of material things, and then, relying on His goodness, their existence, clearly and distinctly known insofar as they are geometrically intelligible, extended things, divisible things in motion, that is, exchanging places with one another in accordance with the laws of nature decreed by God. The ultimate unintelligibility of motion without a void need not concern us here; it didn't worry Descartes, though it did some of his critics. Nor for that matter did he worry, it seems, about the problem of the substantiality of bodies whose very quintessence is only spread-outness in space. So, although the principle of individuation of Cartesian bodies may seem to us (as it did to some of Descartes's contemporaries) tenuous enough, we may take it here as read, returning briefly to that problem in later chapters. We 'know' clearly and distinctly if we follow Descartes (or pretend to follow him) the existence of bodies insofar as we distinguish them by shape and size: geometers' bodies. But what of the richer things around us, with their colours and odours and noises and all? Austin's pig, one supposes, was not only pig-shaped, a well-fed Hampshire shape, let us say, but black and white belted, smelly in a unique porcine manner and equally characteristically porcinely grunting. No, says Descartes, *that* sort of thing about the world we never know really clearly and distinctly, but only in a rough pragmatic way—sufficient for a child to tell 'piggy' from 'horsy' or for a farmer to tell a Hampshire from a Large White Yorkshire hog. That sort of thing, confused as it is, does for the lowly needs of practice, but is irrelevant to science. Aristotle had objected to Democritus that things are distinguished by more than shape and size: a saw must be hard enough to cut, a threshold solid enough to take one's tread, and so on. Now Descartes in turn replies to the upholders of real qualities that they have hypostatised modes into substances, and with their alleged substantial forms have transferred to the corporeal, whose whole essence is extension, properties they have glimpsed in their own confused awareness of *in*corporeal things. Moreover, they were confused in that awareness, which, given the discipline of Cartesian method, *could* be clear, because they had not weaned their minds from the seductive sensory impulses of a prenatal, infantile and childish state. Indeed, that *is* the discipline of Cartesian method: *abducere mentem a sensibus* (*AT*, vii, p.3). All we know of bodies that is not intelligible, that is, geometrical, is confused; all our sensory information apart from that concerning shape and motion, though necessary to the life of the embodied mind, misleads the intellect, and hence, if we believe Meditation Four, may, if we don't take care, mislead the will as well.

What, then, of our knowledge that we *are* embodied, somehow unified substances even though composed of two, a thinking thing that could exist without its body, and a body that will exist, though decaying, when its mind departs? There are three common notions, which serve as models for all our other knowledge, Descartes reminded Elizabeth, following on a list of four in his earlier letter of 21 May 1643: mind, body and the union of mind and body. The first we know clearly and distinctly, the second, too, as far as 'primary' qualities go. But what sort of knowledge have we of the third? The knowledge, Descartes tells us, of everyday experience—and we know what that's worth in Cartesian terms: not much except as a pragmatic second best. The first two items, in other words, we know by natural light, but the third only through that 'natural impulse' which Descartes has warned us in the Third Meditation has so often misled us, not only in the search for truth but in the choice of goods. It seems predestined, therefore, that the interrelations of mind and body, the events of our lives as united minds and bodies, that our human histories, in short, and therefore our human *being*, can be comprehended only in this relatively obscure, non-scientific and instinctive rather than in that luminous, intellectual way. As Descartes emphasises, the union of body and mind is accessible to us, not through science, but through the experience of everyday life; and it is precisely the experience of everyday life that has been definitively undermined in the programmatic doubt of Meditation One, followed by the demonstration in Meditation Two of its incurable confusion. For the piece of wax not only confirms the prior intelligibility of mind over body, it does so by giving free rein to our natural impulses, and showing us, even if perhaps we were not dreaming, how thoroughly muddled is our reliance on our sense-related everyday impulses.

In what way, then, does the third common notion rank along with the others? Meditation Six notoriously does not tell us much; in the *Principles*, however, where he is plainly trying to deal with a number of difficulties raised by readers of the *Meditations*, Descartes does attempt to sort this out. At I, 66 he tells us

> There remain the senses, passions and appetites, which can indeed also be clearly perceived, if we take great care not to judge about them further than what is contained in our perception, and what we have intimately in consciousness (*AT*, vii, 1, p.32).

In the French, 'distinctly' has been substituted for 'clearly' both in the caption and in the accompanying text, as it has in the text of I, 68. In the original, however, Descartes is very exactly separating the clarity of our 'senses, passions and appetites' from the distinctness that they lack. The pain a patient feels in his amputated limb is, by all accounts, as clear as may be—as clear as the red is in the rose; but the confusion suffered with respect to the location of the sensation marks precisely the want of distinctness, that second indispensable criterion for the ideas out of which Cartesian science is constructed. In I, 68, on the other hand, Descartes admits, with exacting—and fateful—care just what is distinct as well in our 'senses, passions and appetites': to wit, their existence 'only as sensations or thoughts'. The sentence containing this telling phrase is worth looking at carefully. It reads:

> In order then that we may distinguish what is clear from what is obscure, it must be noticed with the greatest care, that pain and colour and other things of this kind are clearly and distinctly perceived, only insofar as they are seen as sensations [*sensus*] or thoughts (*AT*, vii, 1, p.33).

Two points should be noted here: first, it is only in their sheer subjectivity that perceptions, passions and appetites are clearly and distinctly perceived. When we ascribe them to bodies, even to our own bodies, we forfeit distinctness. And, second, we even forfeit clarity: we can distinguish the *clear* from the obscure only by limiting it to its pure subjective, immediate evidence. The third common notion, therefore, not only attains distinctness in a peculiarly restricted way; it holds even its clarity at peril. What is plainly felt, however 'clear and evident' the everyday experience of it, not only tends to lack distinctness, and lacks it unless held in check by the recognition that it is *only* a feeling; by forfeiting distinctness, it forfeits even its clarity. However vivid, however urgent the lights that dazzle, the pains that dismay, they are in their very being purveyors of obscurity unless 'they are seen as only sensations or thoughts'. There you have it: unless controlled by Cartesian discipline, the third common notion is inherently deceptive. The remainder of I, 68 supports this reading, as, indeed, does the summary of philosophic method in I, 75.[1] And finally, the concluding sentence in the original confirms the contrast between the infantile reliance on sense from which the third common notion derives and the wiser reliance of the philosopher on his 'mature reason'. The French adds, on his reason 'when he is in a state to conduct it well'—a proviso that may lead me to the second context in which I want to look at Cartesian passions: the context of Descartes's intellectual development as mediated by his correspondence with Elizabeth. For presumably between the composition of the Latin text and the French translation, it was Elizabeth who had suggested to him that reason, though by right sovereign, may be disordered through disease. Well, well, Descartes replies in effect, I never thought of that! (*AT*, iv, pp.269, 281–2).

5

As I remarked at the start of this chapter, Descartes sometimes associates his theory of the passions with the treatise about animals he has not completed. Yet if we look through the works and correspondence, we find the statements he makes about passions (and feelings in general) in men and animals oddly inconsistent with one another. I want to suggest that at the time he published the *Discourse* Descartes did hold a consistent if erroneous view of the nature of (other) animals, and of human beings, that it was a by-product of his principles in physics as well as metaphysics, that it was Princess Elizabeth who urged him to reflect in detail about the life of the emotions, that this led him into a confusion from which he found—indeed, I would argue, could have found—no egress within the framework of his own physics and metaphysics, even had he not succumbed so early to the rigours of the Swedish winter.

The best known evidence for Descartes's early view is of course the *Discourse*; both its modernity and its absurdity are even more strikingly displayed in his exchange, *via* Reneri, with Pollot in 1638.[2] Pollot had sent him, *via* his friend, a number of comments on the *Discourse* and essays, among them the following:

> Experience makes us see that beasts make their affections and passions understood by their sort of language, and that by several signs they show their anger, their fear, their love, their grief (pain? *douleur*), their regret for having done wrong . . . it is clear that animals function by a principle more excellent than the necessity stemming from the disposition of their organs; that is, by an instinct, which will never be found in a machine, or in a clock, which have neither passion nor affection as animals have (*AT*, i, p.514).

Although he illustrates the alleged moral sense of animals with a particularly silly report from the *History of Animals* about equine incest, Pollot's comment seems sensible enough. That (other) animals have feelings seems as clear as anything. Indeed, Pollot's preceding remarks about the mind-body relation are also very reasonable. To the comments about animals, Descartes replies:

> It is certain that the resemblance that exists between most of the actions of animals and ours has given us, from the beginning of our life, so many occasions to judge that they act by an internal principle similar to that which is in us, that is, by means of a soul that has feelings and passions like ours, that we are all naturally imbued with this opinion. . .

. . .'*que nous sommes tous préoccupez de cette opinion*' (*AT*, ii, p.39). Kenny renders this 'deeply imbued by nature' (*K*, p.53); but plainly this could be 'nature' only in the sense of that natural lower impulse, formed rashly in infancy and retained by unconsidered habit. Whatever reasons we might have to deny this childish notion, however, Descartes continues, it would be hard to publish them without exposing oneself 'to the laughter of children and weak minds'. But—again here comes the path of Cartesian discipline—

> for those who wish to know the truth, it is essential to distrust above all opinions in favour of which they had been thus prejudiced from infancy (*AT*, ii, p.39).

Thus to reach wisdom is to set aside common notion three in favour of the knowledge of one and two. What Descartes advises here, moreover, is just the move of science-fiction philosophising that has become so prestigious in our day. Turn your back, not only on childhood, but on reality itself, and substitute the fabrications of technology for the arrangements of nature! This is the contrivance Descartes proposes:

> Suppose that a man had been brought up all his life in some place where he had never seen animals except men; and suppose that he was very devoted to the study of mechanics, and had made, or helped to make, various automata shaped like a man, a horse, a dog, a bird and so on, which walked, and ate, and breathed, and so far as possible imitated all the other actions of the animals they resembled, including the signs we use to express our passions, like crying when struck and running away when subjected to a loud noise (*AT*, ii, p.40, *K*, p.54).

In this situation, dealing with a manufactured man, and unable perhaps to tell him from a real one, our truth seeker would test the human versus the divine manufacture by the two methods specified in the *Discourse*: language and the multiplicity of talents. Now, Descartes asks, what judgment would such a man make about the animals among us,

> especially if he was gifted with the knowledge of God, or at least had noticed how inferior is the best skill shown by men in their artefacts compared with that shown by nature in the composition of plants. Nature has packed plants with an infinity of tiny invisible ducts to convey certain liquids in such a way as to form leaves and flowers and fruits. . . (*AT*, ii, pp. 40–1; *K*, p.54).

Note that our automaton maker has not been raised without plant life around him, only without non-human animals. And note also that for plant physiology a mechanism is obviously adequate! Nobody thinks plants have souls like ours; so what could they be but machines? Now suppose our man has got this far; thinking about the automata we make and those vegetable machines made by God or nature, he would further confidently believe, Descartes goes on,

> that if there were automata made by God or nature to imitate our actions, they would imitate them more perfectly, and be incomparably more skillfully constructed than any which could be invented by men (*AT*, ii, p.41).

How then will he interpret actual animals when he comes at long last to see them? He would notice 'in their actions the same two things which make them differ from us, and which he had already been accustomed to notice [that is, to notice the lack of] in his own automata'. Such a man, then, Descartes writes—and equally, we might add, a man brought up on twentieth-century analytic philosophy, who has not even flora to look at, but only arguments—such a man, faced with 'the animals that are among us'

> would not judge that there is in them any real feeling, or any real passion, as in us, but only that they were automata, which, being made by nature, were incomparably more accomplished than any of those that he had previously made himself (*AT*, ii, p.41).

Our mythical man, then, can reasonably avoid those prejudices that we, poor deluded fools, have sustained since childhood 'only through custom', prejudices founded entirely on external appearances, which are never adequate to prove that there is anything corresponding inside. And we see, Descartes is sure, that a judgment like his will be much more reasonable than the one we have so far been accustomed to. The *Discourse* presents in effect the same argument in more condensed form, and the reference to automata under the hats and cloaks in Meditation Two reflects the same line of reasoning; but the science-fiction hypothesis of the letter to Pollot reveals so sharply both the anti-natural bent of Cartesian thought and, in its similarity to currently fashionable arguments, our continued subjugation to it, that it seems a specially valuable source.

6

Whichever source one prefers, the lesson is plain. Nothing could be clearer, more rigorous, or—to any one with any experience of animals, whether agricultural, scientific or just domestic—more ridiculous. But there it is: that *was* the doctrine of the *bête-machine*, which denies feeling of any kind to beasts—and relegates the human as well as the animal body to the status of an automaton. 'Nature' in the sense of the living scene made up of untold styles of life, nature in the naturalist's sense, is not only inferior to the geometer-mechanist's extended universe; it is illusory. There are really pure mind and pure matter, as our knowledge of God assures us, and, third, a muddled everyday sense of the togetherness of my mind and my body, which, however, philosophic discourse reveals for the crudely pragmatic tool it is, appropriate not to knowledge but to the circumstances of our present (unintelligible though undeniable) psycho-physical existence. Of course Descartes had begun, in Meditation One, as Gouhier insists, from common notion three, as every one, in his pre-philosophic prejudice, begins (Gouhier, 1978a, ch. 12, pp. 321–44). That is clear from the very fact—so regretted by Descartes—that we have all been infants. But where he got to from this beginning was: the relegation of that clear but non-distinct sense of psycho-physical existence to its everyday function, and the elevation of the (alleged) knowledge of mind, body and their distinction to the rank of philosophic truth.

Nor, second, is the reason for this move on Descartes's part far to seek. As Gilson established definitively many years ago, the aim of Descartes's new method was to alter in the framework of the traditional ontology just so much as was needed to establish the foundation of the new science of nature (Gilson, 1930). That was a radical move enough, far more so than he himself ever knew. It meant the reduction of finite substance to just two kinds: mathematicising mind and the essentially geometrical matter accessible to such mathematical apprehension. Reason on the one hand and extension on the other: the one is both instrument and object of understanding, the second object only; but how beautifully they collaborate in the establishment of a nature entirely open to explanation in mechanical terms! Substantial forms (except for our odd case), real qualities, incomplete substances: all that litter must go. For science, both on the subject and the object side, all is now clear. For the purposes of practice, indeed, Descartes admits, he needs tentative rules, consonant with those of the society in which he lives—but that is of comparatively little interest. It is the transformation of physics into mechanics that matters most. Medicine and even morality will eventually follow, the former in the style indicated by the theory of the circulation (in Descartes's reading), the latter, as the original conclusion of *Principles*, Part One, indicates, through reliance on 'mature reason', liberated from the psycho-physical confusions of childhood and common life.

Meantime, what most preoccupied Descartes was the clearing away of scholastic rubbish from the image of the natural world, and the liberation of natural knowledge for a purely mechanical perspective. Over and over he insists, in his published and unpublished work and in his correspondence, that he can solve all problems about physical (including physiological) occurrences by applying mechanical principles only. *Except* for our everyday consciousness of mind-body union, substantial forms are otiose: the Peripatetic philosophy has never solved a single philosophical problem. Real qualities, like their cousins substantial forms, were invented, Descartes remarks, as hypostatisations of a muddled notion of *in*corporeal substance. Once we know clearly the essential difference between mind and body we will no more claim reality for such airy nothings than we will attempt to imagine little winds or airs to embody pure separable mind. Notoriously, the Aristotelian tradition put all sorts of barriers in the way of a mechanical-mathematical physics; only the heavens were left free for the application of mathematical reasoning. But once heaven and earth were one, why should not all creation be open to mathematical explanation, and its handmaid, mechanical experiment? Granted, there are knotty questions about Descartes's method in science that I cannot go into here.[3] In general, however, we may at least assert that, on the whole, his confidence in the universal application of mechanical-geometrical principles pervades his discussion of physical (and physiological) questions throughout most of the correspondence as well as in the *World*, the *Principles*, the *Description of the Human Body*, and so on. Further, and as I have just stated, it was from the twin liberation of mind and material universe that his eventual reform in medicine and even in morality were to flow. In replying to Elizabeth's question on 'how to fortify one's understanding so as to discern what is best in all the actions of life' (*AT*, iv, p.291; cf.iv, p.280, 11. 13–14), he enumerates four truths 'most useful to us'. These are: (1) the knowledge of God, (2) knowledge of the soul, 'insofar as it subsists without the body and is much nobler than it' (*AT*, iv, p.292), and last, the greater importance of the interests of the whole over our own; 'we must... think that none of us could subsist alone and each one of us is really one of the many parts of the universe' (*AT*, iv, p.293; *K*, p.172).[4] And enumerated in the third place has been 'that vast idea of the extent of the universe that I tried to convey in the third book of my *Principles*'. Thus, even morality is assisted by Cartesian physics:

> For if we imagine that beyond the heavens there is nothing but imaginary spaces, and that all the heavens are made only for the service of the earth,

and the earth only for man, we will be inclined to think that this earth is our principal abode and this life our best. Instead of discovering the perfections that are truly within us, we will attribute to other features imperfections which they do not have, so as to raise ourselves above them. We will be so absurdly presumptuous as to wish to belong to God's council and assist Him in the government of the world; and this will bring us a mass of vain anxiety and distress (*AT*, iv, p.292; *K*, p.172).

Elizabeth, as we shall see, is quick to retort in the spirit of John Donne, and Descartes replies in puzzlement (*AT*, iv, p.315). How *can* his physics bring anything but solace?

7

Thus Descartes for his own part, I submit, was sublimely satisfied with his conceptual reform, both for mind and matter—and of course for God's relation to the universe, which is essential to our knowledge of their real separateness as well as of the (human, anomalous) substantial union of the two. It was the Princess Elizabeth who forced him to face the more concrete problems of mind-body interaction, the *im*practicality of his naive mathematician's vision and its uncomfortable consequences. If we look at the correspondence on her side as well as his we find this conclusion irresistible—or so it seems to me. She did not, it is true, question his view about animal-machines (and by implication our body-machine), but her questions about Descartes's efforts to deal with concrete problems of mind-body interaction, though always couched in a context of the utmost admiration and respect, were so telling as to compel him to reveal, willy-nilly, the nest of puzzles entangled in the compulsions of practice, which his mathematician's understanding, together with the relatively easy circumstances of his life, had so far allowed him to evade.

Unfortunately, I cannot go into the details of the correspondence here. The exchanges in question start with Descartes's advice about a slow fever he has heard the Princess has been suffering from. In each letter he puts forward conventional claims about sovereign reason, to which she replies each time with pressing practical qualifications. Finally he confesses, in response to her request, that he must examine the passions in some detail—as he indeed proceeded to do.

What I believe, further, is that it was this *excursus* that induced the confusion contained, as we shall see, in Descartes's last statements about the passions in animals and men. In short, Elizabeth's slow fever provided the occasion for Descartes's foray into a subject-matter he had not troubled with before—confident as he was in the liberating power of his mechanics and in the adequacy for his everyday life of the tentative ethic summarised in the *Discourse*. And it was a subject-matter that defeated him, that might have defeated the Cartesian tradition in its infancy, had seventeenth-century metaphysics not seemed so alluring and seventeenth-century 'philosophical psychology' such a tedious appendage to it.

But that is to move on too hastily. I must refer here again in some detail to the letter in which Descartes specifies the four items, the knowledge of which he finds conducive to the cultivation of felicity, and to the exchange with Elizabeth that follows. After the list, he adds three further points. We also need knowledge of particular truths in each case, we need to pay attention to the customs of the society we live in, and we need practice.

Elizabeth, in her reply, asks 'for the explanation that my stupidity needs, concerning the utility of the items of knowledge that you propose' (*AT*, iv, p.302). And then quietly she proceeds to take apart Descartes's maxims. First, God's existence may excuse natural evil, but moral evil, the wrongs done by men's free will, cannot easily be so justified. Second, the confidence in a happy hereafter may lead us to seek death. Third, Descartes's vast universe threatens 'that particular providence, which is the foundation of theology, of the idea we have of God' (*AT*, iv, p.303). And fourth, to see that we are part of a larger whole does not help us to balance the probable evils and goods involved in making choices in such a wider perspective. To weigh the particular truths involved in an action, further, would take much more exact knowledge than we have—and finally, when we take into account also the *mores* of our place of residence, we may find ourselves compelled to follow some very unreasonable courses just in order to avoid even greater inconvenience. Descartes's reply to this gently annihilating document is feeble, no more than a thin reaffirmation of what he had earlier written. But it is also in this letter that he announces his intention of examining the passions in more detail, and indeed sets out to do. Referring to his treatise on animals, he begins:

> You know already how I think various impressions are formed in their brain: some by the external objects which act upon the senses, and others by the internal dispositions of the body, either by the traces of previous impressions left in the memory, or by the agitation of the spirits which come from the heart. In man the brain is also acted on by the soul which has some power to change cerebral impressions just as those impressions in their turn have the power to arouse thoughts which do not depend on the will...

Notice the smooth transition from cerebral impressions, to memory (present in animals, one supposes, in purely corporeal fashion—those 'traces' that still plague psychology—) to 'thoughts,' which ought, according to Descartes, to be unique to us. He goes on:

> Consequently, the term 'passion' can be applied in general to all the thoughts which are thus aroused in the soul by cerebral impressions alone, without the concurrence of the will, and therefore without any action of the soul itself; for whatever is not an action is a passion (*AT*, iv, p.310; *K*, p.178).

Here is the general doctrine of action and passion to be enunciated in the *Treatise*. And Descartes then distinguishes the general from the special use:

> Commonly, however, the term is restricted to thoughts which are caused by some extraordinary agitation of the spirits. For thoughts that come from external objects, or from the interior dispositions of the body—such as the perception of colours, sounds and smells, hunger, thirst, pain, and so on—are called external or internal sensations. Those that depend on the traces left by previous impressions in the memory and the ordinary motion of the spirits are dreams, whether they are real dreams in sleep or day dreams in waking life when the soul does not determine itself to anything of itself, but idly follows the impressions on the brain (*AT*, iv, pp.310–11; *K*, p.178).

Then comes the account of imagination that I referred to earlier, and which, again, is adhered to in the *Treatise* itself:

> When the soul, on the other hand, uses the will to determine itself to some thought which is not just intelligible, but also imaginable, this thought makes a new impression on the brain, which is not, from the soul's point of view, a passion, but an action; and this is what is properly called imagination (*AT*, iv, p.311; *K*, p.178).

A kind of spirit writing! Then there is a further distinction, of disposition from passion—a distinction difficult to deal with in Cartesian terms, which allow no potencies, worked up or otherwise—but he is talking here, I suppose, about ordinary usage, not ontology:

> Finally, when the normal behaviour of the spirits is such that it commonly arouses sad or cheerful thoughts or the like, this is not attributed to passion, but to the nature or humour of the man in whom they are aroused; and so we say that one man has a sad nature, another is of a cheerful humour, and so on. So there remain only the thoughts that come from some special agitation of the spirits, whose effects are felt as in the soul itself. It is these that are passions properly so called. (*AT*, iv, p.311; *K*, p.178).

That sounds straightforward enough, if anything about the action of a body on a soul or a soul on a body can be straightforward. But it turns out that in fact actions of the soul, both of imagination (as just described) and judgment, intervene in this process—and that is how we move, I presume, from the mere movements of animals, and of our own bodies, to passions proper. Descartes writes:

> Sometimes also people confuse the inclinations or habits which dispose to a certain passion with the passion itself, though the two are easy to distinguish. For instance when it is announced in a town that enemies are coming to besiege it, the inhabitants at once make a judgment about the evil which may result to them: this judgment is an action of their soul and not a passion (*AT*, iv, p.312; *K*, p.179).

It is here that individual differences come into play. As Descartes puts it:

> though this judgment is to be found in many alike, they are not all equally affected by it; some are more affected than others in proportion to the greater or less habit or inclination they have towards fear (*AT*, iv, p.312; *K*, p.179).

A Cartesian account of habit, however, as we noticed, will be difficult if not impossible to carry through. The very concept calls for Aristotelian implementation—God, clarity and distinctness forbid!—or lapses into the murky realm of common notion three. A third way will be to rely on the weasel word 'motion'. For 'motion' has allegedly been purged of its scholastic ambiguity and means change of place. Yet we speak—Descartes speaks—of movements of the soul, that non-spatial, non-locatable being. Thus, in the present context, he continues:

> Their souls can receive the motion that constitutes the passion only after they have made the judgment (*AT*, iv, p.312; *K*, p.179).

Yet if passions are modes of soul, as Descartes insists they are, how can a motion 'constitute a passion'? Motions belong to bodies, not to minds. Here is the very kind of *metabasis eis allo genos* that Descartes so deplores in scholastic, and everyday, thought. And then again we have the action of imagination as somehow parallel to judgment. For if the souls of those in question have not made the judgment, Descartes continues, they have

> at least conceived the danger without making a judgment, and then imprinted an image of it on the brain, by another action, namely imagination.

In this case, the soul

> acts upon the spirits, which travel from the brain through the nerves into the muscles, and makes them enter the muscles which close the openings of the heart (*AT*, iv, pp.312–13; *K*, p.179).

The soul, therefore, has now acted on the body—'imprinting an image,' 'acting on the spirits'—, and the body, reciprocating, 'acts', still indirectly, on the mind. For the spirits have now been forced, by the soul's imaginative action, to enter the muscles of the valves. And this in turn

> retards the circulation of the blood, so that the whole body becomes pale, cold and trembling, and

—now we have it—

> the spirits returning from the heart to the brain are agitated in such a way that they are useless for forming any images except those which excite in the soul the passion of fear (*AT*, iv, p.313; *K*, p.179).

Note the teleological language: 'useless except for. . .'. And note also that now, in *Meditations* style, or indeed in that of other Cartesian texts, images are formed in the brain. Far from being acts of the soul, they have turned, in the space of a paragraph, into cerebral, that is, corporeal motions. And they 'excite' in the soul—whatever that may mean—the passion, a surrogate motion, so to speak, if we retain the causal-corporeal context, or alternatively, if we want to achieve clarity and distinctness, a pure subjective feeling, for which, as geometer-physicists, we infer a mechanical-causal frame.[5] Taking this paragraph as a whole, finally, we have to conclude: that passions, strictly speaking, far from being direct effects of body on mind, are effects of body on mind consequent on actions of mind both in itself (judgment) and on the brain (imagination). In terms of this account, we would suppose, animals are indeed passionless; vivisect all you like, you are not causing pain, only motions—which, for some odd reason, are contrived to imitate the motions that, in us, accompany pain. After all, we kick and scream, too, sometimes, without knowing we're doing it.

8

Elizabeth, I regret to admit, never objects to this fundamental account, with its appalling implications, although she does, after reading the treatise that eventuates from Descartes's reflections, wonder about some of the detailed bodily motions that are supposed to produce certain responses in the soul. Insofar as the correspondence continues to raise philosophical points, they concern chiefly her dissatisfaction about the relation between God and our freedom, a dissatisfaction which Descartes, as a philosopher rather than a theologian, is quite incapable of putting to rest. For the present purpose, however, we need pursue the exchange no further: with Descartes's interest in the passions established, we may look in conclusion at some of his last pronouncements on them, especially in the context of the question of their existence or non-existence in animals. Without entering here on any detailed analysis of the *Passions*, I may, I think fairly, point out its fundamental incoherence in the light chiefly of the basic doctrine of Part 1. When one looks at it closely, Cartesian mind-body interaction really does break down. And finally, I want to look at three letters, one (probably) to the Marquis of Newcastle and two to Henry More, which illustrate the ambiguities introduced into Descartes's *bête-machine,* once a detailed study of the human case has undermined the easy dogmatism of the 1630s.

We have already noticed the context of action and passion in general, within which Descartes carves out the space of the passions strictly speaking. In Article 27 he comes to the definition of these; they are

> perceptions or feelings or emotions of the soul, which we relate particularly to it, and which are caused, sustained and fortified by some movement of the spirits (*AT*, xi, p.349).

And he proceeds to justify this definition in the next two articles. What is supposed to preserve automatism intact, evidently, is the relation of the passions to the soul itself. We have perceptions of things outside us, of our own bodies, and perceptions referred in particular to the soul. While strictly animals have *no* perceptions, it is the third kind they most conspicuously lack; their brains could presumably follow through the same sequence of motions as ours and, thoughtlessly, 'initiate' appropriate movements—as other automata do. But there would be no self-reference. Even in our case, Descartes believes, many movements occur without thought through the pure mechanism of the body. People often fail to distinguish purely bodily events, internal as well as external, from actions—or passions—of the soul. So, he adjures Elizabeth, we must be careful to differentiate between hunger and such bodily appetites and desire: only the last is a passion (*AT*, iv, pp.311–12). A remark, probably to Arnauld, in 1648 seems to clarify this point. We should distinguish, Descartes says, between direct and 'reflex' (reflective?) thoughts. In response to a question about infantile amnesia, he has distinguished between corporeal traces and those sufficient for memory, that is, accompanied by a purely intellectual awareness of novelty—thus, incidentally, contradicting the ascription of memory to animals in the letter of 6 October 1645. Again, in any detailed explanation of mind-brain relations there is a slippery back and forth between what is and is not corporeal—souls are always thinking, but yet in a way not always; animals remember yet in a way do not. But that is by the way. Descartes goes on:

> Finally, I make a distinction between direct and reflex (reflexive) thoughts corresponding to the distinction we make between direct and reflexive vision, one depending on the first impact of the rays and the other on the second. I call the first and simple thoughts of infants direct and not reflexive—for instance, the pain they feel when some wind distends their intestines, or the pleasure they feel when nourished by sweet blood. But when an adult feels something, and simultaneously perceives that he has not felt it before, I call this second perception reflexion, and attribute it to the intellect alone, in spite of its being so linked to sensation that the two occur together and appear to be indistinguishable from each other (*AT*, v, pp.220–1; *K*, p.234).

On the one hand we may notice that here, as often (in speaking of movements of the soul, for example) a physical analogy is made to carry a thesis about mind.[6] And on the other hand it seems that Descartes already needed, and used without calling it such, something like Harry Frankfurt's concept of second-order desires, or rather, more generally, second-order awareness, as the mark of human uniqueness (Frankfurt, 1971).

Now such a distinction, like the old idealist one between consciousness and self-consciousness, appears at first sight metaphysically neutral. It would fit perfectly well, one supposes, with the automatism/intellect duality of the *Discourse* and *Meditations*. When applied in detail, however, in the account of mind-body interaction, it becomes increasingly implausible: witness, for example, the inconsistent account of 'memory' just noticed. Indeed, the story told in *Passions* I, articles 31–7, about the operation of the pineal gland, can only be taken as a joke. In perception, the pineal gland 'acts immediately on the soul', making it see an external object (*AT*, xi, p.356); and similarly for the passions: the spirits of the brain open or keep open the cerebral pores that lead to the nerves:

> For from this alone that these spirits enter into these pores, they excite a particular movement in this gland, which is instituted by nature to make the soul feel this passion (*AT*, xi, p.357).

Apart from any other problems, what did Descartes think the pineal gland was doing in other animals? Was it put there to [illegible] us by a non-deceiving God, as some people were to [illegible] sils were set as a temptation into the rocks? Be that as it may, movements also go on not connected with the soul:

> In the same way that the course the spirits take towards the nerves of the heart is sufficient to give the movement to the gland, *by which fear is placed in the soul*, thus too through this alone that some spirits go at the same time towards the nerves, which serve to move the legs to flee, they cause another movement in the same gland, by means of which the soul feels and perceives that flight, which can in this way be excited in the body by the sole disposition of its organs, and without the soul's contribution to it (*AT*, xi, p.358; italics mine).

Just a short step to the James-Lange theory this time! If one is already an absolutely convinced dualist, I suppose this might not sound wildly implausible. But with the best will in the world (which I confess to lacking) it is hard to work. For example, Descartes himself speaks in Part III of 'impressions joined to that of good and evil in the brain' (*AT*, xi, p.398). Surely if there is anything the soul does 'by itself' it is perceiving good and evil! In other words, once one seriously tries to cash in Cartesian intellectualism and/or automatism, the cerebralisation of mind as well as the psychologising of body (as in the remarks on animal memory) are bound to follow.

9

The basic difficulty becomes clearest, finally, in the language in which Descartes writes both (probably) to the Marquis of Newcastle and to Henry More about animals. Let me look briefly in conclusion at these passages.

In a letter of 23 November 1646, Descartes explains why he cannot share the opinion of Montaigne and others 'who attribute understanding and thought to animals'. There are two expressions in this text that deserve mention. After recalling the actions we too perform without thought, he continues:

> I think also that if we had no thought we would eat, as the animals do, without having to learn to; and it is said that those who walk in their sleep sometimes swim across streams in which they would drown if they were awake (*AT*, iv, pp.573–4; *K*, p.206).

And he continues:

> As for the movements of our passions, even though in us they are accompanied by thought because we have the faculty of thinking, it is none the less very clear that they do not depend on thought, because they often occur in spite of us. Consequently they can also occur in animals, even more violently than they do in human beings, without our being able to conclude from this that they have thoughts (*AT*, iv, pp.573–4; *K*, p.206).

'The movements of our passions', then, occur without thought and may therefore occur also in animals. At first sight it seems, therefore, that passions are also ascribed to animals. But this would be inaccurate: it is the *movements*, which Descartes has tried to separate from the passion in our case, that can also occur in animals. So, though slippery, this *may* be read as less than a counter-use to the automata sense. Even with that reading, however, there is still the question of passions in us—feelings caused, if indirectly, by extreme agitation of the spirits as distinct from thoughts—that is, from perceptions whether externally or internally caused or even caused by the soul itself. The 'passions' hang there as a kind of anomaly perched between the thoughts we harbour and animals lack and the mere physical movements their bodily machines, just like ours, are contrived to carry out.

The next paragraph of the same letter is even more difficult to square with Descartes's earlier view. In contrasting vocal expressions taught to animals with true speech, he says:

> I add also that these words or signs *must not express any passion*, to rule out not only cries of *joy* or *sadness* and the like, but also whatever can be taught by training to animals. If you teach a magpie to say goodday to its mistress, when it sees her approach, this can only be by making the utterance of this word *express one of its passions*. For instance it will be an expression of the *hope* of eating, if it has always been given a titbit when it says it. Similarly, all the things which dogs, horses, and monkeys are taught to perform are only expressions of *their fear*, *their hope*, or *their joy*; and consequently can be performed without any thought (*AT*, iv, p.574; *K*, pp.206–7; my italics).

Here it is not the movements accompanying passions, but the expression of passion that must be eliminated in examining cases of pseudo-speech. Yet the recurrent references to hope, fear and joy clearly ascribe these emotions to the animals in the case—as Descartes in the famous passage in the Replies to the Fourth Objections had emphatically refused to do. Here, it seems to me, the doctrine of the *bête-machine* and, with it, the doctrine of the pure automatism of the bodies of all animals including ourselves, has clearly broken down.

Similarly, in the first letter to More, Descartes concludes his usual abjuration of the infantile prejudice about animals with the remark:

> I am not disturbed by the astuteness and cunning of dogs and foxes, or all the things which animals do for the sake of food, sex and fear; I claim that I can easily explain the origin of all of them from the constitution of their organs (*AT*, v, p.276; *K*, p.243).

Now clearly, 'food and sex' can be interpreted as purely corporeal: one thinks of Freud's famous *Project*. But fear? It is less than a decade since Descartes had insisted that a sheep does *not* fear a wolf; it is only a question of the light reflected in its eyes. And again in this letter he refers to 'natural impulses of anger, fear, hunger' and so on (*AT*, v, p.278). True, he had distinguished hunger from desire for food; but how can anger, any more than fear, be interpreted as other than a feeling? In the next paragraph, moreover, he remarks:

> I do not deny life to animals, since I regard it as consisting simply in the heat of the heart; and I do not deny sensation, insofar as it depends on a bodily organ (*AT*, v, p.278; *K*, p.245).

Granted, this statement typically degrades life to heat; but how can Cartesian animals be held to *sense*? Sensing is either just motion, and so non-sentient, or it is thought: even when I sense or see (that is, seem to see), that is something I do as *res cogitans*; it is a mode of mind.

In the letter to More of 15 April 1649, further, there is an equally odd remark. More had asked, charmingly, 'Don't dogs nod with their tails as we do with our heads?' (*AT*, v, p.311). Descartes replies by dismissing tail-wagging as 'a movement accompanied by a passion'. (*AT*, v, p.344; *K*, p.251). So, it appears, animals *do* have passions. Admittedly, Descartes's response could be short for something like the following: when *we* nod, we think assent; dogs wag their tails in a similar motion—imitating our movement of assent, but without thought or judgment. So the movement that in us would be accompanied by a passion: a passive yes-saying in the Soul—in their case has *no* such accompaniment. But that seems a very far-fetched reading.

One last small paradox in the correspondence with More: On 5 February Descartes admits that his inference about animals is merely probable, 'since the human mind does not reach into their hearts' (*AT*, v, p.277). But in August he remarks flatly, also to More: 'I never decide about questions on which I have no certain reasons and I never allow conjectures into my system' (*AT*, v, p.402). So much then for the *bête-machine*, one would have supposed.

These are slight texts, if you like, on which to hang my argument. But together with the exchange with Elizabeth they suggest the place at which the Cartesian enterprise, motivated by the hope for a new physics, reached the limit of its explanatory power: in the concrete life of feeling, which Descartes, mathematician, physicist, expatriate and would-be recluse, had done his best to avoid, and in the way in which attention to that embodied yet sentient aspect of our own experience confounds the attempt to cut ourselves off from the norm of animal existence in which, without the artifice of Cartesian method, we would find ourselves spontaneously at home.[7]

Notes

1. There is a qualification omitted in the French: II, pp.25–8: '*quamvis nondum sciamus quae sit causa, cur ita nos afficiant*'.
2. *See* also e.g. *AT*, iii, p. 472.
3. *See* chapter 3 below.
4. This is not a usual Cartesian theme. One wonders whether it renders the Thomistic view of natural law, but that is mere surmise.
5. Note that we *know* the cause: *see* note 1 above.
6. *See* for example one of the notes copied by Leibniz:

   > If we should compare the modes of mind with the modes of body, we would say that perception is nothing but, as it were, rest in the body; perception of the thing, like motion; perception of the thing by understanding, like circular motion; by doubting, like quivering motion; extension, like the magnitude of the thing thought; duration in either direction, like relation in either direction (*AT*, xi, p.650).

7. For a demonstration of the way in which even Descartes's mechanism is rendered incoherent by his view of the mind-body relation, *see* Gabbey (1984).

3 *Truth and Fiction in Cartesian Methodology*

1

The preceding chapters have established, or ought to have established, two general conclusions about the Cartesian enterprise. Both have to do with Descartes's opposition to scholasticism, though equally with the positive issue of that opposition. First, as we learned, *via* a reading of Gueroult's interpretation of the *Meditations*, Descartes's aim was 'to lead the mind away from the senses', to liberate the intellect from its dependence, learned in infancy and reinforced at school, on what the senses seem to tell us about our world. And that means at the same time to break the mind's habit of making, irresponsibly, hasty and confusing existential judgments based on sense. As the *Principles* emphasise, there is nothing wrong with sense taken as subjective. What seems seems. But the seemings of sense provide inadequate evidence of what there is. It is that kind of evidence, and the hasty judgments based on it, that the Deceiving Demon is called on to suspend. We will deny that there *is* earth, sky and so on. The common-sense-x-scholastic judgments called in the Third Meditation 'adventitious' which lead us to judge that something *like* what we sense is *there*, outside, somehow: *those* are the questionable affirmations the Demon leads us to suspend, or rather, for the time being, to deny.

This therapeutic denial has, at the same time, the positive effect of liberating the mature intellect from its dependence on sense and sense-based judgment to the clear and responsible inspection of evidence and the affirmation, ever after, of only such judgments as pure emancipated thought shall authorise. Hence the Fourth Meditation's imperative: keep the will always within the bounds of the understanding. Only the intellect, which has loosed the shackles of impeding flesh, can go straight to the evidence, affirm what is affirmable and deny what is to be denied.

It follows also from this view of Descartes's undertaking, as, again, Chapter 1 has emphasised, that the locus of truth has shifted from the judgments, or propositions, beloved of the School, to clear and distinct ideas: to what J.L. Marion, following Hamelin, calls 'atoms of evidence' (Marion, 1975, p. 135). As will become plain in what follows, Cartesian method cannot be understood in terms of any propositional logic, whether classical or post-Fregean. It is another game altogether, some aspects of which the present chapter will investigate. Frankfurt has argued that Descartes's defence of reason falls short of a correspondence theory (Frankfurt, 1970, p. 25). I believe, on the contrary, that the claim of Cartesian reason — though qualified, indeed, by the incomprehensibility of God's omnipotence — goes radically beyond, or better, perhaps, bypasses Thomistic adequation, and cuts free mind loose from its ties to a sensed reality. 'Correspondence' fails, not because it goes too far in claiming that things are as they appear, but because the 'correspondence theory' rests on a confused conception of the relation of thought to sensory 'evidence', and allows our power of evidential insight to remain entangled in a web of habit from which it needs to, and can, with God's help, cut itself loose. The (in)famous alienation of the modern mind from nature *is* its Cartesian liberation.

The second conclusion, which in turn provides the problematic for this chapter, was incidental to the explicit theme of chapter 2. Descartes's study of the passions arose, not from his own intellectual need, but at Elizabeth's instigation; the impasse he arrived at in consequence displays the limits rather than the positive power of his method, and of the ontology on which it rests. But incidentally to our argument about the passions we found Descartes asserting as one of the practical consequences of his philosophy the solace to be derived from a mechanistic interpretation of nature. It was the turn to mechanism, we found, which, on Descartes's view, was to free our reason in practice as well as theory from the superstitions of the past and the prejudices of infancy. A modern, but much firmer, analogue of Stoic reason would be established, Descartes believed, by the overthrow of the muddled Peripatetic view of nature and the establishment of a clear, coherent mechanistic physics (and eventually physic) in its stead.

This thesis, too, has both its negative and positive aspects. Against scholasticism, Descartes insists on abolishing all forms of change except local motion only. Thus while preserving (at least in an impoverished form) the concept of substance, he wants to ban substantial change. True, each finite mind is created *ex nihilo*, but so, at the beginning, was nature. Thus Descartes can, on principle, he believes, give an account of generation and development without recourse to substantial forms or other traditional explanatory principles, which, in fact, on his view, have never succeeded in explaining anything at all (*AT*, vii, pp. 597–8). Such 'forms' were devised, he holds, through the illegitimate extrapolation from human mentality, the only place in the created world where there *are* substantial forms, to other non-ensouled entities (e.g. AT, vii, pp. 441–3; iii, pp. 420, 434, 661–8, 694; v, pp. 722–3). But if substantial change is an unnecessary concept, so are qualitative alteration and growth. Local motion alone, of the four Aristotelian types of change, is adequate to explain all the events that make up the natural scene.[1]

It seems to be the claim that local motion alone constitutes natural events that most plainly characterises mechanism, or what came, in Britain, to be called 'the new mechanical philosophy'. We shall be concerned with other versions of this general conception when we come to Gassendi. Meantime it must just be noted that, from a later perspective, there is an odd twist to the Cartesian version of mechanistic thought. Descartes still accepts the traditional concept of causality in terms of degrees of being, as in the proofs of God's existence, yet reads cause and effect in nature in the language of impact alone. Locke's concept of power, I suppose, if one can make any sense of it, rests somewhere in between the older emanative view and the modern when-then causality that seems to us most readily associated with mechanistic physics. This question, too, we shall return to later, in the context of Descartes's ontology.

Whatever its ontological foundation, however, the advance Descartes claimed to be making here was radical indeed. He was substituting for the complicated would-be explanations of the School, with their forms and quiddities and acts and potencies, a single account of nature in terms of position and changes in position. For a complex muddle of categories he would substitute — geometry. In the *Rules* he had initiated the project of a universal mathematics, not literally a mathematics, but a unified science containing only concepts as clear and simple as those of arithmetic and geometry.[2] It turns out, however, that for all entities except God and the mind, mathematics, and in particular geometry, indeed, more especially analytical geometry, offers the unique instrument of knowledge. The first move Descartes makes is the clear-cut separation of mind from body; the second is the geometrisation of nature.

As we shall see more clearly in the following chapter, and as commentators in the French tradition have demonstrated with increasing subtlety (e.g. Gilson, 1913; Gouhier, 1924, 2nd ed. 1972; Marion, 1981), Descartes has no intention whatsoever of effecting by these twin alterations an overthrow of the traditional cosmology. He is not a 'modern', like Hobbes, sweeping away (except for substance, be it said) an accepted, and acceptable, theistic conceptual apparatus.[3] He wants *only* to effect a reform sufficient to permit to the mathematical mind access to a readily mathematicisable nature. Together, the mind-body break and the reduction of the external world to extension provide the wherewithal for this undertaking.

Short of its ontological foundation, what is this enterprise? I have no intention, and no competence, to set forth the details, or even the physiognomy, of Cartesian physics.[4] It is the method, and epistemology, of the project that I want to look at here. There are oddities about it that have led to conflicting interpretations. Although I shall touch on a few of these to begin with, the resolution I shall favour leans very heavily on the work of J.L. Marion. This holds both for the interpretation of the *Rules*, where my own earlier view is immensely strengthened by his commentary, and for the interpretation of Cartesian 'fictions', where I shall be following what seems to me a radically new reading of the Cartesian texts.

2

Descartes, everyone knows, was after certainty, a certainty never before achieved, witness the fact that in the past, on every subject, experts have disagreed. And as Descartes points out, when two people disagree, neither can have the truth (*AT*, x, p. 363). If one of them did, and both were rational, he would of course persuade the other. This shilly-shallying of opinions Descartes is out to alter, or rather to put a stop to, once and for all. He will find, he is confident, indeed, has found, a sure and unshakable foundation on which to build the sciences. If the 'quest for certainty' characterises philosophy until, and even well into, the twentieth century, it is nowhere more conspicuous than in the writings of Descartes. He will have no truck with anything merely conjectural; only unshakable evidence will do.

On the other hand, there are two areas in which he appears to contradict the restriction of his method to what cannot be doubted. Instead of moving from certainty to certainty, eliminating all conjecture, in writing about physics he admits hypotheses into his reasoning, and, more sweepingly, he devises descriptions of the world itself and of the human body which are, in both cases, not by admission only, but by boast, 'fables'. How do guesswork and fiction fit into Cartesian methodology? That is the question I wish to raise and, I hope, answer in the following sections of this chapter.

To raise it, however, one must first be clear about the nature of Cartesian method insofar as it does seek indubitability. Only then can one discover where the hypothetical and fictional moments fit into it. The first point to notice—and this cannot be too heavily emphasised—is that the Cartesian road to knowledge is not, in the logician's sense, the way of proof. Descartes himself stressed, in the Replies to Second Objections, that he had employed in the *Meditations* the method of analysis, or resolution, the way of discovery, in contrast to the method of synthesis, or of composition, the way of exposition.[5] Admittedly the *Principles* combine both methods, since in part at least they summarise results already achieved. But Descartes's great discovery, in his youth, had been the discovery of the method of discovery, and that is 'analysis', not 'synthesis'. As Ian Hacking argues in contrasting him with Leibniz, Descartes did not know what a proof was, and didn't care (Hacking, 1980). What he cared about was something quite different from logicians' fun and games; what he cared about, what he believed he was introducing to the world, was a way to move to new knowledge, to all the knowledge possible to us, indeed—to move to that new knowledge from a first firm and indubitable step, *via* intermediates just as firm and certain. Whatever this method is, it is not, in either a classical or modern sense, deductive. If we are to understand at all the reform Descartes intended to initiate, we must rid our minds of any conception of him as an *a priorist*, in the sense of someone who sets up axioms and demonstrates theorems that flow from them. Hacking is right about that; Descartes has no interest in proofs, no feeling for proofs; his fundamental concern is different: to apply his mathematical tools to the discovery, previously undisclosed, of the essential nature of nature.

In such a project what matters is not the formal relation of premises to conclusions, but the ordering of thoughts—*methodos*, the way one is on, and the sequence of steps one takes on it. Far more clearly than in the popularising *Discourse*, the scheme for that method was laid down, probably about 1627, in the unfinished *Rules for the Direction of the Mind*.[6] As Victor Cousin put it in the preface to his edition of Descartes,

> They surpass perhaps in lucidity the *Meditations* and the *Discourse on Method*... One sees here still more openly the fundamental aim of Descartes and the spirit of that revolution that has created modern philosophy and placed forever in thought the principle of all certainty (Cousin (1826) in Marion (1975), p.18).

Anyone who has once read the *Discourse*, and indeed the *Meditations*, in the light of the *Rules*, must agree with Cousin's statement (whatever one may believe by now of the eternity of Descartes's principle of certainty; that's another question!). For what emerges so lucidly from that fragmentary text is not only the serial nature of Cartesian method, the importance of ordering, so much insisted on by Gueroult in his reading of Cartesian metaphysics. What is exhibited so clearly there also is the character of the units of which the series is to be composed. Much more subtly than in the *Meditations*, let alone in its Lockean bowdlerisation, but still recognisably the same, the new way of ideas is there given its first and classic statement. The new beginning so often celebrated as stemming from Descartes consists essentially in the aim of building a stable edifice of knowledge, a construction in which the choice of materials, so to speak, the selection of the right building blocks, is all-important. Clear away all the old rubbish, select the very simplest items to start with: simple natures, and build with them step by step, from the easiest insight to the more advanced, never turning aside for any speculative trimmings, however elegant or subtle. Eschew conjectures in favour of certainties, however simple; order these rightly, and you will achieve a unified science that will endure for all time to come. As every reader of the *Meditations* knows, Cartesian knowledge is built of, and only of, clear and distinct ideas. But what a clear and distinct idea is, is best understood, it seems to me, as to many others, in the light of the exposition of *intuition* and allied concepts in the *Rules*, Descartes explains in the body of the Third Rule what he means by this crucial term:

> By *intuition* I understand, not the fluctuating faith of the senses or the fallacious judgment of a badly compounding imagination, but the conception of a pure and attentive mind, so distinct, that absolutely no doubt remains about what we are understanding; or, what is the same thing, the undoubting conception of a pure and attentive mind, which is born of the light of reason alone, and is more certain even than deduction, because simpler, even though we have already noted that the latter cannot be badly performed by man (*AT*, x, p.368).

There will be other steps along the way, movements of mind, alternatively described as deductions, inductions, enumerations—more of them shortly—but intuition is the norm for knowledge, what it ought, as much as possible, to be. And what *is* intuition, in the light of the above brief, two-sided description? It is the performance of a 'pure and attentive mind', set free, as we have seen, from the snares of sense, free, equally, of any lurking doubt, on the one hand, because of its source: it 'springs from reason alone', and on the other, because it is a conception so plain that it leaves no doubt about *that which is apprehended.* In other words, it is an act of mind directed toward a simple, wholly lucid and therefore indubitable target. Again, to quote Hamelin and Marion, it is an *atom of evidence*. It has *objectivity*, not as corresponding to an other than mental reality in which somehow our cognitive powers are situated, but in itself, as an intellectual insight into a content clear and distinct, evident, in its own intentional bearing. Thus the alienation of mind from nature that Descartes is seeking is not, or not yet, a turn to some inner,

Kierkegaardian subjectivity, but a turn to *evidence*. It is meant to give us, for the construction of a unified science, a unit, not, admittedly, out in the world of things, but somewhere between *mere* subjectivity and things-quite-other-than mentality, a unit of significance. And yet the signified is here wholly at one with its sign. The *cogito* will be of course the instance *par excellence* of such a unity: there *can* be no schism between myself thinking now about my thinking *and* that thinking. But each intuition, each clear and distinct idea, exhibits, ideally at least, that coalescence of intention and intended, of thinker and thought.

3

I could go on, as I have done elsewhere, to talk about the movements of thought that are needed by our finite minds in their present location at one (somehow) with pieces of extension, in order to complement, or to complete, the moment of clear and attentive, undoubting thought (Grene, 1983, pp.64–91). But I think the nature of Cartesian method as projected in the *Rules* can best be clarified through reference to their interpretation by J.L.Marion in his commentary, *Sur L'Ontologie Grise de Descartes* (1975). None of the major English language commentaries on Descartes published some years ago refer to this work;[7] yet it provides, in my view, an absolutely authoritative reading of the *Rules*, which puts that text for the first time into a much plainer relation to the published works, as well as to the major philosophical tradition.

There has always been at the least a terminological puzzle about the *Regulae*. On the one hand, why does Descartes use the concept *intuition* here and later drop it in favour of *idea*? And on the other, why does he jumble together in so slovenly a way, as it seems, three distinct cognitive processes, deduction, induction and enumeration? 'Enumeration', it is true, is the name for a specifically Cartesian device—the sorting out of classes of thoughts or judgments, such as that we examined in the arguments considered in Chapter 1. And it does serve perhaps as a tag for the Cartesian version of induction. But how could so careful a thinker as Descartes 'confuse' deduction with induction? Marion's answer to both puzzles is as illuminating as it is original. Descartes was adopting the terminology of the

School in order to reread it in his radically new direction. Granted, the detailed comparison Marion executes is between the Cartesian text and the texts of Aristotle himself, whom Descartes presumably did not study at first hand. But the tradition Descartes was reared in—and was to modify, ontologically, but never to abandon—was, if at nth hand, Aristotelian. And the comparison works astonishingly well. Rather than trying to present Marion's argument in any detail, I shall attempt to give something like the gist of it, first, by quoting a later Cartesian text that Marion also quotes, and then by considering very briefly and sketchily what happens on his reading to the key scholastic (='Aristotelian') terms.

Commenting on Herbert of Cherbury's *De Veritate* in a letter to Mersenne of 16 October 1639, Descartes remarks that he has never, like Herbert, tried to examine what truth is, since it seems to him 'a notion so transcendentally clear that it is impossible not to know it' (*AT*, ii, pp.596–7). What is there to explain? And if one explains what 'truth' nominally means to someone ignorant of the language, and says that strictly 'truth' means the conformity of thought with its object, one must qualify this by pointing out 'that when one attributes it [i.e. truth] to things that are outside thought, one means only that these things can serve as objects to true thoughts, whether ours, or those of God' (*AT*, ii, p.597). Marion remarks:

> A text astonishing for its precision, which expresses perfectly the transformation (or rather disappearance of form, the aformation) of the given and individual thing, which, by abstraction, is reduced to what thought can admit for its object (Marion, 1975, p.62, n. 70).

In other words, the real individual thing, the individuated *atomon eidos*, the form, that is the target of Aristotelian science, is here abandoned for the objective of the intellect, what a true thought can place before the mind. Aristotelian form is the very quintessence of the individual, existent thing. Descartes rejects this alleged foundation of knowledge. It is too subtle, too complicated, too diversifying in the varieties of knowledge it produces, or claims to produce. For it he substitutes the unit of evidence, an indivisible, not in the real world, but present, intellectually, for the mind's inspection. Now this may seem at first a paradoxical move. What Descartes wants, we are supposing, is to change just enough in the scholastic tradition to effect a mathematical *physics*: to permit the geometer's mind to go directly, instead of *via* sense-perception, induction, definition, syllogistic demonstration, to the nature of extended things. But as Duhem pointed out, it was precisely the direct, tied-down empiricism of Aristotelian method that prevented its initiation of a mathematical science of nature in the modern style (Duhem in Ross, 1936, pp.81–2). Too many diverse qualities, relations, states could be apparent to the inspector of a given concrete situation. A distancing from experience, from the nature of the concrete thing, was necessary if mathematical concepts were to be applied directly and purely to the understanding of the physical world. And it is just such a loosening of thought from experience that the Cartesian turn acknowledges—in order, more directly, *via* an intellection unmediated by sense, to approach reality in its mathematicisable and evident nature. If the nature of nature as described in the Fifth Meditation is ever to be discovered, of course in its due order, then, *eidos*, the *form* of the tradition in its individuality and concreteness, must go. And a new indivisible, the atom of evidence, the single, intelligible target of a clear, unsullied act of attention, must take its place. In all the Cartesian created universe, indeed, only one form remains: the human mind, which, in this life at least, serves as the 'substantial form' of that particular piece of extension that happens to serve, for the time being, as that particular mind's body (*See* e.g. *AT*, vii, pp.356, 587; iii, pp.503, 505).

I have wandered away from Marion's terse comment on this particular text, but not really far from the point. That is: that in the *Rules* Descartes has quite self-consciously used against itself the discourse of Aristotelian methodology. Intuition, in his sense, as the act of an undoubting mind, replaces *nous*: the unification of the intellect with the *eidos* it is engaged in understanding. The apprehension, or what is the same thing, the enactment of what Descartes will later call a clear and distinct idea becomes not only, in parallel to Aristotelian *nous*, the unique starting point (*arche*) of science, but its chief component, its target at every stage along the way. But at the same time this constantly reenacted moment of truth is shorn of its Aristotelian rooting in real *things*. The object of thought—the *true* object of *true* thought—can be directly mathematical only if it is held at a distance from the concrete *eide* with which, both in ordinary life and in the too common-sensical Aristotelian tradition, we are continually engaged. We were all infants once, and in our everyday life as well as in our confused scholastic heritage are still inclined to think like infants about some all-too distracting this-such-here-now. A radical turn to maturity is needed, a turn *against* the *eidos* of and in the thing, to the evidentiality of the pure intentional *object*. It is the difficult road to such maturity, of course, that will be initiated through the discipline of the *Meditations*.

Intuition, then, is transformed to its peculiar Cartesian, intentional and intellectual, less than wholly ontological status. As Marion puts it, it is 'a-formed', from an Aristotelian point of view, one would want to say, 'de-formed'. (A better pun, in fact, since it carries the notion of distorting form as well as of abolishing it.) But what of deduction, so oddly equated with induction? In the absence of *eidos*, Marion argues, this move, too, was bound to happen. For the movement of a Cartesian inquiring mind there is no proper middle term. The genus falls out, so to speak, with the species, and only *epagoge* or 'induction', the counting of cases, in short, enumeration, remains. The scholastic vocabulary has served its turn, for Descartes, by undermining, on his reading of the fundamental act of understanding, its own distinction. There remains only the careful step by step course along the paving stones of Cartesian intuition, with enumeration our possible next move when the single next step is not yet univocally clear. So deduction gives way to induction, which *is* enumeration, and there is only a twofold method: intuition of the simplest notions at the start, and, indeed, intuition always wherever possible, with enumeration sorting out alternatives at junctures where the mind cannot yet plainly move without assistance from one clear and attentive, undoubting conception to the next.

Such is Cartesian method, going, certainty after certainty, straight to the confrontation with its object, and empowered to do so precisely by its abandonment of the rootedness in the things themselves that had characterised the science of the past. But Cartesian objects are not yet Kantian appearances. They are characteristically neither things in themselves, like Aristotelian *eide*, nor radically cut off from them, as Kantian phenomena will be. It is their peculiar in-between objectivity, and the intellectual certitude that is intrinsic to it, that most clearly marks the Cartesian project as the starting-point of modernity. It is this objectivity, finally, that carries with it, constantly and unshakably, from one step in discovery to the next, the certitude Descartes not only demands, but believes he has achieved.[8]

4

There is, Descartes himself insists, no place for 'probability' here, no place, one would have thought, for conjecture or hypothesis. Yet Descartes himself just as plainly admits the hypothetical nature of some part of his physics, and more than that, he carefully contrives both his 'world' and his 'man' as fictions: a new world, a new man, indistinguishable, indeed, from those we see around us, but nevertheless invented, devised by René Descartes for our instruction. That both these 'fables' remained unpublished in his lifetime does not cancel out the seriousness of the project. Indeed, the fictional nature of his cosmological method is stressed again in the *Principles*, the most systematic formulation of his physics that he did publish. So we have urgently to ask about Cartesian science, how it can proceed *via* certainties only, yet also *via* hypothesis-mongering and story-telling.[9]

There have been various answers to this question. Fusing hypotheses and fictions, Alquié has argued that, at the period when he was writing *Le Monde*, Descartes's method was a hypothetico-deductive one, even anticipating the conventionalism of Duhem or Poincaré. 'A made, forged, machine-built universe', he says, 'could only be a feigned world' (Alquié, 1960, pp.113–14). And it is just such a fictional procedure that seems to characterise the hypothetico-deductive method. You invent a story—any old story—and see if the facts fit it. F.Mentré has presented a similar interpretation of the *Principles* themselves (1904, cited in Rodis-Lewis, 1971, ii, p.496, n. 23), and Larry Laudan has recently put forward a parallel view for the methodology of both Descartes and Boyle (Laudan, 1981).

Nothing, it seems to me, could be much more implausible. True, the texts are there. Descartes does admit to using hypotheses.[10] He does celebrate his world, his man, as fables (*AT*, xi, pp.48, 97, 119–20). Yet in every case, or almost every case,[11] so far as I can tell, he explains the use of invention as ancillary to the indubitability and stability of his fundamental principles.[12] And that is not the so-called H-D method, whether of conjecture and refutation or conjecture and confirmation. It is a method of clear and distinct ideas, supported by fictional devices which give imaginative aid, where necessary, to its underlying certainties. True, when the experiential, or experimental, evidence is very direct and clear, Descartes admits, one may present statements unrelated to the principles of physics. But even this, I believe, would be for Descartes a temporary situation only. Given the principles of his physics, observations once made out of relation to them would take on a different sense. And, as he insists over and over, one really needs the whole of his physics (which, unfortunately, he had better not publish) to see how principles and consequences really hang together. It is the advance from certainty to certainty, never faltering into probability, that matters. Hypotheses in physics, like the hypothetical, or hyperbolical, doubt of Meditation One, are instruments of such certainty, never a substitute for it.

There are a number of convincing, indeed, in my view, overwhelming, reasons to take this stand. I shall mention three, the first of which is very general, while the second and third offer what seems to me a plausible interpretation of the role of hypotheses and fictions in Cartesian method.

Before I go on to present these arguments, however, I must make a para-Cartesian point about the issue that seems to be involved here. Without wanting to present a caricature of the arguments of such scholars as Alquié and Laudan, I cannot help seeing them as suggesting a scenario somewhat like the following. The method of modern science, it is said, is hypothetico-deductive. Descartes is one of the initiators of modern science. Even though his physics did not amount to much compared to Newton's, he did help to get things going.[13] He certainly did talk about using hypotheses, and even about supporting an hypothesis by finding that observable consequences follow from it and from no alternative theory.[14] In that case he was plainly anticipating in his conception of science good logical empiricists or even, at least as Alquié sees it, conventionalists like Duhem or Poincaré. Maybe I am erecting a straw-man here; if so, my apologies; but all the same he has enough life-likeness, I believe, to need some knocking down. So let me say briefly how I see the relation of Cartesian to modern scientific method as contrasted with the H-D model. That model, I believe, following Polanyi, MacIntyre and others, has really had very little indeed to do with the growth of science (Polanyi, 1958, 1966; MacIntyre, 1981; Grene, 1985). The devising of hypotheses from which phenomena may be deduced—such as the earth's movement or its non-movement, the blood's crossing from arteries to veins and back or flowing back and forth on a single side—such a procedure may help to explain the phenomena in question, and even, if no other conceivable hypothesis can do the job, to explain them necessarily. And indeed Descartes knew this form of argument very well and used it to good purpose, for example, in his controversy with Harvey. Some circulatory phenomena, he held, could be shown to follow from either his account of the heart on Harvey's, but some followed only from his furnace theory and not from Harvey's pump version (*AT*, xi, pp.241–5). Moreover, the H-D model as *the* form of scientific explanation was adopted in the seventeenth century by Thomas Hobbes, who, however, did not himself contribute conspicuously to the explosion of scientific knowledge in his time, much as he admired it. And it was of course revived by the Vienna Circle, in Hobbesian form especially in the physicalist period. But from Austria and England to Chicago and Los Angeles that was chiefly a philosopher's pipe-dream. What science does live by is not any one logical schema, but progressive problem-solving, sometimes approaching formalisability, more often not. And in that respect Cartesian method is indeed very like the procedure of a modern laboratory scientist. Here is the problem, let's solve it, then the next one, and so on. One question at a time, in the right order. But there the similarity stops. For Descartes believed he could accomplish such ordered problem-solving with *certainty*. Only the simple, clear, indubitable was to be admitted to the scope of scientific inquiry. Thus Cartesian science is still contained in the tradition of belief in an *episteme* that is different in kind, in cognitive foundation, in authority, from mere opinion. Ian Hacking has described in *The Emergence of Probability* the turn, with Hume, from this sharp division to a probabilistic view, in which the higher kind of knowledge is assimilated to the lower (Hacking, 1975).[15] Locke still divided knowledge sharply from mere probability or 'judgment', as he called it, and so, for that matter, did Kant. Answering Hume or not, about the causal principle, Kant failed to grasp, or to admit, the radical turn to the conjectural as the sphere of scientific knowledge. But once, willy-nilly, Hume's argument on induction is assimilated, Descartes's alleged progress from solution to solution disappears. Instead we have a (relatively) orderly series of (relatively) successful guesses, rather than a succession of certainties. Here Descartes differs radically from the present-day scientific problem-solver.

That is by the way: just to keep the persistent, but irrelevant, ghost of the H-D method from plaguing us when we seek to understand what Descartes is doing with his 'hypotheses' or his fictional world. Let me proceed, then, to the three points about Cartesian methodology that I want to make.

5

The first, and general, point may be briefly put. It is only to restate what I have already stressed. The warp and woof of Cartesian methodology, the very medium in which it has its being, is *evidence*, luminous, indubitable, unshakable evidence. The Cartesian corpus, when one studies it, simply exudes confidence in such clear, convincing evidence, in intellectual certainty. Whatever role we assign to the hypothetical in Cartesian science, it cannot, it dare not, undercut that first and last and intermediate fact. Hacking, for all his insight in the comparison with Leibniz, goes wildly astray, I find, in attributing Cartesian hypotheses to the philosopher's despair of finding what knowledge is, or recognising it when he has it (Hacking, 1980). Most of the great philosophers, Plato, Aristotle, Spinoza, Leibniz, have claimed in their different ways to possess some path to certainty; but no major thinker is more simply, serenely confident of this than René Descartes. Even when he uses sceptical ploys, he is untouched by them. As Gilson has put it, he borrows the tropes of scepticism, not, like Montaigne, to verify ignorance, but, on the contrary, '*pour vérifier la vérité*' (Gilson, ed., 1967, p.209). Anything approaching *un*certainty, whether doubt or conjecture, is abhorrent to his nature and *a fortiori* to his method.

His strictures on Galileo, for example, confirm this point. About the *Two Great Systems* there is some relatively sketchy evidence, and a good deal more about his reception of the *Two New Sciences*. About the first: in April 1634, he replies to Mersenne's report of Galileo's work, 'denying' what his friend tells him of Galileo's views (*AT*, i, pp.284 ff.). In August he gets a chance, for a day or two, to glance through Beeckman's copy, and he writes to Mersenne of Galileo: 'he philosophises well enough about movement, although there are few things he says that I find entirely true; but so far as I can tell, he goes farther astray when he follows already received opinions that when he is further from them'. And he proceeds to describe some cases in which he has himself anticipated Galileo's views (*AT*, i, p.304). In 1638, when he receives a copy of the *Two New Sciences*, he has a number of comments to make. He writes to Mersenne in October, giving repetitious detailed comments and criticisms. 'In general,' he writes:

> I find that he philosophises much better than the vulgar, in that he leaves as far as he can the errors of the School, and tries to examine physical matters by mathematical reasons. In that I entirely agree with him and I hold that there is no other means at all of finding the truth. But it seems to me that he lacks a great deal in that he constantly makes digressions and does not stop to explain one matter altogether; which shows that he has not examined them in order, and that, without having considered the first causes of nature, he has simply sought for the reasons for some particular effects, and that he has built without foundation. And in so far as his manner of philosophising is closer to the true (method), so much the more easily can one recognise his faults, as one can better say when those go astray who sometimes follow the right path, than when those go astray who never enter it at all (*AT*, ii, p.380).

There follow numerous detailed objections. For example, Galileo treats problems about weight, Descartes objects, without having determined what weight is (*AT*, iii, p.385). (One wonders here about Descartes's own claim to be able to treat light, in the *Dioptrics*, while omitting his own theory of its real nature (e.g. *AT*, ii, pp.201, 424–5)). He denies the constant of acceleration (*AT*, ii, p.387) and on the next page remarks sweepingly: 'That is to say, in a word, that he has built everything in the air' (*AT*, ii, p.388). On the same page (*AT*, ii, pp.388–9), he concludes that there is not much in Galileo's book he would like to have done. The best part, he says, is on music, and he (Descartes) has done that too! After treating of some other matters, he returns to the constant of acceleration, remarking that it may hold sometimes, but not, he believes, always. And finally, he comments in general: 'I'll say to you that the explication of all the things Galileo deals with is very easy on my principles' (*AT*, ii, p.399). Some weeks later, further comments follow in the same vein. Of Galileo on the balance and the lever, he complains, that he explains how, not *why*, as Descartes does (*AT*, ii, p.433). A bit further on, he again insists that the constant of acceleration holds only for some velocities (*AT*, ii, p.435); and further, M. de Beaune is probably wrong in mechanics 'because he follows Galileo' (*AT*, ii, pp.442–3). But the basic trouble, for Descartes, as we have already noticed, is that Galileo, though commendably mathematical, fails to work in the proper order, as Descartes does, but dips in here and there. The tree of natural knowledge must be properly sequential, from root to branch.

6

Well, then, let me face up at last to the question, what this purveyor of certainties means by employing hypotheses and/or fictions in the development and exposition of his science. My second and third points attack this problem more directly. However, I still want to try to keep separate at least for the moment hypotheses and fictions—even if some 'hypotheses' turn out to consist in one sort of fiction. I shall look in particular at two pieces of evidence: the discussion of hypotheses in an exchange of letters with J.B.Morin in 1638, and then the more sweeping case of Descartes's 'fables', especially in the light of J.L.Marion's interpretation of Cartesian science as a code (Marion, 1981).[16]

After the publication of the *Discourse* and accompanying essays, in 1637, Descartes responded to numerous comments and criticisms on his work, a number of which involve the question of his use of hypotheses. On 22 February 1638, for example, he wrote to a Jesuit, presumably one Father Vatier, expressing his delight at the Reverend Father's appreciation of his book (*AT*, i, pp.558 ff., *AT*, i, p.305). Both about the *Dioptrics* and the *Meteors* he explains that his method here is hypothetical, only because he could not at this stage expound the whole of his physics. On the same day on which Descartes was writing to Vatier in these terms, Jean Baptiste Morin, professor of mathematics at Paris, was himself writing to Descartes, expressing doubts similar to those the good Jesuit seems to have put forward. At the start of his letter he places questions about two closely related passages, one at the close of the *Discourse* and the other at the beginning of the *Dioptrics*, where Descartes has explained, or better perhaps, excused, his use of 'suppositions or comparisons' in the latter work, having already remarked that he could not here supply the larger context of his physics, in which everything would assume its proper and more than suppositional place. The opening paragraph of Morin's letter deals with the passage at the close of the *Discourse*, in which Descartes apologises for calling some of the matters introduced in the essay 'suppositions,' and explains that in this context the conclusions, which are effects, are 'demonstrated' by the premises, which are their causes, and 'reciprocally, the latter are demonstrated by the former, which are their effects'. Yet this is not a vicious circle, Descartes insists, since the causes serve 'not so much to prove...as to explain' (*AT*, vi, p.76). Morin writes:

> ...since you have reserved the knowledge of the universal principles and notions of your new physics (the publication of which is passionately desired by all the learned) and since you found your reasonings only on comparisons, or suppositions, of the truth of which one is at least in doubt, it could be sinning against the first precept of your method, which is very good, and which is familiar to me, to assent to your reasonings (*AT*, v, pp.537–8).

That first precept, modified from the *Rules*, reads:

> never to receive anything for true, which I do not know evidently [i.e. with clear evidence] to be such: that is to say, to avoid carefully precipitation and prejudice [*prévention*]; and not to include in my judgments anything more than is presented so clearly and distinctly to my mind, that I [would] have no occasion to call it in doubt (*AT*, vi, p.18).

Clearly the use of suppositions offends against this rule; that is our problem too. But further, there is the difficulty of selecting among competing hypotheses, which often do equally well, and also the problem of cause-effect circularity. Morin continues:

> And although, according to page 76 of your Method, experience makes very certain most of the effects you treat, nevertheless you know very well that the appearance of the heavenly motions can be derived with just as great certainty from the stability of the earth as from the supposition of its mobility; and thus that the experience of this phenomenon is not sufficient to prove which of the two causes is the true one. And if it is true that to prove effects from a given cause, then to prove this same cause by those same effects, is not a logical circle, Aristotle misunderstood this, and one might say that no such circle can be made at all! (*AT*, i, p.538).

Descartes's reply to the first point sounds at the start modestly 'hypothetical'. He writes:

> You begin with my hypotheses. You say that the phenomena of the heavenly movements can be deduced with no less certainty from the hypothesis that the earth is stationary than from the hypothesis that it moves. I agree readily. I hope that people will take in the same way what I have written in the *Dioptrics* about the nature of light, so that the force of the mathematical demonstrations which I have tried to set out there will not be dependent on any opinion in Physics, as I said sufficiently clearly on p.3 [of the *Dioptrics, AT,* vi, p.83]. If there is some other way of imagining light which will explain all the properties of it that we know from experience, it will be seen that all I have demonstrated about refraction, vision and so on, can be derived from it just as well as from the hypothesis I proposed (*AT*, ii, p.196; *K*, p.57).

In other words, mathematical demonstrations can be used here independently of any theory of the 'real nature' of light. Yet, as will be plain in what follows, Descartes does believe that even his 'hypothesis' is clearer and more economical than its alternatives. And, as he remarked to Vatier and repeatedly tells Mersenne, eventually when he can publish his whole Physics, with its foundation in metaphysics, what are here 'suppositions' will be seen in fact to follow in the right, Cartesian way in the right order and with the right certainty from first truth. In his published work, that will become clear in the *Principles* where, indeed, 'hypothetical' elements remain, but rooted in a non-hypothetical whole, and even in 1637 the conjunction of the Rules of the *Discourse* with the detached segments presented in the *Dioptrics* and the *Meteors* shows clearly enough that the method, given its proper systematic elaboration, would ground these 'suppositions' and remove their present 'hypothetical' character. This letter, too, as we shall see, eventually points in this direction, as a later letter to Morin explicitly does (*AT*, ii, pp.364–5, 12 September 1638).

The question of circularity, thirdly, is put to rest by stressing, as, indeed, the text of the *Discourse* had partly done, the distinctions between 'proof' (in Descartes's sense) and explanation. He continues:

> You say also that there is a vicious circle in proving effects from a cause, and then proving the cause by the same effects. I agree: but I do not agree that it is circular to explain effects by a cause, and then prove the cause by the effects, because there is a big difference between proving and explaining.

Note that 'proof' runs here from effects to causes! 'I should add', he goes on, 'that the word "demonstrate" can be used to signify either i.e., "prove" or "explain"',

> if it is used according to common usage and not in the technical philosophical sense. I should add also that there is nothing circular in proving a cause by several effects which are independently known, and then proving certain other effects from this cause. I have combined these two senses together on p.76: 'As my last conclusions are demonstrated by the first, which are their causes, so the first may in turn be demonstrated from the last, which are their effects.' But that does not leave me open to the accusation of speaking ambiguously, because I explained what I meant immediately afterwards when I said that 'the effects are for the most part certain from experience and so the causes from which I derive them serve not so much to prove as to explain them.' And I put 'serve not so much to prove them' rather than 'do not serve at all', so that people could tell that each of these effects could also be proved from this cause, in case there was any doubt about it, provided that the cause had already been proved from other effects. I do not see what other term I could have used to explain myself better (*AT*, ii, pp.197–8, *K*, pp.57–8).

Again, it seems clear that in the larger context—to be more plainly adumbrated in the *Principles*—the relatively tentative 'explanations' of the *Essays*, a sampler only of Cartesian science, will be assimilated to proven certainties. 'Explanations' are temporary, since 'proofs' can be supplied. Note, however, once more, that while the 'proof' in the case will be stateable synthetically, or demonstratively in the logician's sense, it will have been derived, at least in large part, by the analytic method, or by a Cartesian variant of that method, which 'proves' from what is best known first to the next easiest item of knowledge, and so on. Hence the stress here on 'proof' from effects to causes: start where it's plain you are, and move, slowly and certainly, from step to step. Then, when you get to the cause, you will have proved it: again, as in the *Rules*, in Descartes's terms, the best deduction is inductive! It's the hypothetical 'explanatory' procedure, moving from causes to effects, that you can work into a popular piece, which even women can read! It's not serious science. On the contrary: what appear to be 'suppositions', one may conclude, at certain stages or in certain styles of Cartesian presentation may be assimilated under another arrangement to their permanent place in the 'firm and abiding superstructure of the sciences' on which the master-architect is at work.

There is another side to Cartesian hypotheses, however, which is suggested by Morin's next comment and Descartes's reply. Morin says:

> And as to the astronomers whom you propose to imitate on page 3 of your *Dioptrics*, I shall not at all conceal my opinion, which is, that one who does not make better suppositions than those that the astronomers have made till now, will do no better than they in the consequences or conclusions, and may well do much worse. For wrongly supposing *solar parallax*, or the *obliquity of the Ecliptic* or the *eccentricity of the Apogee, the mean movement* or *period of a planet*, etc., far from drawing true and assured consequences, as you say on the same page 3, on the contrary, they err in consequence in the movements, or places, of the planets, in proportion to the error of their false suppositions, witness the relation of their Tables to the Heavens (*AT*, i, pp.538–9).

And Descartes answers:

> You say also that astronomers often make hypotheses which cause them to fall into grave errors; as when they wrongly hypothesise parallax, or the obliquity of the ecliptic, and so on. To this I reply that these items do not belong to the class of suppositions or hypotheses I was speaking of; I marked out this class clearly when I said that one could draw very true and certain consequences from them even though they were false and uncertain. For the parallax, the obliquity of the ecliptic and so on cannot be hypothesised as false or uncertain, but only as true; whereas the Equator, the Zodiac, the epicycles and other such circles are commonly hypothesised as false, and the movement of the earth as uncertain, and yet for all that true conclusions are drawn from them (*AT*, ii, pp.198–9; *K*, 58).

This is the most puzzling aspect of Cartesian hypotheses. They are not, after all, Descartes insists, of the same character at all as conjectures about what is the case. Rather they are fictions, like the Equator. They may be wholly false and yet serve to mediate truth. Now one might say this, in a way, of Descartes's *World*, which is explicitly declared by him to be invented; we shall see about that shortly. Here, however, in the *Dioptrics*, Descartes is referring to the everyday analogies he will shortly introduce in order to explain how light works: the barrel full of half-fermented grapes, the person tapping his way with a stick, and the racquet-ball player. Surely these are not hypotheses like the movement or rest of the earth, let alone 'fictions' like the Equator or the Zodiac. There is a certain 'hypothesising' involved in explaining fermentation mechanically, in terms of the motions of small parts, but the other two examples are just plain everyday happenings, surely not 'fictional'. What does Descartes mean by invoking everyday analogies and calling them fictions, which bear no relation to truth or falsity as the bad astronomical hypotheses do? What is he in fact doing with these examples?[17]

It will indeed be surprising to Descartes's reader to have refraction explained to him in terms of such singularly irrelevant examples—in this way at least they are 'contrived'. But why? Desmond Clarke has suggested that Descartes's failure as a physicist resides precisely in this kind of reliance on everyday experience (Clarke, 1976, 1982). Yet it seems to me that what Descartes was trying to achieve in these examples was in fact both clear and pertinent to the reform of physics in his time. As I have already stressed, he wanted to teach people to think of all natural (= non-mental) phenomena purely in terms of local motion. Familiar examples in which this could easily be done should help to extend such thinking to the more difficult case of light. Illumination *is* movement; the observation of the regularity of certain visible movements, like stick-tapping or tennis-playing, or the mechanical reading of a familiar process like wine-making—where there is clearly movement of some kind: such observations may teach us something about the movement that is light. Of course, applied literally to light, on the other hand, these analogies, like all analogies, would be 'false'. So they are put forward, not as propositions true in themselves, but as devices to help the reader understand. In this sense, then, the 'fictions' Descartes uses here may be assimilated to the tentative and temporary place he has already suggested for hypotheses, relative to the whole structure of his physics (x-metaphysics).

That is clear also, I believe, from his reply to Morin's final remark in this opening objection. After comparing his own, less hypothesis-ridden astronomy with the traditional, Morin returns to the problem of causality: 'to prove that the cause of an effect is its true and unique cause, it is necessary at least to prove that such an effect cannot be produced by any other cause' (*AT*, i, p.539). Descartes's answer appears in what looks like classic hypothetico-deductive form, though with a realistic rather than conventionalist twist. 'It is true,' he writes, 'that there are many effects to which it is easy to fit many separate causes; but it is not always easy to fit a single cause to many effects, if it is not the true cause from which they proceed (*AT*, ii, p.199, *K*, p.58, revised). The way to find the true cause, however, is to find one cause from which many effects follow, and Descartes claims that all the causes of which he has spoken belong to this class. He then proceeds to compare his hypotheses in the *Dioptrics* and the *Meteors* with those of others: 'Compare', he challenges Morin,

> all their real qualities, their substantial forms, their elements and their other countless hypotheses with my single hypothesis that all bodies are composed of parts. This is something which is visible to the naked eye in many cases and can be proved by countless reasons in others (*AT*, ii, p.200; *K*, p.59).

The 'suppositions or comparisons' of the *Dioptrics*, therefore, seem to be cases used to support this single hypothesis, which, far from being fictional, is believed by Descartes to be true. He goes on:

> All that I add to this is that the parts of certain kinds of bodies are of one shape rather than another. This in turn is easy to prove to those who agree that bodies are composed of parts. Compare the deductions I have made from my hypothesis—about vision, salt, winds, clouds, snow, thunder, the rainbow and so on—with what the others have derived from their hypotheses on the same topics! I hope this will be enough to convince any one unbiased that the effects which I explain have no other causes than the ones from which I have derived them (*AT*, ii, p.200; *K*, p.59).[18]

Again, this sounds like (realistic) H-D reasoning. In other

words, Descartes sounds here like a good modern scientist, of the very kind dreamt of by modern philosophers of science. But the next, and qualifying, clause in turn puts that appearance in its place: 'although I leave open the (project of) demonstrating (the true cause) in another place (*AT*, ii, p.200; *K*, p.59)[19]—where, once more, 'demonstrating' here will be Cartesian proof, from effects to causes, with the hypothetical feature of the 'proof', the merely explanatory, supplanted by the proper certainty.

In the next paragraph, moreover, Descartes expands on this remark, and explains that he has not here touched on the essential nature of light, because he has dealt elsewhere with this topic in the context of 'the general causes on which it depends' (*AT*, ii, p.201). Thus it seems clear that the hypothetical character of his reasoning in these *Essays* is the product of the relatively popular nature of that work, and of the absence of the proper grounding in first principles that would remove their tentative character and the necessity of using everyday analogies or 'fictions' to support them. In such a larger context, it would be clear how the effects here explained really follow from their true causes, since we would have arrived at a clear understanding of the general principles from which all such effects flow. And again, finally, what this basic reform in physics will do, when systematically stated, is to substitute for 'real qualities, substantial forms, elements and things like that', the plain and simple thesis that bodies are composed of parts, and consequently that natural phenomena are best accounted for in terms of the relative position of their parts. The true, mechanical account of nature is what matters. Short of a total exposition of the principles on which it rests, however, it can be propounded, in relation to certain phenomena people want to explain, through using 'comparisons and suppositions' that help them to understand in this new and clear way. The general principle itself, too, is here stated as hypothetical, to be 'proved' elsewhere; the 'comparisons and suppositions' drawn from familiar examples, however, are hypotheses in the sense of fictions, in that they are invented here for pedagogical purposes, to guide the reader's mind in the right direction. They entail in themselves no truth claims whatsoever.

The sense in which such 'suppositions' are fictional, as distinct from the underlying 'explanatory' hypothesis, is well illustrated by a comparison with sociobiological explanation, as analysed by Richard Boyd and Nicholas Sturgeon.[20] You have a puzzling phenomenon: altruism. You explain it by a theory: genetics taken at the level of the single gene with its tendency to perpetuate itself. What story you tell about how it happened in this particular case is merely illustrative. It is the underlying genetic theory that is the correct explanation. Similarly with Descartes: what matters is that the phenomenon you are investigating is explicable in the language of extended substance and its changing relations: that is, of the relative location and relocation of the parts of bodies. 'Just-so stories' are pedagogical constructions, fictions, like the Equator or epicycles, to help us understand what is really going on: and that is *partes extra partes*, no more. Thus there are two kinds of 'hypotheses' involved: the underlying theory, which 'explains' the puzzling phenomenon, and the 'fictions' invented or the stories told in its support. But of course the true theory, in the Cartesian as distinct from any twentieth-century case, will itself flow smoothly from the methodic search for certainties. Cartesian explanations in their full context, in other words, will turn out to fit well enough into the method of certainty-succeeding-certainty that the *Rules* elaborate, the *Discourse* summarises, and the *Meditations* illustrate in their first fundamental steps.

7

So much for the discussion of the text I wanted to look at as illustrative of Descartes's use of 'hypotheses'. We found that he introduced 'hypotheses' as tentative explanations in partial presentation of his physics, short of their 'proof' in a fuller context, and also 'hypotheses' as conventional devices, stories, so to speak, or 'fictions' intended as auxiliary to explanation. Second, however, there is a much more massive use of 'fiction' in his work, which has more profound implications for the nature of his method and of the science based on it. We have to ask, not only why Descartes plays with hypotheses when his whole method is intended to eliminate them, but why he explicitly sets forth his *whole* cosmology, his *whole* physiology, as a *fable*. There are, I believe, at least two reasons for this, one very obvious and at first sight superficial, the other more global and extremely important for the interpretation of the whole Cartesian project of intellectual reform.

First, any account Descartes gives of the origin of either the world or man that is *not* the account of *Genesis* is, of course, in an obvious sense fictional. Whatever he knows as natural philosopher, he believes what Revelation, hence Scripture, tells him. Nor in his view do these 'two truths' contradict one another. Descartes's gratitude to the Jesuits for the teaching on which his very life is founded is no hypocritical gesture. Yes, he was cautious; when Galileo was condemned, he put aside the publication of his global theory and tried a more modest route. But his faith and his respect for the Church were real. Indeed, even this obvious point has its philosophical grounding. On the philosophical level, too, Descartes *knew* (viz, believed he knew!) that our rationality, the very root of our certainty, depends on God's omnipotence and the creation of the eternal truths. That is a complex issue that I cannot go into here (*see* Frankfurt, 1977; Rodis-Lewis, 1971, pp.125–40; Marion, 1981, *passim*). It should suffice here to point out that our rationality is, first, never allowed to contradict relevation but only to complement it, and second, never absolute in the sense of self-founded, since it rests, like everything there is, on the inexhaustible but evident omnipotence of the creator. So any account we invent will be, however true, literally a fiction compared to the absolutely true account which we accept, even though we cannot strictly understand it, on God's Own Word.

There is, however, a much richer sense in which Descartes's *world* and Descartes's *man* are fables, a sense close to the very core of his mechanistic doctrine, central, it seems to me, to his method, metaphysics and physics alike. Bodies, Descartes is convinced, are substances whose essential attribute is extension: their geometry is their being. What we perceive through our senses, however, is qualities, affective states basically dissimilar to those spread-out realities. The aim of Cartesian science, therefore, is to devise a special language that will render our misleadingly rich experience in those more austere terms. Science is a code for putting into figured form what perception has disfigured. But codes are artefacts; in this sense at least, science is a made thing, a fiction. That is, in sum, the thesis presented by J.L.Marion in his second major Cartesian commentary, *La Théologie Blanche de Descartes* (Marion, 1981).

There are, indeed, suggestions for such a reading in the Cartesian texts, at *Principles* IV, 205 (where the analogy is drawn between the decipherment of a code and the 'moral certainty' of Descartes's physical explanations (*AT*, vii, 1, pp.327–8), and especially in the *World*:

> if words, which signify nothing except as established by men, suffice to make us know things, why cannot nature itself have established a certain sign, which makes us have the sensation of light, even though that sign has nothing in itself resembling (light)? (*AT*, xi, p.4; cf. *AT*, vi, p.113; viii, 2, p.359; Rodis-Lewis, 1950, p.213 n).

Marion's reading, however, expands these hints into a comprehensive doctrine.

Again, I shall try to present the general bent of his argument in my own words; indeed, much of what I have already said has doubtless been influenced by my reading of this seminal work. Quite (well not quite, but nearly) apart from its ontological implications (which I shall touch on in the next chapter), his presentation of the intent of Cartesian science, in the section 'From science to its foundation', offers, in my view, a definitive answer to the question of the relation of fiction to certainty in Cartesian method (Marion, 1981, pp.231–340). Needless to say, this is *my* reading and may well fail to render correctly its author's intent. Not only am I unable to report the argument with all its Gallic subtleties; as a blunt English-speaker I am sure I fail to grasp a number of them—and indeed, some that I do grasp, in their rhetorical embellishment, I could happily do without. But the essential argument, insofar as I can follow it, seems to me irresistible.

The straightest path to an understanding of Cartesian science is to look again at the structure of the *Meditations*. We begin with the presentations of sense—that is where we have all begun in infancy, and where Descartes and his confrères were taught to begin in the building of science. But the existential import of such science is unreliable; it is this questionable import that the Deceiving Demon, at the end of Meditation One, enables us to suspend. What seems seems, certainly; but *things* are not what they seem. Thus a radical cut is made between subjective certainty and what there is—or better, at this stage, what there may or may not be. The Second Meditation discovers and stabilises inalienably the region of subjective certainty: the reality of mind in its ongoing, cognitive core. By a delicately constructed, if roundabout, route, the parallel region of certainty about bodies is established, correspondingly, in Meditation Five: not yet their existence, but their essence as pieces of extension, intelligible by cogitation, once the free-ranging will has been confined within the bounds of clarity. Only when this insight has been achieved, can the *existence* of bodies, in the *Sixth Meditation*, be safely acknowledged, and even then, clearly and distinctly—that is, for science rather than for practice—only insofar as things are the objects of geometry. Nature as it exists for us, in our immediate experience, is rich and varied, but obscure. When we turn as mature thinkers from sense to intellect as our source—to what, in the Replies to the Sixth Objections, Descartes calls the third grade of sense, which is not sense at all, but reason (*AT*, vii, pp.436–7; cf.Reed, 1982)—when we make that essential turn, we re-figure the experience nature had itself dis-figured, and read experience in the language of geometry, the language in terms of which, we hope, its Almighty Maker had devised it. Not that Descartes's God is a Leibnizian mathematician. He made the world as He willed to make it; even its mathematics is of His making; but He made our reason, too, and we can (rationally) hope they correspond! It will be here, therefore, if anywhere, that we relocate the correspondence the Schools had alleged they found between sense and real things. What founds Cartesian science is not rootedness in a real, sensible nature with its finite number of natural kinds, including our own peculiar kind, gifted with the power to grasp the sensible forms of things without their matter. What founds Cartesian science, on the contrary, is the hoped-for convergence between our rationality (set free in the *cogito* from the mistaken cognitive claims of sense) and its objective: the geometrical, or geometrisable, essence of what-there-is-out-there. Again, it is the very alienation of mind from nature that liberates the attentive intellect for the clear and distinct apprehension of its objective: the clearly and distinctly evident geometrical relations that constitute the essence of the external world. It is these relations that the inquiring mind devises in the confident hope that the story they tell is at bottom the correct one: the story of God's creation of a world of regularly changing shapes. Basically, the mind has to invent such an account: hence the fictive world, the fictive human body. In detail, some aspects of this account may also sometimes involve 'comparisons and suppositions' not necessarily exactly equivalent to the way it all *really* happened: hence 'hypothetical' ingredients of the kind we noticed in the *Dioptrics*. But what is basic to the whole enterprise is its fictional character in a more fundamental sense: the invention of a language that carries sense-carried subjectivities into geometrised intelligibles, evident truths we may rely on as giving us, not just a fable of our own, but that very language nature has used in 'dis-figuring' her own figures to produce our quality-rich if insight-poor experience. Science gives us a code for reading our experience, a code we may hope is the very code of nature herself.

Let me comment, somewhat at a tangent, on the historical import of this fundamental Cartesian move, and then consider very briefly some of the apparent difficulties of this interpretation of Cartesian science, and their possible resolution.

Much is made of Galileo's remark that 'that great book, the universe, is written in the language of mathematics and its characters are triangles, circles, and other geometric figures without which it is impossible to understand a single word of it; without these, one wanders about in a blind labyrinth' (Galileo, 1965, VI, p.232). Much is made also of the distinction to be christened by Locke (following Boyle and possibly also Fracastoro) as that between primary and secondary qualities, a distinction put forward by Galileo in the same work: 'I think that tastes, odour, colours, and so on are no more than mere names as far as the object in which we place them is concerned. . . If the living creatures were removed, all these qualities would be wiped away and annihilated' (Galileo, 1965, VI, p.345). But if we accept Marion's interpretation of 'science and its code', it is Descartes who achieved the radical geometrisation of nature, not in some passing comment, but in a fundamental projection of natural science as encoding the mathematical relations that show us, with such certainty as our finite minds can master, what nature is. The turn from the School's common-sense to rationality, the turn from natural impulse to natural light, is also the turn from the confusing world of 'real'qualities and substantial forms to the world of shapes and sizes only. The explanation of how the secondary qualities of bodies produce in us ideas of colour, taste, smell and sound, Locke, it seems, will hold to be on principle beyond us. Descartes was more confident that in his full range of discoveries, of fundamental physical principles in turn founded on metaphysical first truths, he had been able to demonstrate how 'secondary' qualities yield to 'primary', how local motion suffices to explain all the phenomena of the external world, from the origin of the heavenly bodies to the fabric of the human body itself. And he accomplished this through showing *how* nature is written in the mathematical language, indeed, through exhibiting nature *as* such a language. Science is a code that construes or deciphers nature's code.

If this project appears more radical than Galileo's remarks, which suggest it but take no step toward its accomplishment, and more successful (on principle, not, be it said, in terms of the actual progress of natural science) than Locke's more timorous primary/secondary distinction will be, it becomes clear also, on this reading of Cartesian methodology, that philosophers did not really have to wait for Berkeley to see nature as a language instead of as a machine (Turbayne, 1962). In fact, Descartes saw nature as the referent of a language, and as itself a language, just insofar as it *is* a machine. Nature has a code for (dis)figuring its shapes into sensations and we devise (figure out?) a code for refiguring our sensed experiences back into the terms of nature's code.[21] Far from being opposed to the machine model, it is the language model that legitimates mechanism as its very source.

8

This seems to me an illuminating reading of Cartesian 'fiction'. My report of it, however, needs some qualification.

First, it is not enough just to say that Cartesian science is fictional because it is a language, hence an artefact. All language is made, yet there is discourse that is not fictional in the sense in which Descartes declares that his 'world' and his 'man' are fictitious. Some discourse tries to, and even does, state facts; it is not always story-telling. To say, 'Imagine a human being fabricated in a factory rather than born of a human mother' is not to practise the same kind of discourse as in saying 'Today is Tuesday'. The Cartesian code of science is not just language, it is a specially made-up language, not exactly a private language, but one invented for a specially trained, specially rational professional audience that, being steeped in Descartes's writings, will have learned its use. Indeed, the concept of a 'code' carries with it that feature. The Cartesian method will teach its users to suspend such statements as 'See this red rose' in favour of statements about the motions of the parts of this flower, which cause these particular sensations of colour on our part through these particular physiological responses (and of course the conscious states responding to these responses in this particular mind—but that's no longer physiology). It is this physicist's language (as in the description of Eddington's 'real' table!) that Descartes has set out to invent. Relative to everyday experience (and scholastic would-be learning), it devises a fictional account, which, however, in the light of reason, we know to be true.

Second, there is a question, at first sight at least, about how the code of science is to be read. If Descartes does really invent his geometrical language as a de-coding of nature's code, must it not, to work properly, be precise, literal, in every part of every expression? Descartes is confident that he is discovering something—indeed, something fundamental—about the *real* external world. Yet his fables, and even the less hypothetical moments of the essays, give us a kind of leeway that one supposes a successful decoding ought not to permit. I find this point unsettling, but a suggestion of Marion's about a text in the *Rules* may help to deal with it (Marion, 1981, p.238). Descartes there suggests that at a juncture where enumeration is needed—for the study of colour, in the example he is using—we may correlate different colours with different geometrical diagrams:

like  for blue

or 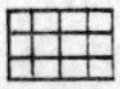 for red, for instance (*AT*, x, p.441).

Now obviously this is not some kind of proto-wave-theory; Descartes was to be a firm particle theorist (though of course not an atomist!). Light results from the motion of small parts of bodies which he calls 'subtle matter'. But here the use of shapes is purely conventional, a guide for sorting out a complex subject-matter. Extensive relations here do not literally refer. And neither do they in Descartes's own new geometry: the analytical kind. Graphs are not pictures. They use extensive relations to explain the regularities of an extended nature, but not in simple one-to-one relation. A sine curve, for example, does not correspond to some sine-shaped thing out there in the world. If it represents motion, it might be said (with due precaution in view of Descartes's odd view of time) to translate temporal into spatial relations. It is a metaphor. Granted, for Descartes the relation of sign to signified is still close: a Cartesian curve does represent spatially what are at bottom also relations of shape—since everything but minds, finite and infinite, are in truth shapes and their relations. Still, there is a kind of gappiness, a minimal fictionality, so to speak, between Cartesian geometry and the nature that is its target. The code does not refer, item by item. It is not a naming code. It codes for motions, for operations, for change. But at the same time its units are of the same nature as what it codes for: units of shape and size.

Finally, there is a problem, central, indeed, to Marion's own account, and which it will be our task to reflect on in the next chapter. If Descartes's aim was to provide a grounding, within the traditional cosmology, for mathematical physics, that physics at its base is firmly grounded in his ontology and in the philosophical remnant of theology that his ontology demands. For the code of nature which Descartes hopes his code of science has re-invented is of course a code instituted by God, whose ways transcend our understanding as radically as our understanding acknowledges and depends upon His goodness and His truth. As Marion puts it, the project of the code is a foundational one: the Cartesian method of evidence, which frees the mind to grasp its mathematical objectives, also demands a foundation for those evidential certainties. We need to know that our code *is* nature's; otherwise for all his ingenuity the mathematician too will be back in a blind labyrinth. How can we be sure that our code is *the* code? It is God's code—a kind of supercode ('*surcodage*') that really gets things going (Marion, 1981, pp.327 ff.). And how can we know *that*?

Descartes, Marion argues, has set for modern philosophy both the problem of the foundation of knowledge and the *im*possibility of solving it (Marion, 1981, pp.444–54). It is this problem, both Descartes's ontological achievement and his ontological plight, that we have next to consider.

Notes

1. R. Lenoble (1971), p.292, n.2, points out that the denial of other forms of change is implicit in Descartes's summary of the *Meditations, AT,* ix, p.10. All substances are created and destroyed by God; 'decay' at death is the rearrangement of the parts of extended substance; the same would hold for birth and growth.
2. On the relation of the *Regulae* to the *Geometry, see* Lachterman, 1984, 1985.
3. *See* my essay, 'Hobbes and the modern mind' in M. Grene (1976) pp. 155–65. A very different, but illuminating, view of the relation of Cartesian physics to the tradition is given in Machamer (1978) pp. 168–99. Machamer's view of the place of 'hypotheses' in Cartesian science, as well as of the use of traditional formal (and, surreptitiously, final) causality in the Cartesian program, also differs from mine. I have not complicated my argument by taking account of his; it is well worth studying, and I hope that my conclusions would not be fundamentally at odds with his. I do think he errs, however, in taking *perceptio* in Descartes to mean exclusively *sense*-perception (as in the piece of wax argument, for instance). Another, and more unusual, view worth noting is that of Desmond Clarke (1982).
4. *See* the outstanding anthology edited by Stephen Gaukroger (1980). For an illuminating discussion of Descartes's methods in physics, *see* G.Rodis-Lewis (1971), I, pp.185 ff., the analysis of Descartes's treatment of the rainbow in the *Meteors*. In general, Rodis-Lewis's exposition of Descartes's science in relation to his philosophy and its development provides an excellent introduction to the problems of interpretation in this whole difficult context. One of the best statements of the nature of Cartesian method in its claim to certainty is that of Gouhier (1972) e.g. p.273, p.275, and the conclusion of the original edition of that work, p.277.
5. Although in general Descartes's use of the (relatively standard) distinction between these two methods is beyond dispute, his account here does present problems for the reader, especially of the (surely botched!) French translation of the Replies to Second Objections. The matter is explored in detail, and definitively, it seems to me, by P.J. Olscamp in his introduction to the Liberal Arts edition of the *Discourse, Dioptrics,* etc. (Olscamp,ed.,1965). *See* also *AT*, i, p.563, for confirmation of the odd use of *a posteriori* (and *a fortiori* and *a priori*) in the Replies.

6. E.M.Curley (1978) stresses the change from the *Rules* to the *Meditations*; *see* also Schuster, in Gaukroger (1980) for the 'instability' of the *Rules*; also Kraus, 1983. But *see* Marion (1975) p.182, for a table of parallels between the *Rules* and *Meditations*.
7. *See*, for example, E.M. Curley (1978); Bernard Williams (1978); Margaret Wilson (1978); also Michael Hooker (1978). For a devastating, but characteristically esoteric, not to say idiosyncratic, critique of the first three (and two other recent works on Descartes), *see* Caton (1981). Caton does refer to Marion's later work, *Sur la Théologie Blanche de Descartes,* (1981), and takes 'white (= blank!) theology' for a joke. Perhaps so; there is indeed something farcical in the contemporary style of French philosophising, as there is also, as Caton insists, something bead-game-like in analytical philosophical historiography. But, as will be (tediously) clear in this and the next chapter, I find the modish aspect of Marion's work relatively superficial, although his argument (in both books) seems to me very serious indeed.
8. Pierre Pellegrin (1982) has put forward a highly original reading of Aristotle's biology and in particular of the meaning of *eidos*. I hope that my reading (and Marion's) is not inconsistent with it. In any event, however, it is the scholastic Aristotle Descartes was confronting.
9. For the role of hypotheses in the *Principles*, *see Principles* III, 15–17, 19, 43–7; *AT*, viii, 1, pp.84–5, 99–102; cf. *AT*, III, p.45, IV, p.690 and discussion of exchange with Morin, below. David Lachterman has reminded me that the problem of 'hypotheses' in science should be seen, in Descartes's time, against the background of Osiander's notorious preface. I hope we may take that as read, and still see a genuine methodological problem in Descartes's own thought.
10. *See* note 9 above; also *Discourse on Method*, *AT*, vi, p.45; *Studium bonae mentis*, *AT*, x, p.202.
11. For a seeming exception, *see* e.g., *AT*, v, p.275; all his physics is necessary, except where it is known '*per solam experientiam*'.
12. *See* e.g. *AT*, i, p.305; he cannot answer any questions in physics without his principles; similarly, to Vatier, *AT*, i, p.563, or *AT*, ii, 437, where he says he needs his *Monde* to answer Mersenne's questions about subtle matter.
13. For a recent discussion of Descartes's hypotheses and his experimental method, *see* Sakellariadis (1982) as well as the paper by Machamer referred to in note 3 above. For another suggestion about the relation of Descartes's 'fables' to his method, *see* D. Garber, in M. Hooker (1978); also D. Clarke (1976, 1982).
14. *See* e.g., the discussion of Morin below.
15. Hacking's chronological claim (beginning probabilism with Hume) is weakened, I am afraid, by the case of Gassendi; *see* ch. 6 below.
16. Other cases might also be used to illustrate Descartes's conception of his method; instructive, for instance, is the letter of Descartes to Plempius for Fromondus, 3 October 1637, *AT*, i, pp.414 ff., included in part in *K*, pp.35–40. Point 11 (*K*, 39) bears on the question of 'suppositions'.
17. *See* also the similar formulation in Replies to Fifth Objections, *AT*, vii, pp.349–50.

18. *See* also the reply to Fromondus referred to in note 16 above.
19. Kenny puts it: 'None the less, I intend to give a demonstration of it in another place' (*K*, p.59).
20. Reported in a lecture given by Richard Boyd to the Council for Philosophical Studies Summer Institute in the Philosophy of Biology at Cornell University on 16 July 1982.
21. French rhetoric is infectious!

4 *Substance at Risk*

1

If Descartes's method was to initiate a unified science, that science in turn was firmly grounded in ontology. Indeed, his whole physics, he insisted, was contained in his 'first philosophy' (*AT*, iii, pp.233, 297–8).[1] True, the science of nature is geometrical, but the mind's grasp of the essence of bodies is itself subtended by the knowledge of *res cogitans*, *res extensa* and the Infinite Mind that made, and maintains, them both: the knowledge acquired on the well-ordered path of the *Meditations*. The emphasis placed in the preceding chapter on Descartes's methodology in its scientific aspect was not intended to play down, let alone to deny, the firm grounding of his physics in his metaphysics. Indeed, it is clear that Descartes had sketched out his metaphysics in a draft of 1629–30, before he embarked on his *World*, let alone the *Discourse*, *Dioptrics*, and so on (Gouhier, 1972, pp.77–9; Rodis-Lewis, 1971, pp.112–120). If one may fairly argue, as I have done, that the turn to a mathematical, mechanistic physics played a central role in Descartes's programme, the reform of—though *within*—traditional ontology necessitated by that program provided at the same time its indispensable foundation. In short, Cartesian science-and-ontology together form a seamless whole. It is the basic concepts of that ontology and the peculiar place they hold in the history of Western thought that I want to consider in this chapter.

2

Before I go on to do that, however, it may be useful to stress more explicitly the ontological grounding of Cartesian physics by comparing Descartes's position with that of his friend and principal correspondent, Father Mersenne (cf.Schuster, 1980, pp.56–7). Most readers of Descartes think of Mersenne as the faithful friend of 'the illustrious man', who distributed his works to interested parties for their comment. So he was, and so he did, but that is by no means the whole story. Father Robert Lenoble's careful account of Mersenne's interests and achievements paints a different picture, of a figure at the centre of an intellectual life that goes well beyond the Cartesian perspective, in ways that make his science appear more 'modern' than Descartes's (Lenoble, 1971, but cf. Marion, 1981). Short of that contrast, even the contrast in their personal destinies is instructive. Descartes, a young gentleman of independent means, has sought out a retreat in the Netherlands from the importunities of his friends and relations. Through extensive correspondence and a few personal friendships, he maintains contact with the learned world, but always with his primary attention on the work he hopes to achieve. He hesitates to publish, but gradually develops a desire to persuade the world to adopt his teachings (Gouhier, 1972). He remains a good Catholic, and indeed his life's work can be viewed with some verisimilitude as belonging either to the new science or to the new apologetics, better, to both at once. At the same time, with one exception (and that chiefly in correspondence),[2] he refuses to mix in explicitly theological matters. I shall return to that point shortly.

In contrast, Mersenne, the son of humble parents, though seemingly destined to rise in the Church, has chosen to enter the strict and ascetic order of Minims, and to follow all his life the austere rule of that Order. From 1619 until his death in 1648 he is based at their monastery in the Place Royale in Paris. At the same time he publishes widely on all sorts of subjects, from 1624 until his death in 1648. The five treatises published in 1634 appear to be representative. They are: *Questions inouyés ou Recreation des Scavants; Questions Harmoniques, dans lesquelles sont contenues plusieurs choses remarquables pour le Physique, pour le Morale, et pour les autres sciences: Les questions Théologiques, physiques, morales, et mathématiques; les Mechaniques de Galilée* (translation from the Italian of an early work of Galileo, with additions from other sources); *les Préludes de l'Harmonie Universelle, ou Questions curieuses utiles aux Predicateurs, aux Théologiens, aux Astrologues, aux Medicins, et aux Philosophes* (Lenoble, 1971, xxviii–xxxi). And so it goes on. For us, it is difficult to find a central theme for such diverse materials. Perhaps the very diversity is the theme. But not quite. Wherever Mersenne looks, it is the cause of God he champions. Earlier, he had taken part in the quarrel about Fludd and the Rosicrucians; he is especially keen to refute pantheistic arguments like those of Bruno. But his very devotion seems to allow him much broader sympathy with the oddest range of writers and thinkers. For instance, although he eventually attacked Campanella for his doctrines, he had welcomed his acquaintance when he came to Paris; and the same went for nearly every one. In particular, Gassendi—one of Descartes's bitterest opponents—had been his dear friend before he met Descartes, and stayed in Paris to the close of Mersenne's final illness when Descartes (who had been on a visit there) fled in view of the threat of political unrest. And even the questionable Mr. Hobbes was Mersenne's good friend: witness Hobbes's tribute in Latin verses, composed more than two decades after Mersenne's death (Lenoble, 1971, pp.596–7). But in all these diverse friendships, too, there was a focal point: the new science. Every one interested in that was of interest to him: he shared Hobbes's enthusiasm for Galileo—with none of the reserve expressed by Descartes, and certainly with none of the disgust of Hobbes so eloquently expressed in Descartes's replies to Third Objections or in his correspondence.[3] In fact, Lenoble argues with some persuasiveness, it was the mechanics of Descartes himself: his project for a new physics, that chiefly motivated Mersenne's devotion to the 'illustrious man'.

But is this not paradoxical: a *dévot* so passionately addicted to the new science that he will talk to just any one about it? Given the nature of Mersenne's interest in mechanism, no. With an effort of imagination, I think we can see how it fits. Nature is the work of God: in seeking to know nature, we are glorifying God. So Descartes also argues, in his own way. But the difference lies in their view of what human reason can and cannot accomplish in this vale of tears. Mersenne can mix in anywhere, in theological questions which Descartes, exponent of *natural* light, eschews. In physics, however, Mersenne believes, we glorify God, not by argument, but by *looking* at His works, by doing experiments and reporting what we *see*.

Mersenne is practically a positivist in his philosophy of science. To Lenoble, writing forty years ago, in the classic period of hypothetico-deductivism, he is *really* a modern scientist, in contrast to Descartes, who mistakenly wants to *found* his physics in first principles. For Mersenne, however, that hope is in error. In this life God's laws are hidden from us; we can only see and tell. (It will, he believed, be different hereafter—for the blessed, of course, one assumes, not for the damned!) So, Lenoble argues, citing much convincing evidence, Mersenne was critical of a good deal in Descartes's ontology. He never accepted the *cogito* (God bless him!) or the proofs of God. He may, indeed, be responsible for much in the Second and Sixth Objections, which he certainly collected. And, it is true, he was a devoted friend. He was everybody's devoted friend, admittedly something of a busybody, but always in the cause of science. It was he who sent the 1637 volume to Fermat, with whom Descartes did not get on (*AT*, i, pp.354–6, 450–4; ii, pp.12, 15–21; also Rodis-Lewis, 1971, pp.192–5), and, indeed, the *Meditations* to those two severest critics, but decidedly not best friends, Hobbes and Gassendi. In the case of Descartes, what he admired was centrally two things. First, he shared Descartes's opposition to scholasticism in the study of nature. Mersenne, too, had had, willy nilly, to abandon the method of his masters, because, as a tool of science, it was simply worn out. And secondly, he shared Descartes's enthusiasm for a mathematical physics. His own enthusiasm, however, was reserved for a pragmatic, positivistic, exploratory physics, not for the founding of our scientific knowledge in ontological principles, even in our knowledge of God's power and hence veracity. Religiosity, one may say, pervades Mersenne's life at every moment (he did *try* to convert Hobbes!). But the very pervasiveness of his devotion forbids the metaphysical grounding of his physics. Descartes, on the other hand, though a believer, needs to find an intellectual basis, not in theology, which is for specialists, but in the philosophical knowledge of the relation of God to mind and nature, for grounding the very mechanical method of his science in a secure and lasting substructure. He has to know it is a rock, not shifting sands, on which his house is built. Again, it is that search for foundations that Descartes has bequeathed to posterity. Many—not only Mersenne—in the seventeenth century were sceptical about that project;[4] but it was the project that set the problematic for philosophical reflection and even, in some fundamental ways, for science in the centuries to come.

3

Descartes is the patron philosopher of the French nation and French scholarship has plumbed the depths of his thought as no English-language literature has done.[5] With respect to Descartes's metaphysical thought, I have found Gueroult (1968), Gouhier (1972, 1978a) and Marion (1981) most illuminating. Although I shall be trying in what follows to set out my own views of some of Descartes's fundamental concepts and especially of their place in the tradition, I must express my debt to all these writers as well as to the superb scholarly work of G. Rodis-Lewis (1950, 1971). My interpretation is not like theirs, and they would all, I suppose, disapprove of it as dismissive and disrespectful; but for what it is worth, my own view has been immeasurably enriched and strengthened by my study of their work.

All of Descartes's thought rests precariously on an edge: on the edge of modernity, on the edge of disaster. Presumably it was that very in-between character that made him so influential. He could be, if not all things to all men, many things to many. But not out of fudging, like Locke. There is a single vision here, coherent yet infinitely rich in its relation to the controversies out of which it has developed. And yet it is also always somewhere in-between. Descartes's 'atom of evidence' gives him a unit of knowledge suspended somehow between the merely subjective and the concrete real. But the concept of the clear and distinct idea into which it is translated, in virtue precisely of its peculiar intermediate character, turns out to be notoriously unstable. Just as plainly, and, indeed, in symbiosis with the methodology, the fundamental concepts of the ontology on which Cartesian method rests are perilously balanced between old and new. It took the genius of a Descartes to achieve that equilibrium in the 1640s, an achievement that is certainly worth studying on its own, as one of the most dazzling accomplishments of our philosophical tradition. Both Gouhier in his *Pensée Métaphysique de Descartes* and Marion in his *Théologie Blanche de Descartes* have brilliantly analysed the detailed relation of the philosopher to his scholastic predecessors, in the former work to St Thomas, in the latter to Suarez and other, lesser, figures. Any reader who doubts the subtlety of Descartes's argument in taking issue with, though without abandoning, that tradition, I refer to those authorities.[6] On the other hand, it is rather the relation of Descartes to the (then) future, Descartes as our destiny, that forms (as I suggested in Ch. 1) the chief context of my own interest. I shall discuss in Part Two the relation of Descartes's thought to that of some of his contemporaries or near contemporaries; but before leaving his own work, I want once more to look at it, this time at its metaphysical foundation, in relation to the destiny of modern thought.

What I shall do here, therefore, sketchily enough, is to examine some aspects of Descartes's ontology, and try to show how he had both retained and reduced traditional concepts to produce the conjoint power and instability that mark his metaphysics.

The first theme I must stress, however, and indeed have already anticipated, is as a matter of fact not a transitional one, but the frame for all the rest: and that is, Descartes's view of the relation between reason and faith. In this respect, he remained an out-and-out Thomist, faithful to the teaching of the Jesuit academy at La Flèche. Reason is one source of truth, revelation another; but since our reason itself is of God's making, the two, though separate, are in essential agreement. God is truthful; what He has made and what He has said cannot but harmonise. 'Cannot but' is not quite right, however, since in God there is, for Descartes, no necessity. Still, in our feeble language—in my case, indeed, in the yet feebler language of the unbeliever, who cannot even properly *know* that two and two are four (*AT*, vii, pp.140–2)—in our feeble language, 'cannot but' may perhaps reflect the Being-Beyond-Necessity from Whose Veracity that harmony of *Creatum* and *Verbum* may be said to flow. I shall return shortly to the problem(s) of Cartesian Deity. For the moment, the point is simply that for Descartes, as for any good ex-pupil of the Jesuits, faith and reason, theology and philosophy, are separate yet harmonious ways to truth. This is what I want to emphasise before going on to look at some of the basic metaphysical concepts whose traditional form is, in Descartes's hands, indeed reshaped.

On this matter, of course, as on the methodology, Cartesian commentators have disagreed, though, in my view, with even less reason. Without alluding to specific names or arguments, let us just look at some of the possibilities here (*see* Gouhier, 1972, pp.11–37; *AT*, i, p.144; ii, pp.466–7).

Occasionally, Descartes has been viewed as a neo-Augustinian, or even a Platonic, thinker (Leclerc, 1980). He is certainly opposed to the Aristotelian influence in physics and indeed in metaphysics. He seeks to lead the mind away from the senses to reliance on an inner light. Whether, or how, this makes him an Augustinian thinker, I shall consider in connection with the Fourth Objections (ch. 7 below). Suffice it here to point out that, while the first three *Meditations* give us 'the path of the mind to God', the last three give us the path back again to the created world, and after that we may put metaphysics (including God) aside, or rather at the foundation, where it belongs, and proceed from that root to the trunk and branches of the tree of knowledge. Once in his lifetime, Descartes remarks, each man must think out for himself these starting points. But then he will go on to other tasks. That is no Augustinian attitude.[8]

If Descartes is no *dévot*, however, neither is he, as many have tried to argue, a coward and a hypocrite, cringing before authority for fear of the penalties an angry Church might exact. Granted, he did go into voluntary exile in a Protestant country, presumably in order to be free of intellectual distractions, where he could walk about even in cities as if alone, where the climate suited him, and so on. And eventually he was to have enough trouble with *their* ecclesiastical authorities![9] Granted, also, he did suppress his *World* because of the condemnation of Galileo; but he hoped the authorities would eventually change their position, and meantime he did not wholly suppress his views in physics. Granted, further, he did frequently consult Mersenne and others about the bearing of his philosophical arguments on theological matters, he did dedicate the *Meditations* to the Doctors of the Sorbonne, and he did express the hope that the Jesuits (with whom for a time he had feared he was 'at war') (*AT*, iii, pp.126, 572) would actually adopt his *Principles* in teaching. All these matters, too, however, suit clearly enough the Descartes I am here presenting. As in the First, Second and Sixth Replies to Objections, so in his correspondence with establishment theologians, he almost always displays the respect due to professionals in a distinct, though cognate, field. It matters to him, good Thomist that he remains in this respect, to get these delicate relations right, and they can help. Of philosophy, he may say: tear down the crumbling structure and build afresh (*AT*, vi, p.13), but there is no harm in asking a master-architect how to make our new building harmonise with the neighbouring church whose maintenance is their charge—and which is certainly not in line for demolition. As to the dedication to the faculty of the Sorbonne, Gouhier suggests, convincingly, it seems to me, that Descartes had by then come to realise how radical his philosophical reform would look to leading scholars, especially to the Jesuits, and he may well have hoped that the official approval of the Sorbonne would somewhat sweeten the pill (Gouhier, 1972, pp.107 ff.). He is certainly in earnest in his insistence that his philosophy is strikingly well suited to support the cause of God and immortality, and later, in his reply to Arnauld, he will seek to demonstrate also how well the doctrine of transubstantiation can be conceptualised in terms of his *substantia extensa*.[10] By the time it comes to the *Principles*, moreover, he has become—again, to follow Goubier's interpretation—self-consciously the founder of a school, whose doctrines he hopes to propagate. The once-threatened 'war with the Jesuits' has simmered down, and, certain of the truth as he is, he really believes the educational authorities who had given him so excellent a start may see by now how superior his philosophy is to their lingering Aristotelianism and assimilate it in its proper place: primarily, in the case of the *Principles*, as a new physics.

4

Given that secure framework, then, Descartes refashions the traditional concepts of philosophy in order, as he believes, by one and the same move to found a new physics and to stabilise, so far as it befits natural light to do so, an old faith. The order in which, in reliance on his method, he lays that foundation, we have seen in operation earlier. Clearing away the misleading judgments based on sense, the mind can discover, first, itself as thinker, then God, whose veracity guarantees its insights so long as it cleaves to the path of clarity and distinctness, the essence of bodies as extended, the real separate existence of bodies and minds as finite substances, and, finally, in the practical sphere, the life of the (temporarily) unified substance mind-times-body, from whose muddled everyday experience we had set out. The aim of the exercise had been to establish 'something firm and stable on which to build a superstructure of the sciences'. There will be, it is true, as we have seen in the last chapter, a problem about the foundation of the foundation. I shall return to that question (briefly) in connection with Descartes's concept of God. But if it is the foundational, or metafoundational, question that has plagued modern thought in the wake of Descartes's argument, it did not, one can be certain, undercut *his* certainty. He distinguishes in the *Principles* between moral and metaphysical certainty (*Principles* IV, 206; *AT*, viii, 1, pp.328–9); *his* metaphysics, he appears to believe, has attained the latter rank. He *has* found the secure foundation for all knowledge, future as well as present. Again, the subtlety and richness of the metaphysical structure Descartes erected out of his clear and distinct ideas are not to be denied. Nor do I wish to deny them, and I trust that this has become clear in the preceding chapters as well as the present one. Yet in looking straight at Descartes's ontology in its major features, and looking as an historicist, that is, as someone who interprets our own philosophical tasks in the light of our own intellectual history, I can see Descartes only as effecting not so much the stabilisation of metaphysics he thought he had produced as its radical unsettling. He leaves only so much of the traditional cosmology as, bereft of his own unique vision, cannot stand alone. Let us look at these moves of his with respect to some basic metaphysical concepts: substance, attribute, degrees of reality, and God.

We have already noted that Descartes's method is marked by the substitution of an 'indivisible' ('atom') of evidence for the Aristotelian 'indivisible form' (*atomon eidos*). For Aristotle and the Aristotelian tradition, it is the form of the concrete existing entity, identifiable by means of the thing's being of such-and-such a kind, that connects knowledge to its roots in the diversified real world. Aristotelian substances are this-suches, and it is the 'such' in each case that ties down the 'this', making it an individual, independently existing, substance rather than just a particular this-character-here-now. In the central argument of the *Metaphysics* Aristotle suggests several meanings for the term 'substance'. 'Matter' and 'universal', however, fail to qualify. Substance, it turns out, may be taken to be the compound of form and matter: a dog or a tree or a man is this general possibility-for-organisation actually organised in-this-way-and-no-other. Or substance is the form itself, the organising principle that shapes tissues and organ-systems into this canine or arboreal or human life cycle. And it is form, Aristotle claims, that is *more* basically substance than the compound. The form, however, is not a universal; it is the form of the kind, of dog, or tree, or man, but the form in its function of actualising *this*-such: this dog or tree or man. Such, or something like it, is the 'substantial form' Descartes was so keen on abolishing from nature, from everywhere except for that one anomalous case, the human mind-times-body in this life.

Now of course for physics it was essential to get rid of Aristotelian forms.[11] They were only a nuisance. But what happens to substance in their absence? Shouldn't it go, too? Yet the basic Aristotelian belief that everything there is is either a substance or an accident (in Cartesian language, mode) of a substance seems in the seventeenth century to be part and parcel of every thinker's intellectual baggage: what Descartes calls a 'common notion'. Even Hobbes uses substance-accident vocabulary, but argues that the only substances are bodies. Well, then, given that Descartes,too, though anti-form, is still a 'substance metaphysician', could he too have gone that road? Of course not. As the *Rules* make clear, it was the discovery of the 'real distinction' (sc. between mind and body) he had started from: science is the work of mind set free from body. They must both be substances, and Infinite Mind, the First Substance of all, must guarantee their proper meeting in the mathematical physicist's knowledge of the world God made. Besides, Hobbesian science is based on a *hypothetical* materialism, as I have already suggested, exactly like the physicalism of the Vienna circle in this century. That will not do for Descartes. Certainty and permanence are what his science demands and his ontology must provide them: God, mind and body, all must play their parts.

But, again, we must ask, what *is* substance, bereft of form? Three features of Cartesian ontology need to be noted in this connection: the definition of substance, the peculiar nature of Cartesian attributes, and the role of levels of reality in Cartesian thought.

5

As far as definition goes, Descartes appears happily to accept a bowdlerised version of the Peripatetic view. A substance, as distinct from a mode, is what exists independently. But what a 'gray ontology' it is! Independence? God, Descartes notoriously stresses, not only made the world: he has to remake it at every moment. God's *concursus*, of course, was not a new notion: it is one of the features of Judaeo-Christian theology Descartes happily and unquestioningly assimilates. But the paring down of kinds of substances to three and the austere account of the nature of the finite ones—as well as the stress on omnipotence in Descartes's God, of which more hereafter—all this makes the juxtaposition of substantial 'independence' and God's moment-to-moment intervention so strange a feature of his metaphysics as to point straight to its Spinozistic resolution. Descartes's faith, off in the background, may stabilise his own acceptance of his own ontology. But for those who come to it not so equipped, this heavily dependent independence can serve only as a problem, not a solution. Indeed, combining Descartes's theory of perception[12] with his account of substance, one can see the demise of substance metaphysics as foredoomed. Either its apotheosis with Spinoza: one substance, not 'substances', or its burial with Hume and the propensity to feign: those are the clear alternatives ahead. The conception of 'substances' as the real things around us, to which events and characters are somehow attached: that notion seems to be over, in one direction or another, and to have been predestined to such an end by the Cartesian account. Such was the view, at any rate, of my generation in philosophy, who read Cassirer's *Substance and Function* in our youth (Cassirer, 1953). David Wiggins's careful argument in *Sameness and Substance* (Wiggins, 1980) may lead to a rethinking of this simple historical story; but if so, perhaps, to an appendix rather than a revision. Maybe we do need to revert to a concept of substance truly like the Aristotelian: to restore precisely the suchness of this-suches, the *atomon eidos* Descartes had so effectively abolished. Something of the kind is suggested also by some recent thinking about metabiological problems. But this is not the place, nor am I the person, to effect such a reform.[13] Suffice it to say that, given the impoverishment of the very concept of substance in Descartes, together with his theory of God's *concursus* on the one side and his view of perception on the other, the notion of a world full of well-organised substances stably related to one another had not long to last.

6

It seems unlikely that Descartes ever glimpsed this danger, or that he ever saw his concept of substance as in any way novel. The distinction between substance and mode, with substance independent and modes dependent, was just what everybody knew. What he was proud of, however, was his conception of the attributes of substance. Traditionally (before the beginning of 'our' science), what science wanted to know, had always wanted to know, was the *essential nature* of substances. One wants to grasp not only that this is a such-and-such, but what-it-is-to-be a such-and-such. And the formula for such a way of being may be complex and elusive. Ultimately, I suppose, one has to rely on *nous*: on the rational insight into the right starting point that will get a particular science started. That is just the kind of rigmarole, Descartes believed, that kept traditional science from getting off the ground at all. Essential natures are not all that complicated. Each (kind of) substance has *its* attribute, which is single, and clearly and distinctly intelligible to a 'pure and attentive mind'.[14] Indeed, there are only two (our understanding of God's nature is another matter!). There is thought, the essence of mind, and extension, the essence of bodies. And since God has made thought, the essence of mind (especially of geometricians' minds) with the power (given the right discipline) to understand the essence both of itself and of bodies, all seems as right as right can be.

Yet, especially about body, there were problems from the very start. Not, of course, that there were not problems about mind as well, especially about the relation of mind to body, but those problems are not so clearly dependent on the single-attribute idea. Allegedly, God created each mind at conception, with its thoughts to occur, modally, forever after. And I suppose those who (unlike the present writer) can conceive of a separable mind identify it sufficiently with themselves to be able to think of it as 'me', as distinct, say, from my present thought of Cartesian attributes. However, these problems have been touched on earlier and will be so again. In the present context, it is the question of Cartesian material substances that is most obviously troublesome. If body is just extended substance, how is it different from just exten*sion*? (e.g., *AT*, vii, pp.173, 364). What does the 'substantiality' add to the extensiveness? Descartes insists that everyone knows the difference. Extension is the attribute of body, and body is extended substance. But the distinction seems not much more than verbal. In fact, of course, it turns out that extension and its alterations are inadequate for the science of nature, even for Descartes; force has to be invoked, although Descartes's manner of invoking it seems less than adequate.[15] But even apart from that oddity of Cartesian physics, the very thinness of corporeal 'substantiality' is patent from the start (*see* Rodis-Lewis, 1950, ch. 2, pp.37–66). How many bodies are there? Minds are countable, since God creates each one at conception. But how many extended substances there are it is hard to say. It seems they were all made in one creation (*see* n.1, ch.3 above). But since they are infinitely divisible, and the products of the divisions are bodies, too, it is hard to imagine, or, indeed, to understand, how they can be counted, or separated one from another. Sometimes Descartes speaks as if their substantiality were relative: as when, backing off from the problem of 'incomplete substances', he points out that a hand, taken in itself, is a substance, but, relative to the whole body, is not so (*AT*, vii, p.222). But that's just the trouble! If we want to count bodies, they must be clearly and distinctly separable. On the other hand, we cannot count bodies as an atomist can, since, in Descartes's view, the very concept is self-contradictory (an *in*divisible *body*—when 'body' means divisibility, *AT*, iii, p.191). Nor, as some say, could an atom (if there could be one) take up more or less space. Indeed, Descartes insists, 'for a true part of matter, the determinate quantity of space it occupies is necessarily included in the distinct thought one has of it' (*AT*, iii, pp.191–2). And that different bodies are in fact really distinct (and, one supposes, not just relatively so) is insisted on in the *Principles* (I, 60; *AT*, viii, 1, pp.29–9). At the same time, however, Descartes insists also that even their small parts are substances (*Principles* II, 55; *AT*, viii, 1, p.71) and that seems to lead us back to a kind of substantial relativity. So where is the 'distinctness'? And yet, he goes on to adjure Mersenne in the letter just quoted, 'The chief aim of my Metaphysics is to make intelligible what are the things we conceive distinctly' (*AT*, iii, pp.191–2)!

This in turn suggests another problem about Cartesian corporeal substances. Even if we could count them, separating each by the space it occupies, how would we account for corporeal *change*? All change is local motion; in a plenum all motion is relative, hence the famous vortices. But that means bodies changing places, not themselves changing. Quite apart from the question, why they should change, *how* can they change? They are really just units of extension. But they cannot alter their precise extension, and so change shape or size, since that is just what distinguishes them from one another. Descartes did write a bit, in the *Description of the Human Body,* about development (*AT*, xi, p.252 ff.), remarking, however, that he had not yet done enough experiments to have the whole problem worked out. In general his account is indeed (crudely) mechanical, like his account of the circulation, but relying also, like the latter, on that famous innate heat in the heart, and also on the behaviour of his three material elements, of differing coarseness or 'subtlety'. He certainly never comes near to Roux's eventual *Entwicklungsmechanik*. But in our present, ontological context, the question is, how could he? In terms of the sole attribute of extensivity, a given body cannot change. If it gets bigger—if it takes up more space or space of a different shape, it is *ipso facto* a different body. Yet, if God made the whole of (material) creation in one initial act, how can new bodies be added? If we cannot count Cartesian bodies, neither can we account for their development. Again, it will make more sense to think of Nature as an Infinite Unity expressing itself infinitely through minding *and* extensiveness (incorporation?) But that, of course, will be a betrayal of just the precarious balance Descartes was so proud to have achieved and in whose stability he so profoundly believed.

7

Finally, there is another feature of Cartesian ontology related to his concept of substance that we need to consider. We must ask, what remains for Descartes of the traditional conception of levels of reality, this time, not so much an Aristotelian as a neo-Platonic residue in his thought and in that of his time. I have already pointed out in passing that the concept of causality in Descartes, though intended to operate in a mechanistic physics, still retains an older, 'emanative' cast. That is evident to all readers of the Third Meditation in the twist he gives the causal principle: the cause must contain, either formally or eminently, at least as much reality as the effect. Now I have been used, I must confess, to taking Descartes's procedure at this stage as chiefly a device for turning the reader's attention from the first clear and distinct idea to the second. This is, once more, analysis, not synthesis: discovery, not demonstration. What is important is the step from the *cogito* to God, however accomplished. On the other hand, these maxims are said to be clear by natural light. It would not do, at this point in the *Meditations*, to assert them objectively (in the modern sense of that term), with respect to things in a world we do not yet *know* to exist. But they do qualify as 'common notions': as part of the equipment of reason innate to our minds and ready to be applied when the right moment comes. Besides, levels of reality talk recurs in the Fourth Meditation: we are beings somewhere between perfection and nothingness, and of course in the Fifth, in the third proof of God's existence. It is clearly part and parcel of Descartes's way of philosophising, not *only* a device for moving attention from one point to another in the order of thought. To be is, for him, to fit into a cosmic scheme in which Being possesses degrees of more and less. And once more, this is a feature of Christian philosophy that it never occurred to Descartes to question. For instance, when some of his readers raised the problem of mind-body interaction that seemed to them to follow from the discovery of the 'real distinction', Descartes could reply: that at least he did better than the Schoolmen, since he was talking about cause and effect relations between two substances.[16] They, he charged, much more implausibly, thought modes, like their alleged 'real qualities', could affect substances. But causality is always, if not from greater to lesser reality, at least between realities on one level, never from less to more. Ideas can act on motions, since they are both modes; minds can act on bodies, or bodies on minds, since they are both finite substances. And of course God, who is Infinite Reality, can act on us or on our thoughts, and on bodies or their shapes and motions, while in the other direction there is no path.

Levels of reality talk in general, and talk of levels of causality in particular, sounds very odd to modern ears. Things are or are not—how can some be more real than others? Causes are necessary and sufficient conditions for effects; what has 'degree of reality' to do with it? Degrees of reality discourse works, in fact, only if, as Spinoza will put it, by reality and perfection one means the same thing. The existence of finite things is indeed all or none; it is that kind of 'being' that is suspended by the Demon (I will pretend there is no earth, no sky, and so on), and that is reinstated in Meditation Six. But the Being of a thing, its nature, and hence its power, is a matter of degree: a matter of its proximity to or distance from the source of all Being. This is the old concept of reality, and of causation, which, once more, simply belongs to the fabric of Cartesian thought. To speak of a 'theory of emanation' here, however, it should be remembered, is to make a merely externalist, retrodictive, claim. Descartes seldom uses the term 'emanation' and would not recognise any 'theory' in the case at all (*see AT*, iv, p.608; cf.i, p.152; cf.Beyssade, 1979, pp.108–9). The well-ordered series of degrees of being, with their hierarchical causal relations, belongs, again, to that fund of common notions which everybody shares and on which the philosopher is free to draw. As we see matters, this conception sits very oddly with the billiard ball causality we associate with a mechanised nature. For Descartes, however, as we have already noticed and will consider more particularly in a moment, it is entirely essential. Ideas and things harmonise thanks only to the veracity and goodness of the Infinite Power that makes and remakes them. Nature's code is decipherable only if God has so decreed. All order, all intelligibility, flows from that Source. The lesser perfections of mind and body meet in knowledge, thanks to the higher reality of God.

But what has Descartes done with the well-ordered universe of degrees of reality and of power? There used to be God, angels, human beings, 'nobler' beasts, ordinary domestic animals, plants, nasty creatures like mice and flies, some generated by dirt and decaying matter—each kind at every level in its own unique place. Now of all the variety of creation, with its many levels and many kinds at any level each in its special place, what is left? Three levels, and, altogether, five kinds. There are: one infinite substance, two kinds of finite substance and the modes of each of the latter. Descartes has cleaned out the lumber room of scholastic thought so thoroughly as to leave what seems a barely habitable shelter. Nor will it stand for long. The 'firm and stable' something he had set out to produce, and the very foundations of the structure he had erected, proved unstable indeed. That is the irony of Descartes's influence. What has held us captive in his thought is its innovations: the alienation of mind from nature, with its consequent subjectivism, and the denial of life, with its reductivistic consequences. But Descartes's concept of substance and the notion of a hierarchically ordered series of causal powers associated with it: these concepts, which furnished the ontological foundation for his proposed reform, had become, through his own originality in transforming them, too abstract, too impoverished, to survive. The albatross of modern thought has been, not Descartes's own ontology, but items adopted from it and read into new contexts, contexts generated at least in part by those very items taken without their original and idiosyncratic setting. The ontology itself, in its pure unsullied form, was soon to fall away.

8

Finally, as we have had ample occasion to remark in passing, Descartes's ontological founding of his method depends in the last analysis on the conception of God, on God's role as Founder of the foundation. Again, from within the tradition, Descartes effects here a radical change both in method and in content. He effects what Gouhier in his *Pensée Métaphysique de Descartes* (1978a) called a 'metaphysical inversion'.[17] From a careful comparison of Descartes's arguments with those of St Thomas, Gouhier concludes that in talking about God Descartes is reversing the Thomistic method of analogy. He is using an anthropomorphism in reverse. Absolute difference, not analogy, is what must be stressed. This change in method is demanded by, and used to expound, what has been called a new idea of God (Gouhier, 1978a, p.221, after Gilson, 1975, pp.224 ff.). But, note once more, this is a 'new idea of God' conceived within the larger Thomist conception of the distinction and harmony of reason and revelation, retaining with all piety the idea of God as an infinite spiritual substance, the unique cause of all being, supremely good, supremely powerful, supremely wise. Descartes will of course argue, in the *Meditations*, for God's veracity: that is the heart of his foundation for science; but about God's goodness or power he never even argues. Thus, when he wants to invoke deception about existence, he invents a fictive Demon to do the job; when he wants to carry such negations further, to general truths, he invokes 'some God': *aliquis Deus*. God himself, although He could overturn even mathematics, cannot, when we think about Him clearly, be conceived as in any way devious or malicious, any more than He can be conceived as in any way failing in power or wisdom. Descartes's idea of God is new, but the God it is an idea of is the Deity of Christian, indeed of Catholic, faith: the God in whose reality he has been instructed by the religion, as he is said to have put it, of his King and his nurse. What he alters is the conception of our way of knowing God and of the relation of God, so known, to our knowledge of His creation.

In this move, from the analogical method to a stress on absolute difference, Gouhier distinguishes four interrelated strands:

> A God *causa sui* whose supreme freedom is perfect indifference, in whom intellect and will cannot be distinguished *ne quidem ratione* (even in reason), these three theses appear complementary in the profundity of a fourth which makes of this God the creator of the eternal truths' (Gouhier, 1978a, p.230).

For St Thomas, God is without cause. On the analogy of our experience of cause and effect, He could have no cause. For Descartes, on the other hand, there is in God's case a total *dis*analogy to the cause and effect relation. God is pure activity, pure causal power, self-causing, yet not effect for his own causality (*AT*, vii, p.242). He has the dignity of being cause, without the indignity of being an effect. Indifference, similarly, secondly, is for us a feeble kind of freedom. Our freedom is fullest when intellect lights our way. 'Indifference', lack of reason to choose, is what we feel when the light is lacking. With God it is just the other way. His choice is absolutely beyond reasons. He is supreme indifference. Nor consequently, thirdly, can we distinguish in any way at all, in His nature, between such 'faculties' as intellect and will. He is, He knows, He makes be—it is all one. And the deepest reason for all these denials, as well as their most radical consequence, lies in the notorious doctrine of God's creation of the eternal truths. This is not just a daring remark to Mersenne in the spring of 1630, to be hedged on or withdrawn bye and bye. Indeed, Gouhier, Rodis-Lewis and Marion, the last in great detail, have all shown how central this doctrine is, from first to last, in Descartes's ontology.[18] We may take it here, for brevity's sake, in terms of the interpretation of science as a code. The founding of nature's code, to which we hope our code conforms, has simply to be *performed.* It is God's decree from which all rationality, both ours and nature's, has to follow.

The subtle relation of Descartes's arguments to the philosophical-theological concepts of his contemporaries and predecessors are not my concern here—although some aspects of these questions will be touched on in the next chapters. What emerges as central, and centrally illuminating, for the study of Cartesian metaphysics, however, from these analyses, is the emphasis, in this conception of God, on His power. He is the Being on whom the Being of all beings in every way at every instant depends. I have always found the arguments from imperfection in the Third and Fourth Meditations strained and puzzling. What can it mean to argue that, if I could, I would have given myself perfection? I am what I am; my imperfections, my inabilities, belong to the very heart of me. But if the concept I have in view—though only *a contrario*, as what I understand (without comprehending it) that I am not—if that concept is one of complete, infinite power, creative energy, the Being that by its very nature makes beings, than those arguments do in a way make a certain kind of sense. Created things are seen as made by the Power of powers, and in that making are given what lesser power they have, which is their being. It may be objected, if one accepts Gouhier's notion of a metaphysical inversion, that I am here reintroducing analogy:

the analogy between my 'power' and God's. Perhaps. Nevertheless, the method, it seems to me, has indeed been one of putting the idea of God first: an idea of God innately clear yet just as innately incomprehensible, the idea of a God who is Infinite Power, utterly different from our thrownness in a world. When we turn our attention to that idea, as the argument of the Third Meditation teaches us to do, we can then see our limited natures against the yardstick of that incomprehensible Unlimitedness and interpret our imperfection through our failure to give ourselves what, incomprehensibly, that Highest Being is known, as *causa sui*, to give Himself. But all the complications about God's intellect, His contemplation of eternal truths, or their 'presence' in His mind: all those are gone. Only the single inference from Greatest to lesser perfection, Greatest to lesser power, remains.

Is not this 'new idea of God,' however, perilously close to Hobbes's conception of God as *simply* power? Hobbes, in the Third Objections, denied that we had an idea of God. So, he said, Descartes's argument fails. Of course we have an idea of God, replies Descartes indignantly; the argument stands (see references in n. 3 above). Are the two not as far apart as two philosophers can be? Yes and no. Descartes, I have been emphasising, is urging reform *within* an accepted philosophico-theistic framework. Hobbes, on the contrary, is a radical nay-sayer. There is no idea of God because for him 'idea' means image, not a clear and distinct thought presented to reason. Reason for him is only the stringing of names together, and 'God' is a name for infinite power, to be used for frightening men into obedience. The two thinkers are indeed opposite; their mutual misunderstanding is total. Yet, as we shall see later with Gassendi, Descartes vents his indignation especially upon those thinkers to whom, in our view, he seems closest: other mechanists in physics, both Gassendi and Hobbes himself; his own disciple, Regius, when he gets him wrong.[19] And again, he feels himself closest, among his critics, to the arch-conservative, almost evangelical Arnauld. He certainly considered himself as in no way going in Hobbes's direction—and of course Hobbes's ontology, bracketed as it was in people's minds with his 'horrid atheism', was to have little positive influence, while Descartes's arguments, though by no means universally accepted or understood, certainly set the framework for controversy in the decades, indeed the centuries, to come. So I must suppose that the stress on 'power' in these two philosophical theologies was a coincidence of no, or little, historical import. Indeed, although I can see in Descartes's concept of substance, of attributes, of degrees of reality, the precarious equilibrium I have attributed to them, I am not at all sure about the implications for the future of his 'new idea of God'. *Causa sui*, again, will be reread by Spinoza; that is one line of destiny, indeed. And it may be that the creation of the eternal truths, with its relation to the problem of ontological-epistemological foundations, is equally fateful. It is true, that if the foundation must be founded, that is how: in God's *fiat*; and if it cannot be founded, that is why: because God's *fiat* is radically beyond our ken. For me, however, I must confess once more, the instability of Cartesian metaphysics lies primarily in the impoverishment, not so much of the Creator, as of His creation. It is the real distinction and the concomitant double reduction of mind to thought and nature to machinery that have plagued our thinking. As I, and others, have argued too often elsewhere, a world without life is a world in which neither minds, nor anything, can live. The bare unstable Cartesian world does indeed demand a foundation and must indeed fail to find it. Both the need and the failure, however, spring from the paucity and abstractness of the Cartesian real. Even God cannot weld together what clear and distinct thought has so sharply split asunder.

Notes

1. *'je vous dirai, entre nous, que ces six Méditations contiennent tous les fondements de ma physique... Mais il ne faut pas le dire... ceux qui favorisent Aristote feraient peut-être plus de difficulté de les approuver; et j'espère que ceux qui les lirent, s'accoutuméront insensiblement a mes principes, et en reconnaitront la verité avant que de s'apercevoir qu'ils détruisent ceux d'Aristote.* (*AT*, iii, pp.297–8).
2. Descartes discussed the question of transubstantiation in the Replies to the Fourth Objections, and in a number of letters, e.g., *AT*, iv, pp.165 ff., 374ff. *See* the discussion in Gouhier, 1972, pp. 221 ff.
3. *See* Third Objections and Replies, *AT*, vii, pp.171–96; Descartes's opinion of Hobbes is expressed in his letters to Mersenne, *AT*, iii, pp.287–9, 320 and 360. Cf. ch.6 below.
4. *See* the comment by Christian Huyghens quoted in Lenoble (1971), p. 447.

5. Recently also there is much reference in French scholarship to Heidegger on Descartes, chiefly to the passages in the Nietzsche volume, rather than to the classic section in *Sein und Zeit*. This seems to me rather one aspect of a current fashion than a serious addition to Cartesian scholarship.
6. See especially Gouhier (1978a) *passim* and Marion (1981, Sec. 1, pp.27–227).
7. September 1642 (*AT*, iii, pp.436–8), Descartes asks Mersenne to send no more materials about the *Meditations*. In October, he is writing about what makes chimneys smoke, and so on (*AT*, iii, p.587).
8. That Augustinians showed an unusual interest in natural science is well known; I am not suggesting the contrary. But their attitude to observation and experiment seems to resemble rather Mersenne's than Descartes's, in that the sense of studying God's work is always present.
9. Descartes gives an account of his trouble with the authorities at Utrecht in the letter to Dinet (1642), *AT*, vii, pp.582–603, the letter to Voetius (1643), *AT* viii, 2, pp.13–194 and the letter to the Magistrates of Utrecht (1645 and 1648), *AT*, viii, 2, pp.201–317.
10. *See* note 2 above.
11. For a recent account of the relation between Aristotelian and modern physics, *see* S.Waterlow (1982).
12. *See* ch. 8 below.
13. Wiggins takes it that biologists, and philosophers of biology, accept the Aristotelian concept of a this-such (Wiggins, 1982). In general, however, it is just what they vigorously deny. *See* the recent literature on species as individuals (Hull, 1980; Sober, 1984).
14. The 'problem of universals' concerns Descartes very little. *Principles*, I, art. 59, and *AT*, i, pp.154, 196, 216; iii, p.66 are among the scattered references I have noticed. Precisely the delicate question of the relation of 'form' to individuality is missing—as, given the denial of *form*, it must be. Cf. ch. 6 below.
15. For a recent discussion *see* G.C.Hatfield (1979), Gueroult and Gabbey in Gaukroger (1980).
16. The clearest statement of this point is at *AT*, ix, p.213; cf. also ii, pp.367–8 and v, pp.222–3.
17. Gouhier's account is so convincing, and so illuminating for the reading of Cartesian texts, that I shall simply follow it here. Marion (1981) carries a similar line of thought much further; some points made by both commentators will be touched on in the next chapter. That Descartes himself may, at a point different from the tradition, invoke analogy in speaking of God, will be noticed in due course (ch. 7 below).
18. *See* references in ch.3, p.78 Marion gives a detailed table of allusions to the doctrine (1981 pp.270–1).
19. For the relation to Gassendi, *see* ch. 6 below. For the correspondence with Regius, *see* the edition of G.Rodis-Lewis (1959) and the account(s) by Descartes referred to in n. 9 above.

PART TWO

Descartes and his Contemporaries

5 *Descartes and the School*

1

The major context of this essay, it should be amply clear by now, is the all too familiar one of the confrontation of our philosophical problems with the Cartesian tradition at whose close, it seems, we still find ourselves. Our task, in the late as in the early twentieth century, is to find our way to philosophising beyond Descartes. Both Heidegger and (late) Wittgenstein, among others, attempted such new beginnings; yet the dominant mode at least of English-language philosophy remains thoroughly Cartesian. How can we evade this kind of dead-end thinking? Chapters 1 and 2 have provided some hints, but not more; nor have I, as a historian of philosophy rather than a philosopher, some larger emancipative programme ready to hand. Such a glimpse as I have of where a way may lie I shall present, by means of interpretation of another familiar Cartesian text, in my concluding chapter.

Meantime, however, I should like to look, in this and the next two chapters, at a narrower Cartesian context: at Descartes in his own time. Again, as in my reading of Descartes , I shall present only a sampler of the available evidence. Some of this I have already discussed in other contexts, for example, Descartes's correspondence with Morin, professor of Mathematics at the Sorbonne. In general, I shall touch on Descartes's relation to three sets of his contemporaries: to the Scholastics (or Aristotelians), to others who, like himself, were seeking to establish a mechanistic science of nature, notably Gassendi, and to the more conservative group of Port Royal, in particular` to the Great Arnauld. These are some of the contemporary contexts, of course, suggested by a reading of the 'Objections and Replies' published with the *Meditations*, as well as of the *Correspondence.* There are many other connections one might explore: Descartes's friendship with Huyghens, his enmity with Fermat and Roberval, his exchanges with other critics, like More, or with Pollot, who went, it seems, from critic to adherent; with disciples like Regius, or, in cases where there was no direct exchange, his comments on Digby or Herbert of Cherbury. But I hope that the Objections and Replies may furnish a sufficiently interesting diversity of exchanges to serve as our principal starting point for a view of Descartes in his own time.

As they appeared in the first edition, in 1641, the Objections and Replies fall strikingly into three groups. In I, II and VI Descartes is responding to questions from fairly standard Aristotelian thinkers, the first coming (indirectly) from one Caterus, a Dutch priest whose opinion he had himself (indirectly) solicited and II and VI comprising a number of questions collected by Mersenne (II perhaps by Mersenne himself; of that more shortly). Here Descartes speaks, respectfully, as one professional to others. The Third and Fifth Objections, however, from Hobbes and Gassendi, irritate him immensely.[1] The outsider might have thought their commitment to the new mechanism an attractive feature for their fellow mechanist—who has confided to Mersenne that his little piece on metaphysics contains all the principles of his physics. Yet these are the two commentators on the first edition before whom courtesy fails. (The Seventh Objections and Replies, published with the second edition, are another story; of that, too, more later.) The respondent who best understands him, on the other hand, in his view, is Arnauld, author of the Fourth Objections. But Arnauld represents Port Royal, the ultra-conservative Jansenist group. He was even to be banished from Paris because of his philosophical-theological writings. Yet that did not, even then (in 1648), prevent the cautious Descartes—ultra-cautious according to some—from showing his special admiration for this somehow kindred spirit.

What I want to do, then, is to look at these documents, and a little beyond, or behind, them, in order to place Descartes more securely in the context of his own time. And first the Scholastics, or, as he calls them, the School.

2

More than most philosophers, Descartes self-consciously sought to develop his *own* thought, out of his own initiative. That is the deepest motivation of his search for solitude. Not that this means a 'subjective' program, in which his single perspective will be developed in contradistinction to the equally idiosyncratic perspectives of others. Far from being the 'ghost' Ryle thought it or a Wittgensteinian 'secret inner something', Descartes's mind, an instance in his view of mind as he conceived it, proceeds step by step in the right order to enunciate truths that *any* man of right reason would—even will, he came to hope—follow him in asserting. Because of the obscurity and confusion inherent in the mind-body entanglement of this life, because of the misguided ways of infancy and (traditional) early teaching, however, a philosopher must free himself—as we have seen—from those early 'teachings of natural impulse' and strike out, each one, for himself. But the way he follows toward and in his emancipation from prejudice and overhasty judgment will be a way open to any and hence to all. Descartes seeks solitude, therefore, not anachronistically, in a search for some analogue of post-Romantic 'self-expression', but in order to get on, without distraction, in a foundationist enterprise that, once enacted, will serve, not only himself (he will learn to live a long time!), but mankind (so will we all—and be the possessors of nature through our new understanding of its laws). Hence the philosophical project of the solitary thinker (and experimenter, so far as funds permitted) was a project conceived and executed—as far as it went before his death at fifty-four—on behalf of *the* human mind. It was a *mathesis universalis* he was after, both in the sense of a unified science and of a learning available to all men of 'good sense'; both the object of knowledge and the knowledge itself were universalisable.

At the same time, of course, Descartes's search for one coherent and permanent body of knowledge took place not anywhere or any time, but in seventeenth-century Europe, and its relation to its time and place is both intimate and complex. We have already noticed this in a number of respects: his commitment to some of the fundamental tenets inculcated at La Flèche and at the same time his resolve to alter the foundations of Aristotelian thought both in method (in the *Regulae*) and in the metaphysical foundations of physics (*Meditations*) as well as in physics itself (*Principles*). At present we want to look more particularly at his relation to contemporary Aristotelians, a relation which receives paradoxically contrary expression in his works and correspondence and which also, I believe (as I have already indicated), undergoes a personal and rhetorical, though not a substantive, development. Let me take up these two points briefly before going on to think about the School itself in the perspective of Descartes's relation to it.

On the first point, Descartes, like Mersenne, Galileo, Hobbes, Gassendi and many others, certainly did want to do away with some major Aristotelian components of contemporary thought, and especially of contemporary physics. Descartes is quite firm, for example, in the exchange with Morin that we examined earlier, in insisting on the superiority of his explanations of natural phenomena to those of the School. In another letter to the same correspondent he remarks:

> It is true that the comparisons one is in the habit of making in the School, explaining intellectual things by corporeal things, substances by accidents, or at least one quality by another of the same species, offer very little instruction. But as for those which I use, I compare only movements to other movements, or figures to other figures, and so on, that is to say, only things which in virtue of their small size cannot fall under our senses to others that do so fall, and which do not differ otherwise than as a large circle differs from a small circle; I claim that they are the most appropriate means for explaining the truth of Physical questions that the human mind can have, to the point that, if one claims something about nature that cannot be explained by any such comparison, I think I know by demonstration that it is false (*AT*, ii, pp.367–8).

Indeed, in the letter to Dinet published, along with the Seventh Objections and Replies, in the second edition of the *Meditations*, he goes so far as to claim that 'the Peripatetic philosophy has never proposed a solution of a single problem that (he) cannot show to be false and illegitimate' (*AT*, vii, pp.579–80). On the other hand, as we have already noticed, he declares in the *Principles* that he has said nothing not found in the text of Aristotle himself! The latter remark may indeed be put down to a rhetorical purpose: he wants the *Principles* taught (of that more in a moment), and so must attempt to confine their content within the bounds of respectability—*alias* Aristotle. On the other hand, Dinet was the Provincial in charge of the Jesuits of Paris. If it was a question of tact, why did he risk alienating this powerful figure with so extravagant a claim about the incompetence of Aristotelianism? He must *mean* it! Besides, over and over in the correspondence, as in the letter to Morin just quoted, he stresses his hundred and eighty degree opposition to most of the explanatory principles of Aristotelian science. Indeed, the fundamental project of the First and Second Meditations—to lead the mind away from the senses—is, though devious and infinitely careful, just precisely the project of leading his readers away from their Aristotelian starting point. Having worked their way through this intellectual retreat with his guidance, they will, he hopes, have abandoned their Aristotelianism without noticing that that was what was happening (*AT*, iii, p.233: see n.l, ch.4). In short, Descartes must on the whole be taken as opposing the Aristotelian tradition, certainly in physics as well as in epistemology and *partially* in metaphysics. Yet, except for the Seventh Objections (which form a special case), the relation is one of courteous and respectful opposition, somewhere between his enthusiasm for Arnauld and his anger at Hobbes and Gassendi. Through his Jesuit education he shares certain important premises with his scholastic critics and is confident that he ought to be able to persuade them on points where they differ. Those points, moreover, are the very changes needed to make possible a mathematical physics: the reversal of Aristotle's empiricism and of his scientific pluralism, the restriction of change to local motion, the limitation of substance ontology to the needs of this scientific reform.

Such, in my view, is the general relation of Descartes to the School. But that relation, too, has its history, which I noted in the previous chapter, but should mention again briefly here. If Descartes was at first a solitary thinker, who suppressed his *World* because of Galileo's condemnation, and who intended to publish his *Discourse*, *Dioptrics* and so on anonymously, he was nevertheless involved from early on in debate and correspondence about his work. And of course by the time of the *Meditations* he sought criticism to which he might respond *before* publication. So, clearly, the opinions of the learned world mattered to him; and indeed the rhetoric of the *Meditations* itself makes it emphatically clear that he had thought very carefully about the audience he was addressing. With the years in Holland, therefore, something was happening to the alleged recluse. First, on principle, he was concerned to make his program intelligible to others. Second, as a result, he became involved in public controversy: in two of the bitterest cases (Voetius and Bourdin) with scholastic opponents. Third, on the other hand, as Gouhier has persuasively argued, he grew at the same time *more* convinced that his new doctrine (the Truth, after all!) would eventually be taught in those very schools with which, partly and briefly, he had seemed to be 'at war'.

There was a time, between the *Meditations* and the *Principles*, when he considered setting up a table of parallels between his views and those of the Aristotelians, probably of Eustache de St Paul, whose work he considered the best available. Either Eustache's death or—more probably, it seems to me—the notion that the *Principles*, as he was to state them, might win acceptance on their own, led him to abandon that project.[2] Aristotelianism *would* retreat and Cartesianism triumph, as, after Descartes's death, indeed, it partly did (Brockliss, 1981a). So his explicit opposition could be muted and his good relations with the Jesuits in particular cemented. Thus some time in 1643 he writes to Father Dinet: 'I have had these past days much satisfaction in having had the honour of seeing the Reverend Father Bourdin, and in the fact that he has made me hope for the favour of his good grace. I know that it is particularly to you that I owe the happiness of this accommodation' (*AT*, iv, pp.142–3). When he writes to yet another Jesuit, Father Charlet, in February 1645, it is clear that he has become as friendly as can be with his former enemy (*AT*, iv, pp.160–1). And in fact he sent copies of the *Principles* to all three, Dinet, Charlet and Bourdin.[3] (That the conflict at Utrecht proved so much more persistent may be due to the greater ease with which Descartes could be reconciled with Catholic than with Protestant adversaries; but that is pure speculation.)

3

Who, then, were Descartes's scholastic critics, the contemporaries to whom much of his argument had to be directed if his new method and doctrine were to be assimilated to the official teaching of his day? Aristotelians, obviously, in some sense. Even that generalisation has to be qualified, however. For one thing, if, as Alquié believes, and as Mersenne himself seems to have claimed, Mersenne in fact wrote the Second Objections, at least one member of the new, non-Aristotelian, scientific circle is included (Alquié, 1967, p.541).[4] Yet Mersenne, though deep in the new mechanism, is still conventional enough—or confused enough—so that, despite the novelty of his thought in physics, his objections fit in with the general pattern of Objections One and Six. Indeed, as we noticed in the previous chapter, his physics was emphatically anti-foundationalist—and, as Descartes had twice informed him, it was the *foundations* of Cartesian physics that the *Meditations* were intended to provide. More substantively, moreover, it must of course be recognised that the epithet 'Aristotelian' fails to refer univocally to some single, monolithic group of philosophers or doctrines. The doctors of the Sorbonne, for example, to whom the *Meditations* were officially addressed, were far less sophisticated than were Descartes's Jesuit teachers in their attitude to the new science of nature. As Brockliss has shown, it was straight Aristotelian physics that was taught at Paris during Descartes's lifetime (Brockliss, 1981a). The Jesuits, on the whole, took more active account of what was going on in the international scene, and they were subtler interpreters of the tradition itself. The lecturers of the Sorbonne, for example, made no mention at all of the Coimbran commentaries, a standard source of recent and refined Aristotelian exegesis. Even in the Society of Jesus, too, as Descartes was to discover with relief, there could be intemperate members, like Bourdin, who spoke only for themselves, not for the whole community. In short, there is no single view of *the* School as such. So, looking at the overall tenor of Objections I, II and VI, we are admittedly making some very crude historical generalisations; but I hope they give us some not wholly inappropriate sense of the bent and temper of seventeenth-century Peripatetic thought.

A comment appended to the Sixth Objections may give us as good a start as any other at understanding the cast of mind of Descartes's scholastic readers. (I shall return presently to their substantive objections.) They beg that Descartes 'unloose the knot, by which you believe we are held in adamantine chains, so that our minds do not wholly escape the body (*omne corpus*)' (*AT*, vii, pp.420–1). And they continue:

> The knot is, that we understand very well that three plus two make five, that if you take equals from equals, equals will remain; we are convinced by these and a thousand other things, just as you find yourself. Why are we not similarly convinced, by your ideas or ours, that the mind of man is distinct from the body, and that God exists? You may say, that you cannot insert this truth into our hearts unless we meditate with you. But we have read what you have written seven times, and lifted up our minds to the limit of our powers, on the model of the Angels; and yet in spite of that we are not persuaded. Nor do we believe you will prefer to say that all our minds are tainted with a brutish spell, and wholly unsuited to Metaphysical matters, to which we have been accustomed for thirty years, rather than admitting that your arguments, so far as they are drawn from the ideas of mind and of God, are not of such weight, or of such force, that the minds of learned men, lifting themselves as best they can above corporeal mass, can and ought to submit to them. We believe rather that you will make the very same confession if you reread your *Meditations* in that spirit in which you would submit them to an analytical examination if they had been proposed to you by an adversary (*AT*, vii, p.421).

It is a touching picture—of professionals in a rich, long-established discipline, with a lifetime's experience, suddenly challenged, in their authoritative middle, if not old, age, to begin again from a new beginning: to see the world with new eyes: as Merleau-Ponty might have put it, to sing the world, not merely in a new key, but in what seemed to them a new cacophony, or at best a monotone. That Descartes did not in fact abandon, even tentatively, all his former opinions, as he boasted he would do, we have already seen. But clearly the reform he was attempting was radical enough so that even close—angelic?—readings of the *Meditations* were insufficient to turn his readers from their wonted principles to his new beginning. Descartes, it's true, was delighted with this comment, for after seven readings his critics could find no *arguments* against him! That impresses him, he says, more than the fact that they have not yet been persuaded. As Descartes himself well knew, however—why else did he write *Meditations*?—it is not argument but practice and discipline, almost sheer will power, that is needed to turn the mind from its accustomed stance on basic issues—a stance, in the Scholastics' case, Descartes believes, ingrained through childhood experience, of its essence obscure, and reinforced by those very misleading doctrines of the School that his critics still profess and that he seeks to cure them of. He, too, had his sudden insight in the winter of 1619–20: that was no argument, but the vision of a new way to go. Those who yet lack that vision will have difficulty following the new method on its way, especially since it is precisely the cumbersome path of syllogistic argument they practise that prevents their adoption of Descartes's alternative.

But never mind for now Descartes's response to his scholastic commentators. Let us try to understand a little better, not their obtuseness, as it must have seemed to him, but the plausibility of some of their criticisms. After all, it was quite explicitly the conjunction of 'common sense and the School' Descartes was trying to overcome; as the consolidator of common sense, and, some of us might say, also as the inheritor of Aristotle, the School did have something to be said for it. Physics, to get going, undoubtedly needed the turn to the mathematisation of mind and the materialisation of nature for which Descartes in his *magnum opus* was supplying the metaphysical underpinning. But let us try to glimpse if we can the anchorage in reality philosophy was thereby to lose. Not that we should wish to, or could, return to that antiquated cosmology; yet looking at some of its features as exhibited in the Objections may help us, indirectly, to understand our own philosophical dilemma, as well as to place Descartes more concretely within the frame of his time. Including a first, general point I shall list a round dozen, most of them philosophical, some connected with theology (hence only more indirectly with Aristotle), collected from Objections I, II and VI.

4

First, the general point. On the whole, as is to be expected, these critics of Descartes represent a robust and direct realism of a plainly Aristotelian stamp. Indeed, as both our discussion of the *Rules* and of the ontology have already indicated, it was precisely that realism Descartes was seeking to overcome. The School is immersed in *things*; it is to the pure mathematisable *objects* of thought that Descartes wants to turn their attention.

They are the proponents of common sense, who find themselves, as we have all found ourselves in childhood, in a world of real things, or of real kinds of things, including other animals and other people, live, breathing, bodily people as well as live, breathing horses, dogs, cattle or what you will. True, the thought of seventeenth-century scholars was remote, by two millenia and many devious intellectual moves, from the argumentations of Aristotle himself, grounded as these were in the varied experience of a great biologist. What survives, however, in the scholastic apparatus is the rootedness of our attempts to know in the ordered diversity of a real world. Though hidebound, or if you like, calcified, in its methodology, scholastic ontology presents a version of what I have called elsewhere *comprehensive realism*, a realism that moves, not from some secret inner something out to a problematic nature, but within nature—through the disciplined cultivation of that desire to know that all men possess—from the perceived, already orderly manifold to the intelligible ground of its being: discoverable in its being by the human mind whose nature itself contains within itself the potentiality of actualising such knowledge (Grene, 1985). That realism, of course, in any of its traditional forms—Aristotelian or scholastic—is overempirical. Rooted in the diversity of experience, it fails to permit the flights of a mathematising physics. As Thibaut, an obscure correspondent of Mersenne, put it, it is hard to know, when Descartes speaks of 'body as quantity', for instance, whether he is speaking 'in the predicament of substance or of quantity' (*AT*, v, pp. 70–1). For of course Aristotelian mathematics, abstracting from the fuller reality of *things*, treats only of their quantity, whether continuous (in geometry) or discrete (in arithmetic). And quantity is an accidental category; it does not relate to substance, to what things there really, and fundamentally, are.

Thus, for Aristotle, the sciences, like optics or astronomy, that use mathematics for their understanding of nature prove more an embarrassment than an ally. It follows that scholastic science is irredeemably pluralistic. There is a hint of this in an odd comment in the Second Objections. In the context of Descartes's proof of God, the writer—Mersenne?—is worried about the atheist's counter-argument about God's infinity (*AT*, vii, p. 125). Arguing about infinity is difficult, he suggests, because there are so many lines along which it might be sought, or found. There are many infinites, as there are many goods or evils. This is muddled, if you like, since unlike Spinoza the writer fails to distinguish infinite in kind from infinite *per se*. But it illustrates well, I find, the very sort of finitist thinking Descartes had to persuade his contemporaries to abandon. For them, the world is so full of a number of things. In Descartes's wake, we must forget all that and learn to deal with all of nature in one free, mathematical way. For Descartes, in other words, as seems obvious to us though not to all his contemporaries, it is mathematics, for him especially geometry, indeed only geometry, though algebraised geometry, that enables us to deal clearly and distinctly, hence scientifically, with nature at all, and we do this in *one* way in all fields, making sure that we move in the right order, from simple to more complex, so as to preserve clarity and distinctness all along the line.

It is in virtue of this move, also, it should be noted, that Descartes, like Bacon, will make us possessors of nature. Exploration *in* the real world will become exploitation *of* the world: the world's my oyster, which I with high technology will open. Some of us, while acknowledging with due respect and even veneration the vast body of scientific knowledge acquired, and yet to be acquired, in the wake of the Baconian-Cartesian reform, still quake at the prospect of the possessive instinct run rampant. And again, a look at some of the hesitancies of Descartes's scholastic readers to make obeisance to the Cartesian faith (as our friend Thibaut put it) may assist us in our search for a way to break, carefully and with due attention to intervening history, both in science and elsewhere, but nevertheless to break with the dogmatism Descartes succeeded in substituting, in our minds, for the scholastic-cum-commonsensical dogmatism with which his critics responded to his program.

Not, once more, that we can simply turn our backs on Descartes's reform and its three centuries of consequences. It was a move that modern thought, following on Descartes and his successors, has made in irreversible fashion. We cannot, as tightly and immediately as those seventeenth-century Aristotelians could, confine our thought within the limits of an immediately perceptible, finite world. Indeed, beyond Descartes and Cartesianism, Hume and Kant respectively have shown us, (1), that, in science or history or any other non-formal intellectual discipline, we always have to go beyond the evidence and (2), that our intellectual activity is part and parcel of the knowledge such hazardous exploration allows us to acquire. But if we recognise that we are real live animals, trying, through our intellectual practices, however abstract and refined, to orient ourselves in some section of our world, we can see that the primacy of bodily life and of thinking as *embodied* is nevertheless fundamental, in a way analogous, at least, to the way in which these objectors held it to be.

Let us look, then, at some of the more particular criticisms these commentators raised.

5

Second of my dozen: the Cartesian idea, the atom of evidence, as we have followed Hamelin and Marion in calling it, clearly makes no scholastic sense. In fact, its unintelligibility is at the root of most of Caterus's complaints in the First Objections. *Things* are the target of knowledge; ideas are superadded: relatively speaking, nullities. 'What is an idea?' Caterus asks, and answers:

> It is the thing being thought, itself, insofar as it is objectively in the intellect. But what is it to be objectively in the intellect? As I learned it, it is to terminate the act of intellect itself in the fashion of an object. And that is plainly an extrinsic denomination and nothing in the thing. But just as being seen is nothing but the fact that the act of vision tends toward me, so being thought, or being objectively in the intellect, is to hold in itself and terminate the mind's thought; which can happen, even though the thing be unmoved and unchanged, and even non-existent (*AT*, vii, p.92).

So, it seems, an idea is not an act—not an actual thing; it is 'a naked denomination and a nothing' (*AT*, vii, p.92).

Third: Caterus had started by asking, 'Why do I ask for the cause of an idea?' (*AT*, vii, p.92). Now he can explain his question: 'Why do I seek the cause of an idea, which is not an act, which is a naked denomination and a nothing?' (*AT*, vii, p.92). Cartesian causality, it seems, then, is also suspect. Strange. The causal principle as developed in the Third Meditation is, we saw in the previous chapter, both a cornerstone of Cartesian ontology and an inheritance of the tradition. Why doesn't it make sense to a good Thomist like the author of the First Objections? It is, I can only suppose, the routing of causality through ideas that Caterus finds objectionable. As Gueroult emphasises, Cartesian method works only through the acceptance of an entailment that moves from ideas to their objects: 'From knowledge to being, the inference is valid' (*AT*, vii, p.520). That is not to call Descartes an 'idealist'. Given God's veracity, the objects of clear and distinct ideas—the objects of geometry (and of reflection)—may be taken to be real. But the mathematician's mind moves, and must move, from thought to object, not the other way. The School, from a Cartesian point of view, makes that outward move rashly and without adequate evidence: hence the Demon. But from an Aristotelian perspective, the point is that no such move is needed. Causal investigation, in an Aristotelian tradition, consists at bottom in an analysis of the grounds for the being of substances: in each case, ideally, of some least kind of substance, an *atomon eidos*. Such an analysis may look, diachronically, at the origin and endpoint of development: moving cause and *telos*; or, synchronically, at its functional organisation and the content of what is so organised: its form and matter. Indeed, since substances under the moon—which interested Aristotle most—come into being and perish, yet come to be what they essentially *are*, both these approaches are necessary, and conjointly necessary. All four causal approaches are needed, all in well-ordered relation to real things. To introduce ideas into such analyses is simply to introduce confusion—as much as for Descartes it betrays confusion to try to reach out from thoughts less clear and distinct than those of mathematics to some questionable existential target.

What points (2) and (3) amount to, one may suggest, is a difference in the perception of the relation between causality and thought, or the juncture at which one may infer one from the other. Thus, for example, Caterus and Descartes present what look like very similar arguments about this relation, but at characteristically different points. In his brief discussion of the mind-body relation, Caterus alludes to Scotus' concept of a formal distinction—as for instance between God's justice and His mercy—and asks how we can know (as Descartes wants us to know) that two things are different just because we conceive them differently. Descartes replies that formal distinctions apply only to modes, or to incomplete substances (like justice and mercy). His 'real distinction', on the contrary, sorts out two substances, two independently existing 'things'—and here, once God's veracity is guaranteed, our conceptual separation in turn guarantees a real one. But, contrariwise, Descartes questions the Thomists' infinite regress argument to Divine causality. That we cannot conceive an infinite series of causes, he declares, does not entail the nonexistence of such a series (*AT*, vii, pp. 106–7)! If in the case of God (from our idea to His existence) and of the real distinction (from the conception of thought and extension to the existence of two kinds of substance), the inference from thought to object is valid, why not here? I can offer only a speculative answer. In the argument from nature to a first cause, we are starting with just those perceptible things that children (and Schoolmen) *believe* they know about and which they try to explain through their concepts of substantial forms, real qualities and so on. At this level of obscurity, the mind has not yet freed itself from sense, and from the prejudices of infancy and tradition, in such a way as to be able to draw from its conceptions inferences of existential import. Once we *do* understand nature—that is, extended substance—clearly and distinctly, moreover, we understand that it is itself infinite, or better, Descartes reminds himself, indefinite (*AT*, vii, p. 89). So there is in fact nothing wrong with an infinite regress of natural causes, because here, when we understand the matter, we find ourselves engaged in an investigation of the laws that govern an unlimited, a nondelimitable, sequence of motions and cessations of motion.[5] At the level of what will turn out to be Spinozistic modes (of extension!) there is of course an infinite (indefinite) sequence of causes and effects. That we cannot imagine such infinity proves nothing. Thus the power, and impotence, of thought to grasp causality have changed location. For Descartes, thing-bound thoughts cannot reach through, with valid cognitive claims, to a true grasp of what there is. For his scholastic critics, on the other hand, it is thought let loose from its home among the kinds of things there are (including the thinker of such thoughts): it is thought liberated from its rootedness in a complicated, many-featured world that proves unable, on its own, to reach out again to reality, whether it be the reality of itself, of nature or of God.

6

Fourth in my list: although Caterus deals chiefly with problems connected with the proofs of God—especially the passage to God through the idea of Him—he also touches on the mind-body relation. So do they all, Hobbes and Gassendi, too, of course; but what we are looking at here is the relatively Aristotelian, or traditional, resistance to Descartes's 'real distinction'. To anticipate modernity in denying that there *are* minds (or at least imageless thoughts) is one thing; to insist on the rootedness of thought in animate, living bodies is another. And plainly, that is the response of the authors of Objections One, Two and Six; 'body' defined as pure extendedness, as nothing *but* spatiality, is just what they do not understand. The 'body' of any natural thing is its proximate matter: in the case of a living thing, already informed at many levels. A cat, for instance, has the organisation characteristic of cats, but that organisation (= feline sensitive and locomotive soul) *informs* a body already organised into skeletal system, heart and blood vessels, brain and nerves, and so on. And such organs or organ-systems are in turn already organised: their tissues are structured so as to form limbs or heart or brain. And the tissues in turn, at their level, confine the elements they contain so as to make them tissues. The Aristotelian elements in turn can only be analysed into pairs of qualities that inform prime matter. But when we get that far from everyday experience, we are on slippery ground. We can say 'prime matter' and in a way think 'prime matter', but on its own, independently, prime matter cannot *be*. Matter is only potency for form, for actuality. And in the last analysis, only the *actual* is actual! Nor is that a tautology, but the heart of Aristotelian metaphysics (Kosman, 1984).

No wonder the School lost out, you may say. Who could believe such stuff? But who could believe in a 'matter' that is only spread-outness? Space, after all, is, basically, just places for things to be in, and things, far from being hunks of spatiality, are real, rich entities that do things, have things done to them, in the case of the living things so conspicuous in our world are born, grow, alter, age and die. And some of these things, it is perfectly obvious, think, others do not. People and apes and elephants think; oak trees and pebbles don't. But what could thoughts be, in this fleshly, sublunar world, that were not the thoughts of *some* organised living body?

Let us just run through the points raised by all these critics about the real distinction. It was in this context that Caterus brought up the 'formal' distinction of Scotus; how do I know that the alleged distinction between mind and body is not of this sort? (*AT*, vii, p. 100.) And, indeed, I an inclined to think it is! The author(s) of II, in their first comment, ask(s), how you can know that the thinking thing focussed on in the Second Meditation is not really 'yourself, who are a body' (*AT*, vii, pp. 122–3). Descartes, of course, will answer that that is proved in the Sixth Meditation—but is it? That is surely the weakest link in his argument. Indeed, knowing the *Rules*, we can see, with hindsight, that he could prove the real distinction only because he believed it all along. Along with God, it was to prove the essential ontological ground of his method, that great and fateful discovery of 1619. But lacking that vision, why should sensible people accept such counter-evident conclusions?

The authors of Objections VI have a subtler way to make the same point:

> When you say that you *think and exist*, might not some one allege that you are deceived, and that you are not thinking, but only being moved, and that you are nothing but bodily movement, since no one has been able to encompass in his mind your argument, by which you claim to have proved that no bodily movement can be what you call thought? (*AT*, vii, p. 413.)

I can only say this is delightful: why don't we listen to these common-sensical people instead of beating our brains out on the interpretation of the *cogito*? They continue, with a sly gibe at one of Descartes's favourite (wholly unproven) opinions about the interstices of his extended plenum:

> Or, through the way in which, in the depths of Analysis, you have followed all the motions of your subtle matter, are you certain you can show us, most attentive as we are, and, as we believe, sufficiently perspicacious, that our thoughts (can) resist overflowing into those corporeal motions? (*AT*, vii, p. 413.)

It is a neat move to turn Descartes's hobby horse of subtle matter against his own reasoning. Further, in their summing up (*AT*, vii, pp.418–19), they raise again the problem of inferring from our separate *understanding* of mind and body their separate *existence*. For again, as with Caterus, the Cartesian passage through thought to reality is alien to a kind of thinking rooted in things themselves.

Finally, in the first part of the appended remarks, the real distinction between my idea of body and my body itself, is again brought forward (*AT*, vii, pp.419–20). (Alquié asks, how could critics question what Descartes has already explained? Of course they could, and of course we must (Alquié, 1967, p.858)). And in the text of the Appendix we quoted at the start, from those metaphysicians with thirty years' expertise and seven readings behind them, we hear once more:

> However much we reflect, whether the true idea [Latin: *Idola*] of our mind, or the human mind, that is, knowledge or perception, contains in it anything corporeal, we dare not assert that what we call thought does not agree by some principle with any body, affected by what motion you may wish. For since we perceive some bodies that do not think and others, like those of human beings and possibly of brutes, that do think, would you not find us guilty of sophistry, and of too much audacity, if we would therefore conclude that there are no bodies that think? It is hard to doubt that we would have been at once derided by you if we had been the first to forge that argument from ideas, as much for mind as for God, and you had then submitted it to your analysis (*AT*, vii, p.420).

Sound people. And they know their Descartes well! He is, they suspect, so much 'preoccupied and prepossessed' by his method of analysis, that

> you seem yourself to have put a veil before your mind, so that it is no longer free to see that the particular properties and operations of the soul that you find in yourself depend on bodily motions (*AT*, vii, p.420).

Exactly so. The Cartesian *atom of evidence*, far from being the luminous unit of knowledge it seemed to be, was to prove a 'veil' obscuring our natural access to a real world.

7

Fifth, and closely related to the question whether some

bodies think, is the vexed question of the Cartesian *bête-machine*. The authors of the Sixth Objections mention this difficulty, on the one hand, alongside the problem of the souls of Angels (thought by some to be corporeal) and, on the other, in connection with the danger of denying mind to man as well, if 'mechanism' can explain the behaviour of 'apes, dogs, and elephants' (*AT,* vii, p.414). Some people, they remind Descartes, seem to have believed 'that this (sc. thought) could be effected by those corporeal motions ... from which they in no way distinguished thinking'. This repeats their previous point, but they elaborate on it:

> And this can be confirmed by the thoughts of apes, dogs and other animals: for dogs bark in their sleep, as if they are running after hares or robbers, and when awake they know that they are running, and in sleeping that they are barking, since we recognise with you that there is nothing in them distinct from bodies (*AT*, vii, p.414).

Presumably the point is that since it is clear their thought is bodily, they are in some way 'aware' of their performances whether sleeping or waking. They continue:

> But if you deny that the dog knows that it is running, or that it thinks, apart from the fact that you do not prove what you say, perhaps the dog forms a similar judgment of us, namely that we do not know if we are running or if we are thinking, when we perform one or another of these actions (*AT*, vii, p.414).

Note that running and thinking are equally actions: good. Indeed, on some readings of the *Investigations*, a sound Wittgensteinian point! As to the dog's possible judgment of us—that suggestion, if you like, goes as back as far as Zenophanes. Our present writers justify it by remarking:

> For you do not see its internal mode of operation, any more than it sees yours, nor are great men lacking who yield reason to brutes or have in the past done so (*AT*, vii, p.414).

Such an appeal to authority (to the opinion of all, the many, or the wisest, in Aristotelian method) is of course one of the characteristics of the School for which their enemies laughed them to scorn, although it's not so different from the style of academic philosophy today: where argument proceeds from X's article in journal A and Y's in journal B. But their substantive point is the fundamental one: you don't have acquaintance with the dog's mental life any more than he has with yours. The step to subjectivity starts us on a very slippery slide. His critics are, indeed, setting to Descartes a ringing challenge:

> And so far are we from believing that all their [i.e. other animals'] actions can be sufficiently explained by means of Mechanics, without sense, life, or soul, that we would be willing to maintain by any pledge you like that that is both impossible and ridiculous (*AT*, vii, p.414).

Descartes had given his programmatic statement: the wolf and the light in the sheep's eyes (only motion needed; no 'fear'), in answer to the same question from Arnauld (in his case, however, in the spirit of one who *wants* to be persuaded). Here he refers to the fact (as he sees it) that he had 'given a most stringent proof of his view' (*AT*, vii, p.426). This refers, presumably, to the argument of the *Discourse*: if some animals can do some things better than we can, they can't do many; and since they have no speech, which takes very little reason (!), they must have no reason at all (*AT*, vi, pp.56–9). Further, he insists that he has not denied to brutes 'what is vulgarly called life, nor a corporeal soul, nor organic sense' (*AT,* vii, p.426). Their pledge he takes as a sign that they have no proof for their position! Nor do they: the existence of nature, including animals, ourselves among them, is a starting point, not a conclusion. But note: I do not mean by this some arbitrary 'self-evident truth' or *a priori* principle, only the acknowledgement of *where we are*, of our real starting point. Moreover, if Descartes concedes 'what is vulgarly called life', it should be remembered that it is precisely the 'vulgar' view he is trying to defeat. What is vulgarly called 'life', is in fact, in his opinion, animal heat, and in us alone there lurks that other reality, mind with its essential attribute thought and its modes: conceiving, deciding, desiring, feeling and the like. All else is local motion. So be it; I have dealt with some of the problems of the 'animal soul' in an earlier chapter. It should suffice here to applaud those, obsolete as their views were soon to appear, who saw nature as a rich, hierarchically organised nexus of structures and ourselves as part of it.

8

Yet another, sixth, objection, also related to the last two, concerns Descartes's scepticism about the evidential power of the senses and his corresponding confidence in the intellect. The authors of the Sixth Objections write:

> you say that the operations of the senses should be distrusted, and that the certainty of the intellect is much greater than that of the senses. But what if the intellect can enjoy no certainty if it does not first have it from the well-ordered senses? For it [sc. the intellect] cannot correct the error of any sense, unless some other sense first emend the error in question. A stick that is straight looks bent in the water because of refraction; who may correct that error? The intellect? Not at all; but touch. And the same judgment holds of all the rest. For if you have your senses in good order, and they always make the same report, you will reach the very highest certainty of which man is naturally capable: a certainty that may frequently elude you, if you trust the operation of the mind, which often errs in those matters of which it believed that it was impossible to doubt (*AT*, vii, p.418).

One is reminded of H.H.Price's remark: 'we should take off our hats to an animal intelligent enough to walk into a trap' (Price, 1969, p.87). Not that Aristotelian *nous*, properly used, is fallible, as our post-Humean intellects must confess themselves to be. Yet even *nous* was nourished by, and grounded in, the transactions of our sensory systems with the things and events in our perceptible world.[6]

Descartes's reply, predictably, invokes the distinction between sense and judgment. The Cartesian theory of perception, however, forms the subject of my last chapter; I want here just to note the alternative offered by Descartes's critics. Indeed, it seems to me odd that other Aristotelians did not fault the scepticism about the senses in Meditation One. Although everybody knew that 'cold cabbage', as Decartes calls it in his comments on the Second Objections, the Schoolmen, as good Aristotelians or Thomists, surely could not take it seriously. Eustache de St Paul, for instance, in his treatment of perception, simply gives a rather crude version of the *De Anima* and ignores the issue. I wish I knew why Descartes believed his scholastic readers would follow him here; but I have not been able to answer that question, even speculatively, let alone with evidence.

9

Then, seventh, there is the odd question of the atheist's knowledge, which I have noted in passing earlier (*AT*, vii, pp.125, 414–15). If all other knowledge depends on our knowledge of God, do atheists not know that two plus three equals five? Not as science, says Descartes. As Beyssade has shown (Beyssade, 1979, pp.23 ff.), it is not the insight of the moment, which any of us may attain, but Cartesian *science*, the store of propositions achieved by the analytic method and laid up as a possession forever (*firmum et mansurum*) that depends on God's veracity. Here again, of course, the Aristotelians' conception of knowledge is more naturalistic than Descartes's; but then it does not permit the far-reaching flights of mathematical fancy on which Cartesian discovery will depend.

Another bundle of criticisms, some of which I have already alluded to in passing, are more closely connected with theological problems, and less directly, therefore, with the Aristotelian bent of the critics in question. Eighth: as we noticed in the case of Caterus, the proofs of God are worrying (*AT*, vii, pp.91 ff., 123 ff.). Ninth: So are the proofs of God's non-deception (*AT*, vii, pp.125–6; 415–16). There is good authority for the view that God may, and does sometimes, deceive us. (And indeed, as commentators from Gilson to Gouhier have clearly shown, the argument to non-deception is integrally connected with Descartes's 'new idea of God'.) Tenth, the Cartesian concept of freedom is questioned with respect to its implications especially for God's freedom—again, a consequence of Descartes's view of God as pure power (*AT*, vii, pp.416–17)—and in its relation to faith (*AT*, vii, pp.126–7). Eleventh, the problem of 'real accidents' is related in particular to the account of transsubstantiation (*AT*, vii, p.417), which Descartes goes into in more detail in his reply to Arnauld. This was in fact the problem on which Cartesianism was to come to grief with the Church, although Descartes himself insisted that his solution was not only possible, but superior to the usual one. Twelfth, and finally, there was Descartes's doctrine of the creation of the eternal truths (*AT*, vii, pp.417–18). The philosophical importance of this doctrine for Descartes has been touched on, at least indirectly, in Chapter 3.

Such theological problems, however, are even farther beyond

my interest or competence than Descartes insisted they were beyond his. What I have been trying to do here is chiefly to suggest that some of Descartes's more traditional 'Aristotelian' critics did in fact have good reason for some of their hesitations in embracing the new method and its foundational corollaries.

10

The above account has dealt only with objections contained in the first edition. The second edition added a seventh set of objections, with Descartes's replies interspersed and with the letter to Father Dinet appended. Here the spirit of professional criticism and respectful reply has quite evaporated; both parties to the debate are furious. Both go on tediously and repetitiously—Descartes, in part at least, it would appear, in imitation of his critic's querulous prolixity. We had better ask two questions about this confrontation: first, about the circumstances and what they suggest concerning Descartes's relation to the School in general and the Jesuits in particular; and second, about the philosophical insights, if any, which this two-sided tirade adds to those we gleaned from looking at Objections I, II and VI.

About the circumstances, then: this is indeed the juncture at which, Descartes confesses, he fears he is engaged in 'scholastic wars' (*AT*, III, p. 523). He had heard, he explains in his reply to the Objections (and in his letter to Dinet), that a Jesuit, one Father Bourdin, had written about his *Meditations*, and he demands that these criticisms be sent to him, and made public along with his replies. He knows, of course, or so he avers, that if these objections have been formulated on behalf of the Society, they will contain nothing abusive, nothing not marked by the integrity so characteristic of that exceptional and unexceptionable Order! What does he find? A dishonest and abusive document. For a start, he receives a dissertation beginning, 'You have set me many questions.' But he never in his life has set Bourdin a single question. What *is* this? It must be the case that the wretched man does not really know Descartes's work properly and wants to pretend, *via* these alleged 'questions', that Descartes has put forward doctrines he has never in fact enunciated. So there is ill will—surely not that of the Society?—at the root of the whole enterprise. To correct the matter, therefore, Descartes not only interlards Bourdin's text with his replies, but publishes, along with all this, a letter to Father Dinet, the head of the Paris College, explaining the circumstances in which, so much against his will, he has become embroiled, and announcing as well his plan to publish a work, in more scholastic form, with numbered explanatory paragraphs and so on, a treatise, in short, suitable for adoption by the Society in its schools. And the *Principles*, thus announced, will indeed prove deeply scholastic, not only in organisation, but in style. Even the *Meditations*, as we have seen, retain a good deal of traditional vocabulary and traditional thought; the *Principles*, stating the same doctrine in different order, plus explicit Cartesian physics (not only its foundation in metaphysics), are clothed much more conspicuously in proper scholastic dress—ready for the classroom! The same had been true, of course, of the *Meteors*, which, in its treatment of problems, had followed pretty closely the order of Aristotle's *Meteorologica* (Gilson, 1975, pp.102–37). In short, Descartes had always had a shrewd sense of his primary audience: of whom it was he needed to carry along if his work was to be accepted. This time he felt he had been cheated, and feared it might have been the Society itself that was attacking him. But though savage in his riposte to Bourdin, he still endeavoured publicly to exhibit his good intentions—because, as I have already argued, following Gouhier, he hoped, and even hoped increasingly (hence the *Principles*) to see his philosophy—the true philosophy—prevail.

Second: what can we learn philosophically from this ill-natured debate? Some Cartesian doctrines are, incidentally, stated in passing with unusual directness. There is an explicit statement of the relation of what we once knew clearly to our present knowledge (*AT*, vii, p.519); a definite enunciation, *contra* Bourdin, that the inference is valid from knowledge to being (*AT*, vii, p.520); a much more explicit statement than is usual of the way Descartes used the method of (hyperbolical) scepticism (*AT*, vii, p.546), and a useful remark about Cartesian 'reflection', which is no different from any other (non-reflective) thought: thinking is thinking! But it is a long road for a few insights. What Bourdin contributes, on the other hand, is just what one misses in other scholastic critics: a stubborn attack on the method of doubt itself. Indeed, his whole diatribe seems to have this single aim. Even when he raises, as others had, the mind-brain issue or that of the souls of brutes, it is within the context of questioning the method of doubt that he does so. In part—early on—he seems to be providing a caricature of a point made three centuries later in Gouhier's commentary: to the effect that Descartes is not really doubting, but negating each doubtful statement (*AT*, vii, p.456 ff.; cf. Gouhier, 1978a, pp.15–40). Only for Bourdin this would entail in turn negating the negation, the negation of the negation, and so on in an infinite regress of contradictions. The basic problem, however, lies in his conception of the method of universal doubt. Bourdin has failed to grasp (as indeed the authors of the Second Objections had also) that Descartes's method is meant to be one of discovery, not argument—of seeking, not proving from already accepted truths. Bourdin wants logical demonstrations, starting from first truths and moving to conclusions; Descartes wants to give him a *road* to truth—starting from? Where? Not even with sense-perception, the only place we *can* begin, before we get, by a fairly simple induction, to the proper starting points for each special discipline. To a trained Collegian in the Aristotelian tradition (worse yet, an Aristotelian teacher of *mathematics*!) this is an impossible enterprise, an impassable road, or better, a road on which one cannot get a first foothold. But logical proofs, for Descartes, are just what are *not* needed. They don't go anywhere. Like the Red Queen of a later century, they can only run very hard to stay in the same place. So they never solve problems. Clear that old trash away—particularly, suspend your reliance both on sense and on fancy syllogistic formulations—and you will go, step by step, away from the unending to-and-fro of disputation to the careful construction of one universal habitation of philosophic truth. Given this radical difference—which Bourdin, for all his repetitiveness and arch rhetoric, really presents, if only by so thoroughly failing to grasp the difference involved, and hence the need for the ground-clearing work of Cartesian doubt—given this radical difference, it is no surprise that Descartes sometimes replies less than adequately to Bourdin's objections, just as Bourdin in his unending concern with doubt misses, from start to finish, what the *Meditations* are about.

Do the Seventh Objections, then, represent, as those of

Hobbes and Gassendi may seem to do, a case of total misunderstanding on both sides, of non-conversation? In themselves, yes, but then there is the letter to Dinet, and then there are the *Principles.* Why didn't Descartes give up trying to get the Jesuits, or the Scholastics in general, to understand his enterprise, so radically opposed to theirs in starting point and method? Again, one can only answer: because, for him, his new method was intended to establish truths so clear and simple that all would accept them. So why alienate the most prestigious teachers of the day, who, given a chance, will surely come around to seeing things his way? And further, doctrinally, the ontology on which the method rested and in which it issues was not after all *so* radically opposed to theirs. He shared with the School a belief in the harmony of faith and reason, a cabinet full of common notions that he believed all men shared—although they must use them properly, in the right order, making existential claims not *via* the obscurities of sense but only when clear and distinct intellection permit. Then they will be able, with him, to eliminate the rubbish of substantial forms ('rubbish' except for the odd case of our mind-and-body), real accidents, and the like, and begin to elaborate the new mechanical-mathematical doctrine of nature that would make us—God willing, and within God's creation—its possessors. Disputation will give way to certainty, confusion to clarity, and power. Despite Bourdin, before and after Bourdin, that was his hope.

My aim in these reflections, however, has been not so much to repeat once more that general thesis about Descartes's relation to the tradition, as to allow us to listen to some of his more moderate critics, who state, less intemperately than Bourdin, some of the limited positive beliefs Descartes is asking them to abandon; about the corporeal foundation of mind, the intelligence of other animals, the perception-grounded character of knowledge. For such items, I hope I have succeeded in suggesting, they had good reason to be slow in following the Cartesian lead.

Notes

1. An anonymous critic, referred to only as Hyperaspistes, and evidently a sympathiser of Gassendi—certainly an empiricist—also offered objections, to which Descartes replied, but too late for their inclusion. Although Descartes is firm, and sometimes even sharp, in his replies, he does not appear so thoroughly infuriated as by the Third and Fifth Objections.
2. Marion (1975, p.21) conjectures that Descartes abandoned this project because he had already carried it out—in the *Regulae*. Would he have forgotten? On this question, Gouhier's explanation seems more reasonable.
3. The following year, however, in explaining to Chanut his troubles with the Regents of Utrecht, he can remark in passing '...since a Father Bourdin thought he had enough reason to accuse me of being a sceptic, because I had refuted scepticism' (*AT*, iv, p.536).
4. Indeed, Mersenne seems to be claiming authorship of II and VI: to Voetius, 13 December 1642, he writes: '*Imprimis igitur, cum sex istae Meditationes de prima Philosophia saepius, ut se velle testabatur Author, perlegissem, illas objectiones, quae secondo sunt loco, proposui* (*quod tibi vellem in aurem dictum, nec enim ipse novit cujus fuerint*), *quibus enim postea sextus adjunxi, quae jam prae manibus habes...*'.
5. Thus in the exchange with Gassendi, Descartes claims that infinite regress is acceptable '*secundum fieri*', but not '*secundum esse*' (*AT*, vii, pp.369–71).
6. Fortunately, this is not the place to discuss the vexed question of active reason and its possible 'separateness'.

6 *The Gassendi Case*

1

Following a venerable, but still flourishing, interpretive tradition, I have been arguing that Descartes wanted to alter, in scholastic ontology, just those features that had blocked the initiation of a mathematical physics. Epistemologically, such a manoeuvre entailed the method of doubt, the *cogito*, the proof of God as guarantor, and so on. Cosmologically, it demanded the reduction of Aristotelian causality to one only of its four dimensions: local motion. It was a physics of motion and impact that Cartesian metaphysics was supposed to found. Thus in trying, respectfully if cunningly, to move scholastic minds from a sensory to an intellectual starting point, it was to a version of the new mechanism that Descartes intended to convert them. Now others of Mersenne's circle, like Mersenne himself, were also devotedly engaged in this new endeavour: the development of a mechanistic physics, and Mersenne invited two of them, Hobbes and Gassendi, to furnish their objections (the third and fifth respectively) to Descartes's argument. There was also a third, anonymous critic, dubbed by Descartes Hyperaspistes, who replied to Descartes's replies to Gassendi. Descartes replied to him also, but too late for inclusion in the published text (*AT*, iii, pp.397–412; 421–39). But to return to Hobbes and Gassendi: both these men were well-known opponents of Aristotelianism, admirers of Galileo, adherents, and co-projectors, of plans for the new science. Yet while Descartes is courteous enough to most of his scholastic critics, his fellow-mechanists drive him simply wild. He is patently furious at both of them. Why? Is one always angriest at those on one's own side who venture disagreement? Because they're rivals in the same league? Or is Descartes in fact still so steeped in the tradition that he is truly horrified by those more radical than he dared to be? After all, as I have noted in passing, and as we shall see in more detail in the next chapter, it was the ultra-conservative Arnauld who, among all his critics, most appealed to him. For the Hobbes-Descartes confrontation, the latter explanation: that he dreaded those more radical than he, may well be correct. 'What,' asks Hobbes, 'if reason be nothing but the stringing of names together?' For Descartes, with his 'acts of pure and attentive mind', this is either willful misunderstanding or sheer stupidity. And when Hobbes objects to the first proof of the Third Meditation, 'There is no idea of God, the argument falls,' Descartes answers simply: 'There is such an idea; the argument stands.' It is mutual non-communication at its most extreme. Of course Hobbes had also been sending along, *via* Mersenne, bits of physical inquiry that Descartes objected to, and one sympathises with him in his exasperation when he implores Mersenne to send him no more stuff 'by the Englishman' (*AT*, iii, pp.326–7). Looking at the conflict with twentieth-century hindsight, one finds Hobbes, in his Objections, presenting in effect the position of logical positivism in its physicalist phase—almost three hundred years too soon, while Descartes, deeply and subtly a man of his own time, is starting us, carefully, deliberately—and unwittingly—on the long road to that disaster. Descartes had talked of building a house on new foundations. What he really wanted, though, was to throw out a lot of the furniture; those who would raze the very foundations in all earnest shock him to the core. His revulsion against Hobbes seems plausible enough.

Gassendi against Descartes, however, seems at first sight a somewhat harder case. Descartes replied firmly and even dismissively to Hyperaspistes, but not, it seems to me, with the rancor manifest towards Gassendi himself. And indeed, when one reads a little in, and about Gassendi, one understands how deeply he differed from Descartes about philosophy as well as about physics. But he was not a system builder, building, like Hobbes (from Descartes's point of view), in a hopelessly perverse direction. And they did have a good deal in common. They were both devoted to the overthrow of Aristotelian methods in natural science. Why are they, reciprocally, so quickly and totally infuriated? It is partly Gassendi's longwindedness and Descartes's impatience, yet surely it is not just a matter of temperament. There must be a very deep incompatibility here; but it is not entirely clear on the surface just what it is. The question is important, not only for the sake of understanding Descartes, but in our immediate context, of looking at Descartes in his own time. We English-speaking philosophers know Hobbes a bit, and probably some of the vast Hobbes literature; yet the seventeenth-century was not exactly crowded over with Hobbesians. With Gassendists, it was. Prior to Newton, there were two major styles of the new mechanism: Cartesian and Gassendist. As far as our own major philosophical tradition goes, moreover, it seems to be agreed on all hands that it was Gassendi's work that chiefly inspired Books 1 and 2 of Locke's *Essay*. So if we want to understand the place of Descartes in the nascent mechanism of his time, and also the philosophical opposition to his method that helped shape our own heritage, we had better take seriously the Gassendist alternative to Cartesianism.

Again, I shall make a small essay at this truly formidable task simply by looking at, and just a little around the edges of, the Objections and Replies. In this case, that includes also the replies to the replies, which Descartes refused to have printed in the second edition and which were published, with the original Objections and Replies, in Amsterdam in 1644 under the title: *Disquisitio Metaphysica seu Dubitationes et Instantiae adversus Renati Cartesii Metaphysicam et Responsa* (referred to below as *DM*). This lengthy work, now fortunately available in a French translation published with the original Latin by Bernard Rochot, is by no means the least obscure of philosophical documents; it, too, is hard to penetrate. Of course there are sources that have helped. Like every one who ventures at all into the writings of Gassendi, I have benefited greatly from Rochot's edition and notes and from the careful work of Bloch on the philosophy of Gassendi (Rochot, 1962; Bloch, 1971). Howard Jones's intellectual biography is also useful (Jones, 1981). Most of all, however, I have been initiated into the first stages of Gassendism by Lynn Joy's *Gassendi the Atomist: Advocate of History in an Age of Science*, a work that will surely prove a landmark in Gassendi scholarship (Joy, 1983). The argument that follows is deeply indebted to her work—although, needless to say, my errors are my own. In particular, perhaps because I am founding my interpretation chiefly on the *Disquisitio*, I find Gassendi more deeply sceptical than she believes he was. On the other hand, I shall argue, as I believe she does (despite her single-minded subtitle), that there is no one dimension along which Gassendi's thought—in this case, his opposition to Descartes—can be wholly explained. We shall have to look at several, more or less inter-related, lines of difference.

2

Before setting out, however, to enumerate some aspects of the Descartes-Gassendi debate, I must take a stand on the introductory metaquestion: how well did Gassendi understand what Descartes was up to? And to that introductory question I shall add, by way of illustration, a small sample of Gassendi's commentary, which should provide us with some indication, in the flesh, so to speak, or at least in the word, of the style—the philosophical, and human, style—of the *Disquisitio*. (It is a sample from well on in Gassendi's second replies, when enmity has been firmly established; so it doesn't help with my earlier puzzle: why they so angered one another; at this point they already have.)

First, then, how well did Gassendi understand Descartes? Some commentators have thought he wrote, like Bourdin, in uncomprehending indignation, others that he was 'the deepest and certainly the keenest of the critics'. (Beck, 1965, p.44). I must confess that, without disrespect to Arnauld or to our scholastic friends, with their seven readings and thirty years' experience, I am more inclined to the latter than the former view. Gassendi surely knew what Descartes was trying to do and knew why he objected to this programme. Granted, that was not how Descartes saw the matter. In his letter to Clerselier (in the French translation), when he replied to some friends' summary of the *Disquisitio*, he objected, as he obviously would, that Gassendi had insisted on putting into syllogistic form what was never intended for formal demonstration of this traditional kind (*AT*, ix, 1, p.205). And it must be admitted that if Gassendi had thought Descartes had been trying to set up standard syllogistic arguments, he would indeed have been an uncomprehending reader. But consider the circumstances. Gassendi was nothing if not a scholar, who gloried in sheer learning. He knew and respected the literature of philosophy and theology, even where he diverged from its methods, as in logic and in physics. But, as Gary Hatfield has shown (Hatfield, 1985), 'meditations' were still a standard literary form in the early seventeenth century; Descartes is here following, with variations, a well-known genre. And Gassendi must have known that. He must have known, also—in fact, was to write about—the difference between resolution and composition, and so, in effect, between a method of discovery and a method of formal proof. So he is not simply confused. If he misrepresents Cartesian arguments, he is doing so deliberately. Perhaps Descartes had an inkling of this: witness his repeated allegations that Gassendi is indulging in mere rhetoric. Deliberately to distort one's opponent's arguments may indeed be seen as a rhetorical rather than a philosophical move. Yet, I hope it will become clear, this is not a strategy embarked on, in Gassendi's case, out of incomprehension.

Now, to give us a toehold on the text, for a sample from the *Disquisitio*. The passage I want to consider comes from Gassendi's reply to Descartes's reply to Gassendi's initial objections: the third round, or the second of Gassendi's counterattack. So, as I have already admitted, discord between the two has already been firmly established; at what I shall quote, of course Descartes could only be angry. But it's vintage Gassendi, and should give us some sense of the quality of Descartes's antagonist, before we go on to look at their more pervasive differences, or at any rate at some aspects of these.

In his objections to the Third Meditation, Gassendi had presented ten doubts. The ninth (on the second Cartesian proof of God) runs:

> Of another, subsidiary demonstration, from the fact that nothing could be made, or exist, if infinite Being did not exist, and that the parts of time are independent of one another. (*DM*, p.344a)

Descartes has replied that Gassendi fails to distinguish the cause 'according to becoming' (*secundum fieri*) from the cause 'according to being' (*secundum esse*). He concludes: 'And nevertheless I am not surprised that it does not seem to you that I have demonstrated this with the greatest evidence, for till now I have not noticed that you have rightly grasped any one of my arguments' (*DM*, p.345b). Fighting words! In reply to Descartes's reply Gassendi now proceeds to develop six articles, of which the third declares: 'That the demonstration derived from the independence of the parts of time errs at various points' (*DM*, p.347b). Here in turn Gassendi makes six points, of which the last is concerned with Descartes's near-identification of creation and conservation. It begins:

> Sixth, when you conclude as follows: it is indeed one of those things that are manifest by natural light, that conservation differs from creation only by a distinction of reason, this can say nothing if not that you are much blessed, to whose natural light all things are thus manifest (*DM*, p.348b).

Now, however we may interpret them, we are all used to Descartes's pronouncements that p,q,r. . .z are manifest to natural light. Responding in one typical way, we may get into the circle argument (which Gassendi too raises a number of times); or, second, we may play on the fact that in the analytic method propositions are not so much asserted, as used in order to turn the direction of the meditating mind toward the next clear and distinct idea that is due to be presented 'in the order of reasons'—the right order of discovery; or sometimes we mutter something about traditional 'common notions' that Descartes still used because, more than he knew, he was still immersed in the tradition. As for myself, I find the circle fracas, though subtle and occasionally productive of illuminating controversy, largely irrelevant to the study of Cartesian method; but the second and third kinds of response I confess to having been long addicted to. As the present essay indicates, I still think there's a lot in them. What Gassendi shows us, however, here and in many passages throughout the *Disquisitio*, is that we have been faulty in our simple-minded acceptance of Descartes's assurances, and this, as we shall see, on a number of counts. Granted, Descartes's method of discovery, his method of meditation, works by an ingenious sort of seemingly philosophical persuasion: oh, everybody knows that, you can take it (provisionally, of course, not scientifically or ontologically) as given. So the 'causal principles' of Meditation Three, for example, are taken as stepping stones to the next clear and distinct idea—of God as existent—not (yet) as full scientific assertions about the things there are. They are methodological common notions, not yet asserted in all earnest of the real world. And back in Meditation Two, the mind was a thinking thing, not yet a thinking substance—and so on. But a Gassendi, in other words, an intelligent, well-trained seventeenth-century professor of philosophy, steeped in the humanist as well as in the narrower academic literature, can see what most of us have not seen: how crudely and misleadingly Descartes has been using tags from the tradition. What is 'clear by natural light' is by no means so easy to specify as Descartes would have us believe, in particular, in the present case, about the relation between conservation and creation. In the paragraph that follows, Gassendi proceeds to bring out cunningly a number of these difficulties.

First, he takes another gibe (these are recurrent) at Descartes's methodological scepticism:

> For to you, who are deprived of all previous knowledge. . .(p.348b).

Throughout his commentary, indeed, he runs a kind of Rylean spoof: how can you talk to us if you don't know we exist? and so on. Here, the other way, and ironically: of course you know all this by natural light since, denying all previous opinions as you do, it can't be that any one has told you: in your middle age, your mind is happily a *tabula rasa*, and so everything you assert must be presented by 'natural light'. But that's only the beginning. Descartes's dicta of 'natural light', Gassendi avers, express doctrines discovered, if at all, by other and very learned men, not spontaneously, but only after years of careful study. Thus, still embroidering on Descartes's remarkable good fortune, he explains:

> For you who are deprived of all previous knowledge, there occurs quite spontaneously the same thing that does not occur to the most learned and subtle Theologians as well as Philosophers, unless after long study and profound scrutiny of matters divine and human: that should be deemed an incomparable felicity (*DM*, p.348b).

In reality, and this is to anticipate what will be in our century a major theme of Gilson's Cartesian scholarship, Descartes *has* to have learned these dicta about causality, creation and what not from his teachers and predecessors in philosophy. 'Please tell me,' Gassendi continues,

> whether you would have formulated these words even if you had not received them from the scholastics? (*DM*, p.348b).

Thus, apart from his mischievous doubt of Cartesian hyperbolical doubt, Gassendi's first charge here is (the correct one) that Descartes has by no means freed himself from the tradition. But there is worse to come. In this single paragraph, Gassendi mounts a second and third major assault on Descartes's claim.

Descartes has ascribed to natural light his doctrine of the near-identity of creation and conservation. But, first, as we have seen, he must have received these terms from the scholastics. They, however, refer this subject-matter to *supernatural*, not to natural light. So—the second main point—Descartes has seriously misrepresented the teachers he claims never to have heard of, pretending it is reason, not revelation, that is his guide in matters such as creation and God's *concursus*. Claiming to steer clear of theology, he is importing it in large doses and pretending not to. Gassendi writes:

> And was not the fact that they refer creation as well as conservation to supernatural light, in any way a matter for scruple, when you separated yourself from them and referred to natural light alone? (*DM*, p.348b).

Surely this is an offence against his Jesuit teachers. One is supposed to know what belongs to reason, what to revelation. Why Arnauld, with his Augustinian bent, should not have been offended at the demotion of divine to natural light, we shall have to ask in due course. But here we need only note that Gassendi, the scholar, cavils at Descartes's loose usage of traditional concepts.

Further, when we move (injudiciously) to the sphere of natural light, we find ourselves in even more serious trouble with another tradition: not with theologians this time, but with philosophers who, like Descartes at this juncture, claim to rely on natural light alone. Gassendi's criticism here goes in two moves. First step: given that both creation and conservation are manifest to natural light, by what argument is it shown that they differ in no respect at all:

> And since conservation cannot be manifest to natural light, unless creation, which differs from it only by a distinction of reason, be also

> manifest, have you thought yourself persuaded by a pure demonstration, that however conservation is, so is creation likewise? (*DM*, p.348b.)

Descartes has given no such demonstration; he simply alleges that the two processes differ 'in reason alone'. In fact, as Gassendi makes clear elsewhere, they are very different indeed. Natural things, once made, have, other things being equal, a life-course of their own, whereas creation, God's making a creature out of nothing, is not a natural, ongoing process, but the work of a supernatural fiat. But supposing Descartes had persuaded himself somehow of their identity—and he does claim to have done so—then he has not only offended against theology by importing its conceptions into the sphere of natural light, but against the natural light tradition itself, which in fact denies creation. Gassendi continues: 'If that is so' (that is, if you thought yourself persuaded by demonstration that creation, like conservation, both manifest to natural light, differ in no way),

> how did you think it would happen, that that should be declared manifest to natural light, which absolutely all the Philosophers who were said to be guided by natural light alone, not only did not find manifest, but declared to be indeed opposed [to natural light], defending the thesis that nothing is created, or nothing made from nothing? (*DM*, p.348b.)

And he concludes, in a delicious parody of Cartesian reasoning:

> Or did you believe you were legitimately reasoning as follows:
> That is manifest to natural light, which is non-manifest to all the Philosophers who use natural light alone.
> But creation (and following that, conservation, which differs from it only by a distinction of reason) was non-manifest to all the Philosophers who used natural light alone.
> Therefore creation (and following it conservation) are manifest to natural light (*DM*, p.348b).

One must admit, this kind of thing makes Bourdin's attack seem courteous indeed. But for all its tone of ridicule, there are three serious charges here. First, what he claims to have from natural light, Descartes has got from the Scholastics; second, he has got them wrong, moving the evidence of supernatural light to the natural level; and third, what he claims for his natural light is the very contrary of what natural light philosophers, themselves a venerable line of subtle and serious thinkers, have claimed for that source of insight. Indeed, St Thomas himself had admitted that creation is not an event accessible to reason alone: the world could be eternal, for all we know by nature. Aristotle believed it was so. Natural light provides us with principles of causality, not creation. This very point, indeed, the inability to admit creation (something from nothing) was one of the doctrines on which Gassendi had carefully to correct Epicurus. Creation is just what the pure light of natural reason fails, and must fail, to understand.

3

With a half-page sample of Gassendi to help us onward—a half-page out of a 410 page volume—let me now suggest, on the evidence of the whole work, and of Gassendi's work in general (partly as read, chiefly as reported by others), some of the lines along which the two antagonists differed. I shall list seven, some interconnected (as: 1–2, 3–6), but none, or no group, I believe, more fundamental than the others.

First, Gassendi is a humanist, a scholar and a bibliographer, systematically and self-consciously nourished by the wisdom of the past. He not only devoted a quarter century or more to the rehabilitation and exposition of Epicurus—often postponing the writing while he dug further for evidence (he was clearly a man who loved books and libraries). He also took serious account of alternative views: in the (posthumous) *Syntagma* he even included Cartesian method as one of the forms of 'logic'. And he lived, as Dr Joy has clearly shown, in a milieu in which the exchange of ideas, of scholarly and bibliographical information,was the norm. Some of his scientific work appeared as letters; he belonged to an active quartet, with a partly changing membership, who were conspicuous among those called at the time '*libertins érudits*'. (How 'libertine' they were, I cannot say; that Gassendi himself was no libertine, in any sense I can understand, I am certain; of that more shortly). He took a year from his scholarly labours to write the life of his deceased friend Peiresc, himself a bibliographer. In short, learning in the best sense—historical research, and philosophical criticism grounded in historical insight—was the breath of life to him. He has still much in common with sixteenth-century humanists.

Not so Descartes. He has turned his back on all that. As he emphasises in the fragmentary *Studium bonae mentis* (see *AT*, X, p 192), and as is clear from remarks in the correspondence, as well as from his method itself, a person of good sense, untainted by scholarship, would probably do better in philosophical reasoning, he believes, than one overloaded with the prejudices instilled and ingrained in the mind through the trappings of learned controversy. If (as David Lachterman has argued) Descartes has a philosophy of history, it is of a *lucus a non lucendo* cast (Lachterman, 1983). History is misleading, to be abjured. If, more than a millennium before him, Augustine happens to have enunciated a *cogito*, no matter! Who cares what some ancient, however sanctified, has argued? No. What matters is to clear the slate, to start afresh, liberated from the ties of sense—including the reading of dead masters—clearing away what Spinoza will call 'hearsay and vague experience', laying a firm, simple, unshakable foundation for knowledge and building step by step in the right order what will be, for the first time, a permanent superstructure of (God willing!) inalienable knowledge. 'Permanent'? So lasting through history into the future, if you like, and so 'historical'? Yet that will be an unhistorical history, where nothing happens because everything is fixed. Cartesian science will give us—always 'God willing'—in this life a quasi-eternity.

Second, a corollary of the first point, which at first looks contradictory: both are fervent anti-Aristotelians. Indeed, Gassendi's first work was the beginning of what was to have been a many volume exposé of Aristotelian follies: *Exercitationes Paradoxicae adversus Aristoteleos*. He never completed more than the first two books, presumably because the response was so inimical to his enterprise that it seemed useless to continue it, and he turned to his Epicurean project instead. But his opposition to scholasticism in method and in science was plain; so was Descartes's. Would they not be friends through that common interest? There are two parts to the answer.

First, while they both belong to the circle of those who would break the confines of scholastic method, and especially of scholastic physics, the way they go about it differs deeply in the two cases, both in its relation to the philosophy of the past, and (taking the *Meditations* to represent Descartes) in philosophical style. Gassendi, after abandoning the *Exercitationes*, turned to the study of Epicurus. Why? Bloch suggests that, looking for an alternate philosophy to Aristotle's, he chose the Epicurean (Bloch, 1971). That sounds a lame excuse—like picking a warmer coat to put on today because the weather has turned colder. But it is true in a way, for there are good philosophical reasons for the appeal of Epicureanism to Gassendi the thinker as well as Gassendi the scientist. What matters at this juncture, however, is the way in which Gassendi invokes the past in order to find a more viable method and metaphysics than scholasticism offered. He turns to the ancients to assist in a modern problem. The Aristotelianism of his time was 'traditional' indeed, but it was a cramping and impoverished tradition. Yet there have been other thinkers who have shaped our intellectual heritage. We may broaden tradition by heeding their views, too. In terms of a now current fashion, indeed, one may call him a *hermeneutical* thinker. Within history (as we all are), he looks back to the sources of that history, taking a wider view of it than most of its latter-day inheritors have the vision, or the patience, to attempt.

Descartes, in contrast, despises history. Allegedly, he wants a radical new beginning. But—as Gassendi keeps telling him (how could he use those terms if he had not learned from the scholastics? Our example forms just one of many occasions on which Gassendi reproves Descartes for his pretence of knowing nothing)—as Gassendi keeps telling him, he did not in fact 'abandon all his former opinions'. And of course he didn't: is it not the fate of anti-historicists to be more naively steeped in history than those who recognise its power? Descartes, in fact, as we have had reason to stress, accepts a great deal in terminology, in 'common notions', in propositions 'manifest to natural light', that belongs, not only to tradition, but in particular to the Thomistic tradition in which he had been trained. All this, it seems plain, he takes for granted: it is not 'tradition', but 'natural light'! Tradition in any wider, or more reflective, sense he rejects. Humanistic learning, reverence for the ancients, is for him irrelevant. Even his enemies lurk within the scholastic heritage only. And once more, within that heritage (which he takes to be not a 'heritage', but just what is obviously *so*), he wants to alter just enough to make his mathematical physics possible. Rejecting history, he is straitjacketed by history in a way in which a more historically rooted thinker is not.

Very much by the way: I suspect that the influences of Gassendist *doctrine* on Locke fed into a much less Gassendist and more Cartesian naiveté with respect to history. But that is quite another story, which I have neither the time nor the competence to tell.

There is another twist, however, to the present contrast, which must be noted also: i.e., Gassendi's peculiarly scholastic style in the *Disquisitio*. While he, like Descartes, must be counted among the anti-scholastics of his day, he *sounds* scholastic indeed. Especially in the counter-replies of the *Disquisitio Metaphysica*, he does repeatedly reduce the moves of the Cartesian *Meditations* to 'syllogistic' form. For example, in Article 3, Doubt 4, on Meditation Two, Gassendi states Descartes's argument:

> He who knows he is a thinking thing, and does not know whether he is any further thing, like an assemblage of members, a thin air, etc., is absolutely nothing but a thinking thing.
> But I know myself to be a thinking thing, and I do not know whether I am some other thing, such as an assemblage of members, a thin air, etc. Therefore I am absolutely nothing but a thinking thing (*DM*, 300a).

Clearly, Gassendi claims, the argument should have run:

> He who knows he is a thinking thing, but does not know whether he is some other thing, such as an assemblage of members, a thin air, etc., knows himself as absolutely nothing but a thinking thing.
> But I know myself to be a thinking thing, and do not know whether I am some other thing, like an assemblage of members, a thin air, etc. Therefore I know myself as absolutely nothing but a thinking thing (*DM*, p. 300a).

And who, asks Gassendi, 'seeing you pass from what you know to what you are, could tolerate the paralogism?' (*DM*, p. 300a).

Or look at Meditation Three, Doubt 4, Article 3, Gassendi's concluding summary of Descartes's first argument for God:

> If some one, finding himself in a state of ignorance at which he has arrived deliberately, by abstraction, claims to recognise with conviction that he has an Idea by which he conceives (*intelligat*) an eternal, infinite, omniscient,

> all-powerful God, creator of all that is not himself, without the idea's having been received by hearsay or by the contemplation of external things, the authority and conviction of that man are the true principle of a demonstration proving that such an Idea is innate in all men, and that it is not received by hearsay or drawn from the contemplation of external objects. But I find myself in a state of ignorance at which I arrive deliberately . . . etc. Therefore my authority and my conviction are the true principle of a demonstration . . . etc. (*DM*, pp. 327a-b).

Are these the words of some one whose lifework was to conquer the arid methods of scholasticism? Yet this style of argument is repeated throughout the work. Descartes's irritable answer (in the letter to Clerselier) seems amply justified. Descartes had composed *meditations*, in which the reader was to follow with him, through careful thinking and rethinking, the steps along the path of discovery. Syllogisms are just what his infinitely careful 'order of reasons' has—at long last—cast aside, in order to embark on a new, fresh exercise of thought unhampered by the *impedimenta* of a method that was never more than a recapitulation of discoveries already made by other means. Of course Descartes too *could* write in a more scholastic style, when that was appropriate—as in the *Principles*. But any willing and intelligent reader will have understood that the *Meditations* don't work that way. Yet here comes Gassendi, and puts the most delicate, careful many-levelled movement of thought into that old worn-out consequential form. No wonder Descartes keeps insisting that he doesn't understand anything at all!

Why, then, does Gassendi go on like that? If he is not himself among the stultified scholastic enemy, if he is not, as Descartes finds him, just stupid and uncomprehending, why does he write that way? It seems to me there are two good reasons. First, Gassendi was in his youth a professor of philosophy at Aix-en-Provence and was to be later professor of mathematics (= astronomy) at the Sorbonne. Indeed, his *Exercitationes* grew out of his lectures at Aix—where he had first to expound, and practise, 'Aristotelian' methods in detail, and might then, with luck, be allowed to proceed to give evidence of their inadequacy. But he did have to practise such methods; that's the way, one supposes, lecturing was done (*see* Brockliss, 1981b). Descartes, on the other hand, independent gentleman and quasi-recluse that he was, never gave a lecture in his life. He was, of course, a very great philosophical stylist, matched in our philosophical literature only by Plato and the Hume of the *Dialogues*, and he could perfect, at will, whatever philosophical mode suited his purpose: the purpose of persuasion in the *Meditations*, of pedagogy (as he hoped) in the *Principles*. Gassendi, on the other hand, was for some years at least the holder of a chair, who was used to giving instruction in the standard way.

But there is also another side to the story. While the (counter)-objection to Meditation Two raises a solid criticism of Cartesian method, the summary of the first argument in Meditation Three, as well as the closing *consequentia* of the text we looked at earlier, appear, to me at least, plainly meant, quite intentionally and even mischievously, if you will, as travesties of Cartesian argument. As I have already suggested, Gassendi must have known a 'meditation' from a formal argument, he must have known a presentation in 'the order of discovery' from a presentation in the order of demonstration. Indeed, he would have read the Second Objections, with the sample of 'synthesis' Descartes appended to his reply. Moreover, he himself loathed, as heartily as ever Descartes could, the cumbersome heaping of syllogism upon syllogism—what he called 'artificial' in contrast to 'natural' logic. In such circumstances, it seems to me—knowing by now how he has irritated his antagonist and being by now himself annoyed and offended—after being told over and over he has understood nothing Descartes has said—in such circumstances, he is using his competence as a professor of philosophy quite self-consciously to irritate Descartes yet further by proposing caricatures of his every argument. Our sample passage, clearly, moves from biting satire through serious historical counter-argument to full parody. And it's clear Gassendi enjoyed that. He wasn't just mildly puzzled, like the authors of Objections One, Two and Six, nor yet plainly off at a tangent like Hobbes, let alone admiring like Arnauld. Such parodies of Cartesian arguments as that of the first argument for God have got to be tongue-in-cheek. However infuriated he may have been by Descartes's derisive responses, and however heavily he may clothe his counter-replies in the cumbersome robes of scholastic logic, his amusement, the delight of a parodist in his work, shines through the text. Himself a foe of scholastic methods, he uses their weapons to ridicule a fellow-opponent, when his ally, as he ought to have been, turns, for solid philosophical reasons we have yet to examine, into an even more dangerous enemy than the scholastics themselves.

4

Let us try, then, to itemise further the differences in philosophical doctrine and method that divide our antagonists. We have already put first, as pervasive, their positions with respect to the history of thought: let us call these the *hermeneutical* versus the *objectivist* perspective (for objectivism is a perspective, though a self-denying one). My second point—the difference in their opposition to scholasticism—was in part ancillary to the first. Within his hermeneutic approach, thirdly, and, it seems to me, just as fundamentally, Gassendi comes through in the *Disquisitio* as typically and profoundly a Christian sceptic. Thus we may find some further light on the division between our two philosophers by comparing their use of scepticism. Like his friend Mersenne, Gassendi is convinced that God has given us only a very limited insight into the nature of things. The weakness of the human intellect is with him a constant theme. We have no idea of substance, for example, only of the 'accidents' that meet us in immediate experience. So he has a deep sympathy for ancient scepticism. In his early work, and again in the *Syntagma,* he faithfully repeats all the ten tropes. He will have to modify this loyalty a little in support of Epicurus: but not *so* much, after all. Scepticism of course leaves us sensation as subjective: so does atomism. In its Epicurean-Lucretian form, it systematically demands the return to sensation as the test even of the atomic theory itself.

In any event, however his scepticism and his Epicureanism be reconciled, it is decidedly as Christian sceptic that we meet the Gassendi of the *Disquisitio.* Intellectual humility is his hallmark. Thus he agrees, of course, with the conclusion of Descartes's argument in the Third Meditation: there is an all-powerful, all-good Maker to whom we owe our Being and our worship. He is a priest who, so far as one can tell, has never doubted his vocation, and whose every utterance bears the mark of honesty. In agreement with Gassendi scholarship, I see no reason to doubt the sincerity of his faith. But have our little minds, our 'ideas', power in themselves to guide us to that infinite God, so infinitely beyond us? Surely not. We ought not, therefore, to forsake the 'royal road' from experience to a first cause. We must start where we are, in the concrete experience of the things around us, and hope that God will bring our searchings to a fruitful issue. (On that road, it should be remarked in passing, Gassendi has no objection to using allusions to final causes, where they stare us in the face, as in the arrangements of living things, for instance. No dogmatist in any direction, he is not flatly and dogmatically opposed to final causes either.) His scepticism about the powers of human reason is well illustrated, for example, in a letter he wrote about Descartes's *Principles* in 1645. He is surprised, he writes:

> that a great geometer has been able to forge so many dreams and chimeras, and, what is worse, to give them as demonstratively guaranteed ... for every one knows well that a clever man can invent a certain number of things that are mutually consistent up to a certain point ... but to wish to introduce these fictions quite simply into the reality of things and to pronounce that the principles of things in no way differ from them ... that is to refuse to understand what human shoulders refuse to bear (Letter to Rivet, quoted in Berr, 1960, pp. 93–4).

That's Gassendi. To understand our destiny, our places in creation, is to recognise, willingly and submissively, 'what human shoulders refuse to bear'.

Descartes, in contrast, notoriously uses sceptical arguments, extending them so far as to call his own scepticism 'hyperbolical', but at the same time he is using that 'cold cabbage' in order to turn the tools of scepticism to a new use: to eliminate forever the very threat of scepticism. The theme of ancient scepticism, which, it appears to me, Gassendi happily accepts, was the denial of the criterion. Like Hume's 'mitigated scepticism' to come, it entailed the acceptance of everyday judgments, in the recognition that they never yield indefeasible, necessary *knowledge*. Descartes, however, is out to establish just such a criterion: he uses sceptical arguments precisely to undermine everyday judgments until he can re-establish them on a firmer footing—in their right place in the unshakable superstructure he will have erected, step by secure step. Indeed, as we have seen, following Gouhier, it is not so much doubt of the senses, of judgments about the external world, of mathematics, that he is exercising, as it is the tentative *denial* of all these, through their suspension pending their reinstatement on a new and firmer ground. Indeed, I have always found it strange that our sceptical colleagues are so fascinated by Descartes, since, so far as I can tell, there has never been a less scepical philosopher. He was closer, it seems—and as Gassendi well knew—to overcredulity than to scepticism. Gassendi, in contrast, is truly a sceptical thinker; Descartes's dogmatic certainty would offend him as much as his want of any claim to certainty offends Descartes.

5

Clearly, fourth, in the light of their very different assessment of the powers of human reason, Gassendi and Descartes must differ deeply also in their conceptions of methodology. Although they would both play midwife to the birth of mechanism, their obstetrical techniques could not be more unlike. Where Descartes is seeking, in the *Meditations*, foundations for his physics, Gassendi, as the letter to Rivet makes plain, takes a firmly anti-foundationalist stand. Although Gassendi made no major contributions to the new science, he was an experimentalist, both in astronomy and in physics, an experimentalist keen on the importance of patient and accurate observations, of staying close to appearances. Like Mersenne, he admired Galileo, of whom, as we noted earlier, Descartes wrote to Mersenne rather condescendingly: he did not follow the right order in his work—and that, for Descartes, is all-important. Nosing about here and there, drawing up experiments to test this or that: that's not the way to found the new science. But for Gassendi, that *is* the way to go about it. Look carefully, devise means of investigating the phenomena. Although he made no major discoveries of his own, he did yeoman work in both astronomy and physics. For example, he confirmed (in part) Kepler's prediction of the transit of Mercury. And he performed a shipboard experiment aimed at confirming Galileo's statement that 'if the body we are in is in motion, all our movements, as well as that of those things we set in motion, take place, and appear to take place, just as if that body were stationary' (Jones, 1981, pp. 61–2; cf. Joy, 1983,

p. 16). Descartes, too, of course performed experiments. He was, we all know by now, no simple *a priorist*. But he intended to build a single unified science on solid metaphysical grounds—a science tied firmly in place through the proper sequence of clear and distinct ideas. Indeed, he believed himself in the process of building such a science. Gassendi, on the contrary, much more in the spirit of Mersenne, is groping his way carefully from appearances, and always returning to appearances, looking for tentative explanations of restricted phenomena.

It is not, indeed, explicitly their difference in scientific practice that is at the front of the stage in the drama of the *Disquisitio*. But the consequence—or perhaps the ground—of that difference in scientific practice does appear conspicuously. Where Descartes not only seeks, but believes he has found, certainty after certainty, Gassendi is happy to achieve a modest probability. Weak creatures that we are, we should be content with conjecture—not wild speculation, of course, but hunches modestly close to the particular, sense-carried experience that is all we have to go on. Here, one may remark in passing, Locke appears not to have followed the Gassendi programme. Knowledge for him consisted in relations between ideas that were in one way or another guaranteed as certain. Although he found not much of it, he was seeking certainty, and firmly placed probabilities in the second rank, as what we fall back on in cases where we cannot reach the superior condition. Gassendi, well in advance of Hume, appears to have abandoned this claim. Perhaps, sceptically, he is denying knowledge; yet his attitude to conjecture seems a serene and confident one, close, it almost appears, to an acceptance of justified belief as the nearest approach to knowledge we poor mortals can expect.

A fifth contrast is closely related to this. For the foundation of Gassendi's probabilism in the assessment of knowledge claims lies, of course, in his reliance on the senses and imagination—in general, on imaging—as the immediate and ultimate source of all our information about the world around us. And clearly this puts him—as it did Hobbes—in flagrant opposition to Descartes. Where Descartes would lead the mind away from the senses, Gassendi is wholly convinced that, given the human condition, there is no where else to go. Of course the senses err—everyone knows that—but what corrects those errors? As Descartes's scholastic critics, too, had suggested, it is the senses themselves that do the correcting. If you never touched that bent stick, or looked at it out of the water, it would stay bent. Not your judgment, but the same or another sense corrects your error. Even the intellect can operate, in Gassendi's view, only by relying on the images that our senses leave us. Indeed, for him, as for Hobbes, ideas just *are* images. There is a little exchange about this, which confirms the reciprocal misunderstanding. In Meditation Three, you recall, when (as Gueroult argues) Descartes is using partly his own, partly his readers', concepts to open the way for the first proof, he calls ideas 'as it were images of things'—and Gassendi picks this up. You said it yourself, he exclaims. No, says Descartes, I never said ideas were images; you don't understand a word I say! And there had, of course, been the same misunderstanding with Hobbes; in that case Descartes pointed out that 'idea' includes God's ideas—and He has no images! (*AT*, vii, p. 181). Well, did he or didn't he say ideas were images? One can only answer with Hippolytus: 'The tongue is sworn; the mind remains unsworn.' If we have followed Descartes's intent in the *Meditations*, have 'meditated' with him, we know 'ideas' are acts of mind, apprehending content, indeed, but acts, not little pictures. Even this piece of wax, allegedly, I know not through a series of images—which are constantly changing—but through the mind, through judgment, which, it will turn out, is an act of will. To take conception, the act of apprehension of what is clearly and distinctly evident, as a mere picturing, is to have failed altogether to understand the aim and method of the Cartesian enterprise (cf. Costa, 1983). Of course Descartes is righteously indignant. But of course he did use that language on that occasion—whether it was a slip or a self-conscious trick. And, equally of course, Gassendi just as righteously condemns the pretence of human intellect floating free of the senses, claiming its thoughts to be self-evidently true. To hope radically to transcend appearances and to grasp intellectually the inner nature of things is, as he put it elsewhere (Jones, 1981, pp. 39, 51, n. 69), 'no more preposterous than to wish to have wings or to remain forever young'. Philosophically, this is perhaps their deepest incompatibility.

6

The last point connects also, sixth, with a profound disagreement about the nature of mathematics, and especially of its role in physics. Descartes would free our minds from sense, common sense and scholastic prejudice, in order to enable the mathematical intellect to decode the geometry of nature, the geometry that, if God is no deceiver, *is* nature. For Gassendi, on the other hand—and this comes out even in the *Disquisitio*—mathematics is a descriptive technique for abstracting certain relations from appearances. Is it not, in itself, about anything. And it does not, in respect to our reading of appearances, possess any unique problem-solving power. Dr Joy, in her exposition of Gassendi's scientific work, has made this crystal clear. She has shown, indeed, that the separation of mathematics from physics was a major aim of Gassendi's science. Thus in his treatment of Poysson's problem, a popular mathematical puzzle of his time, Gassendi emphasised the confusion produced by the failure to distinguish mathematical from physical points. His argument about the explanation of the different apparent magnitudes around the sun seems to have had a similar purpose. And in his defence of Epicurus against Sextus on the problem of infinite divisibility (Joy, 1983, pp.213 ff.), he relied on the same distinction. The argument is a delicate and complex one, but I hope I am safe in reporting that it includes, among many lines of reasoning, the inference that since Sextus based his attack on Euclidean geometry, yet was arguing about physics, his criticism was misplaced. Epicurus's doctrine had nothing to do with mathematical infinite divisibility, but only with the best sense-supported and sense-supporting inferences about the natural world—not about the games mathematicians play in abstraction from reality. If Gassendi understood as well as I believe he did the Cartesian programme he was criticising, no wonder he was indignant: pure 'mathematical physics' is a dangerous and often misleading enterprise. But this is a paradoxical situation, too. Descartes, founding his own programme for mathematical physics, and, admittedly through his eventual influence on Newton more than through his own science, influencing profoundly the course of the 'scientific revolution', paid little tribute to its other great initiators, Kepler and Galileo. And his own experimental work, as reflected in the

Instigators?

works and correspondence, was in general, I think it's fair to say, not much more than qualitative (cf. Clarke, 1982). Gassendi, on the other hand, took the trouble to confirm Kepler's calculations of the transit of Mercury and Galileo's remarks about relative motion: Galileo whom we remember as insisting that 'nature is written in the mathematical language'. Acknowledging Gassendi's acknowledgement of the primacy of history, we may see here as in so many places the complexity of what from afar and at first glance looks simple. It takes all kinds —in this case at least two—to make a revolution.

7

It may be objected that in all this I have made nothing of Gassendi's 'nominalism'. The final theme I want to point to, however, seventh and last, presumably bears some relation to that topic, yet in a way bypasses it. That is the question of the relation(s) between essence and existence, a recurrent issue in Gassendi's text. Gassendi's arguments on this question are varied and subtle; this aspect of our controversy in fact deserves a detailed study, more detailed than I can give it here.

The issue is best apprehended, however, I believe, by first putting carefully to one side the scholastic 'problem of universals' and its set answers. In the 'problem of universals' as initiated by Porphyry, through Boethius, neither Gassendi nor Descartes displays much interest. Granted, Bloch is justified in calling Gassendi an 'ontological nominalist': his thinking stays close to particulars. Were he to suggest an 'order of doubting', it might be just the reverse of the Cartesian. But he shows, in the *Disquisitio* at least, little concern for the question of general terms, although he was to broach it in his own logical writing. The point here, however, is just that he is not concerned to present a full 'nominalist' methodology. Hobbes' 'stringing of names together' is not a Gassendist turn of phrase. What Gassendi wants to stress is that there are no ideas not derived from sense. The linguistic conventionalism of a full epistemological nominalist like Hobbes is not what interests him. Granted, he throws out in Doubt One on Meditation Five an accusation about the 'universals of the Dialecticians', I assume because Descartes's talk about triangles and such echoes the discourse of Platonic realism. Descartes abjures this accusation, however (*DM*, p. 375b), and Gassendi never returns to it. Indeed, at Article 2 on the same doubt (in his counter-reply), Gassendi's statement about general concepts is not so different from Descartes's own in *Principles* I, 59, where, in textbook style, he has for once to deal with this 'school' question (*AT*, viii, 1, pp. 27–8). He too, incidentally, seems to be accurate in disclaiming interest in the problem. There are only occasional and fleeting references to 'universals' in the Cartesian corpus (e.g. *AT*, i, pp. 154, 196, 216; iii, p. 66). Perhaps one might expect a philosopher who values so highly the power of mathematical thought, who is himself a great mathematician, to reflect on this problem: what is discourse of triangles and circles really about? But after all it's a silly school problem; once one has cultivated one's clear and distinct ideas, what need to bother with subtle arguments about their nature? Get on with what you can *do* with them! Looking at both our controversialists, one might perhaps call Descartes (in the light of *Principles* I, 59) a conceptualist — that's what Alquié does—but then, on *his* account of general ideas, one might have to apply the same tag to Gassendi, who is after all the godfather of Locke's *Essay*. But the question is of relatively little interest.

What *is* of interest, because it offers a kind of searchlight into Gassendi's mind, and *a contrario* into one aspect at least of Cartesian methodology, is the essence-existence dichotomy. As a first run at the problem we may notice three points, one about existence, two about essence.

First, Gassendi in all his thinking stays close to existence. He stresses this approach in his criticism of the wax argument (*DM*, pp. 311b–312a). But the beginning of the first doubt on Meditation Five makes the point in more detail and more directly. You can talk about the nature of man only because and when there *are* men; you can say a rose is a flower only because there *are* roses. Reading this quaintly extreme statement, harking back to the ancient question, 'How can one say the thing that is not?' or forward to Carnap's concern in his early semantic period with the terrible problem of the designatum of negative sentences: reading such statements, one gets a good view, in contrast, of Descartes's enterprise in the *Meditations*. For him, too, existence has a distinctive place. The Demon crowns Meditation One by suspending all existence claims (bar one, as Meditation Two will show). And that was necessary because the way we are used to making such claims flows so directly from the sense-times-school-based confusion that has keep us from achieving science in the past. So we need to turn our minds, for the moment, away from judgments of existence, to liberate clear, evidential thought from the confines of particulars, in order, once thought is so set free and God discovered to guarantee its truth, to return again, in conclusion, to a sounder—and also more limited—set of existential judgments. Then and only then can we claim that nature exists, as geometrical, and even that the not-wholly-geometrical targets of everyday muddled perception and imagination exist, too, in a sort of way, as guides to the necessarily confused practical needs of this muddled psycho-physical existence here and now. In this light, for instance, we can understand Descartes's distinction, against Gassendi, between causes *secundum esse* and causes *secundum fieri*, a scholastic tag, indeed, but one that reflects the fundamental order of Cartesian reasoning: from the end of Meditation One to the opening of Meditation Six, '*fieri*' has nothing to do with the matter. We may return to that context only when we have safely cleared our minds of the muddles that infancy and our teachers have induced. Gassendi, in contrast, though liking the dicta of Aristotelian teachers no better than did Descartes, does not advocate, as Descartes does, an intellectual conversion to liberate our thought from its childhood starting point. On the contrary, to abandon 'artificial' for 'natural' logic, the misleading obscurities of dialectic for a sounder canon (the Epicurean or something like it), is to stay as close as may be to the earth that is our home, to the humble input of the senses. True, for us the stuff about roses is hard to take, reminiscent of the 'logic' of Dewey or Mill. Talking about . . . is not the same as pointing to. . . . This is truly simple-minded empiricism.

Yet, when Gassendi does talk about essences, and in particular, as we shall see, about Descartes's third proof, his criticisms are telling indeed. To begin with (point two of my three), essences are not known: Locke's 'nominal essences' in preview (*DM*, pp. 311b, 353a-b). In particular, as I have already mentioned, Gassendi insists that we cannot know substances. Or as Locke will put it, a bit more modestly, our knowledge of them reaches only a very little way (Locke, 1975, II, 23; IV,

6). For starting with sense, it is the accidents of substances that we know. We cannot reach behind these to the 'inner nature of things'. Thus all knowledge is *inadequate*. This is not a negatively sceptical view, however; we may, and ought to, seek to increase our acquaintance with appearances, with the way things happen around us. But let us never forget our impotence, 'what human shoulders refuse to bear'. We may be careful, ingenious seekers after natural knowledge—as Gassendi himself showed himself to be—we may free ourselves of the shackles of a dead tradition, both by turning back to a more adequate aspect of inherited wisdom, and by groping forward, through observation and experiment, to a more accurate grasp of the phenomena. But freed of scholastic shackles, we can now walk, not fly!

8

Third, if we *do* talk of essences, we had better watch the way we do it. Here, in turn, Gassendi makes three points, the third again threefold. First, there is the argument we have already noticed about mathematics (and indeed, all reasoning about general concepts), as produced by abstraction from experience. In the first doubt on Meditation Five, after presenting a conceptualist (again pre-Lockean) account of the function of general ideas, he continues:

> Now I can say the same of your Triangle or of its nature. For the triangle that you have in mind is as it were a kind of rule by means of which you examine whether a thing merits the name of triangle; but it cannot be said for all that that this Triangle is something real or a true nature outside the understanding: but only that the latter, after having seen material triangles, has formed this nature and has made it common in the same way I have just described in the case of human nature (*DM*, p. 375a).

Nor do these properties of material triangles flow somehow from an 'ideal' one:

> Consequently, it must not be considered that the properties demonstrated of material triangles belong to them because they have been borrowed from the ideal Triangle, for on the contrary they have them in themselves, and the ideal Triangle has them, only to the extent that the intellect, after having inspected the former, attributes them to it, in order to restore them [to material triangles] in the course of a demonstration (*DM*, p. 375a).

Gassendi again illustrates the process with the example of the empirical generalisation, 'All men are rational.' And on Descartes's insistence that he has ideas he never got from sense, he remarks: this means simply that he has constructed them from units supplied by sense—again, an account familiar to us in its Lockean rendering.

Further—second under my third point (take care with essences!), Gassendi in his counter-reply produces an ingenious objection to Descartes's view of the creation of the eternal truths (*DM*, p. 377a). If God *created* the eternal truths, then they are existences, not after all essences, as is generally supposed—and as indeed they are treated by Descartes in his argument. How can any one who proposes such an argument be thought an obtuse, misunderstanding reader? When a conception of intensional discourse is needed, he may himself come out as a naive extensionalist. But he has surely looked with penetration into that Pandora's box, Descartes's view of the eternal truths, and has neatly exhibited one paradoxical consequence of the Cartesian thesis.

But the high point of Gassendi's criticism on the essence-existence question comes, third and finally, in his treatment of Descartes's Meditation Five proof of God. The general point that Descartes is confusing existence with a property (anticipation this time of Kant and the hundred thalers) is made in the second doubt:

> For you are quite right to compare essence with essence, but then you do not compare existence with existence, or property with property, but existence with a property (*DM*, p. 379a).

The 'Instantia', Gassendi's reply to Descartes's reply, articulates this general point brilliantly and explicitly in three separate articles. First, there is the argument that existence is not a property:

> Existence is not a property, and is not determinate with respect to any genus of things (*DM*, p. 380b).

This thesis is supported by a meticulous argument—no sarcasm or parody this time—in which Descartes's confusions in logic are disentangled. Descartes has remarked that he does not see to what particular genus of things Gassendi wants existence to belong. Gassendi replies, that indeed he does not believe that existence belongs to any determinate genus. But, he asks, 'Don't you see what you are doing when you want it to belong to some special genus?' First you take the most general genus, thing (*Res*), or, to give the usual alternatives, *Ens*, *Aliquid*, to be either substance or property: a division into genera, such that every thing belongs to either one or the other. Then properties are further divided into species, and you take existence to be one of these. Here we make a slight detour: at the same time, Gassendi points out, Descartes also uses the term 'attribute' (in the wide sense of what can be attributed, or predicated). This is a confusion, since 'property' is a physical term, while 'attribute' belongs to logic; it is not only a transcendental, like *Res* or *Ens*, but supertranscendent: applying a distinction furnished by the intellect to the broadest genus of being. If Descartes is going to use 'attribute' in the narrower meaning of property, he had better say so. On the other hand, if, as he certainly seems to be doing, he is maintaining that existence is a particular property—here we return to the first step of the argument—then he is really in trouble. For, given the initial classification, we have the following problem:

> Now, from the moment that you claim to make of Existence a particular Property, or a particular attribute, then the term 'property' can indeed be predicated of Existence, and also the term 'thing', given that it belongs to the whole genus to be able to be predicated of the species; but the term 'Existence' can itself never be predicated either abstractly or concretely: neither in speaking of all Properties, since the species can never be predicated of the genus; nor of Thing in general, since what cannot be predicated of the inferior, or less general, cannot be predicated of the superior, or more general. Nor can it be predicated of Substance, since no species can be predicated of the contraposited genus, and of the genus to which it belongs, it cannot be predicated either. Finally, it cannot be predicated of any other property, since no species can be predicated of another that is contained in the same genus (*DM*, p. 381a).

In other words, existence does not function as a predicate. Strange consequences follow if we try to make it do so. Gassendi continues:

> Therefore, just as we do not say, 'Animal is man, Living body is man, Plant is man, Horse is man' in the same way we cannot say: 'A property is an

> existent, or exists; the Thing exists; Substance exists; Wisdom, or some other property, exists.' Don't you really see how the non-existence of so many things results from your claim that Existence belongs to a special genus of things? (*DM*, p. 381a.)

The solution is to take existence, not as a special genus, but 'as an extremely general, or even a transcendental genus' (*DM*, p. 381a). It 'applies to all genera and to all species of things in such a way that if it could not be predicated of things, they would not be and could not be thought to be' (*DM*, p. 381a). But that is not the way that properties, or particular predicates attributable to particular genera, function.

In conclusion, Gassendi tries a thought experiment in its upshot very like the Kantian. 'You want to know,' he challenges Descartes.

> if Existence can be considered as a property of such and such a thing that exists; examine if the thing in question can be deprived of existence, or if one can conceive that it can be deprived, in such a fashion that something remains or can be understood as remaining without change. But you will recognise that that is how it is in the case of all properties: Once the latter are suppressed in fact or by thought, one nevertheless conceives how the substance whose properties they are continues to exist as something quite different (*DM*, pp. 381a-b).

But what if it is existence that is removed?

> Doubtless you see clearly that it cannot [be so removed], since what does not exist is nothing; and in fact if you suppose that something perseveres through its parts, you also suppose that existence is not removed with the parts; but if you suppose that no existence remains, then nothing would remain of the thing (*DM*, p. 381b).

In his original objection Gassendi had couched his criticism in terms of 'perfections' rather than 'properties'; he now returns to that comparison:

> Further, it is from this that I have inferred the difference to be maintained between some perfection of a property, for instance, vision, and Existence itself. For a man, to whom as it were vision belongs, is nevertheless not annihilated if he is deprived of it, but he simply becomes blind, that is to say, less perfect and lacking vision. But whatever be the thing to which existence belongs, if it is deprived of that, then it is truly no longer anything, or it is, as we say, nothing, and not imperfect, or deprived of existence; for what is said to be imperfect or deprived of something, is still

supposed to be something, even though it lacks one of its perfections or properties (*DM*, p. 381b).

We need not linger so long over Articles 2 and 3. Article 2 reads:

There has been, and remains, a paralogism, when the hypothesis is changed from the ideal to the real state (*ex statu ideali in statum rerum*) (*DM*, p. 381b).

This paralogism was introduced in the transition from the first to the second part of this Meditation: when Descartes asked if he could not use the model of inference about the essence of triangles to obtain a new proof for the *existence* of God. And the same fallacy holds throughout the subsequent text. Ideas, however 'clear and distinct'—and of course, as Gassendi has emphasised earlier, different people have different ideas for which they claim those sterling qualities—ideas are but ideas, there is no difference between them:

until we have left the ideal state to enter into the real, or the prison of the intellect for the theatre of nature (*DM*, p. 382a).

In the ideal state, however:

there exists no Criterion that permits you to distinguish whether such and such an idea conforms to an existent object outside the intellect or not; and one is obliged to wait until in the real state (*in statu reali*) experience becomes the Criterion (*experientia Criterium fiat*) (*DM*, p. 382a).

In the second article, Gassendi has displayed Descartes's argument in syllogistic form—no parody this time, but a fair enough rendering. The major premise: what we clearly and distinctly understand to belong to the true and immutable nature of a thing, can be truly affirmed of it. The minor premise: but when we have examined accurately enough what God is, we clearly and distinctly understand that existence belongs to His true and immutable nature. Article 3, examining the minor premise, objects:

You do not give any other proof of the existence of God except that God exists (*DM*, p. 382b).

Again, Descartes is trying to move, illicitly, from his ideas to an existence external to them. 'But to define how one conceives a thing, is that to prove that it exists?' (*DM*, p. 382b).

In conclusion, Gassendi gives a last twist to the screw by turning two of the concluding pronouncements of Descartes's reply back to himself:

> But, finally, you have not in the least diminished the validity of my argument, and you continue to remain in error on the subject of this sophism that you say would have been so easy for me to resolve (*DM*, p. 383a).

and:

> the rest I pass over; since when you say I explain nothing, you yourself explain nothing, and prove nothing, except that it is too much for you to prove anything (*DM*, p. 383a).

9

In what precedes, I have been suggesting some of the philosophical differences on which the reciprocal hostility of Descartes and Gassendi seems to rest. It is, as I confessed at the start, no easy matter to sort out, and I make no claim to having done it satisfactorily. But I hope that, as in the case of Descartes's scholastic commentators, I have given some plausibility to his critic's objections, in this case to the rich perspective of a lingering humanism, supported by scrupulous scholarship, and, at the same time, to the anti-essentialist bent of a nascent empiricism, which still, through Locke and his heirs, exerts its influence on our own variant of modern epistemology and metaphysics—a variant, paradoxically, still under the ban of the Cartesian reform, while at the same time, indirectly but still substantively, Gassendist in many of its doctrines.

It should be added, for the record, that when Descartes visited Paris in 1647 he and Gassendi met and were reconciled. But that does not change our philosophical story.

7 *The Port Royal Connection*

1

In a long letter to Mersenne of 4 March 1641, Descartes both abjures any further exchange with Hobbes and welcomes the Objections of Arnauld (*AT*, iii, p. 318 ff). Warning Mersenne that he wants no more commerce with the Englishman, he nevertheless replies to four of the physical-geometrical questions Hobbes had submitted, and concludes:

> I would be ashamed to take the time to pursue the rest of his errors, for it is the same throughout. That is why I believe I need no longer reply to anything you might send me from that man, whom I believe I ought to distrust in the extreme. And I allow myself to be in no way flattered by the praise you say he gives me; for I know he does this only the better to make people believe he is right when he blames and slanders me. I am distressed that you and M. Beaune should have a good opinion of him. It is true that he has vivacity and facility in expressing himself, which may give him some lustre; but you will soon see that there is nothing at all underneath, that he has extravagant opinions, and that he tries to acquire reputation by evil means (*AT*, iii, pp. 326–7).

He proceeds, briefly, to other problems in physics, then goes on to deal with questions about his manuscript. Fermat is *not* to get a copy, since although 'I believe he knows mathematics. . .in philosophy, I have always noticed that he reasoned badly' (*AT*, iii, p. 328). And, 'finally', Descartes continues testily,

> I sent you this work, in order to have the judgment of the gentlemen of the Sorbonne, and not to stop to dispute with all the little minds that might want to mix in and make objections . . . (*AT*, iii, p. 328).

Poor Descartes! He has still received only four sets of Objections. No wonder, by the time they arrived, he was in a mood to be annoyed by Gassendi's lengthy arguments. What he wanted was the approval of the Sorbonne, and that is just what he was never to receive.

Meantime, however, one young licentiate in theology had, most respectfully, sent his comments. Descartes was delighted. He has not yet drafted his replies, partly because he has been otherwise occupied, and partly because he does not want to hurry. They were to be sent, in fact, on the 18th and 31st of the same month. But, meantime, he expresses his pleasure. Arnauld, he says,

> has obliged me extremely by his objections. I consider them the best of all: not that they are more pressing, but because he has entered further than any one else into the sense of what I have written, something that I had clearly foreseen that few people would achieve, since there are few who wish, or are able, to take time to meditate (*AT*, iii, p. 331).

In short, as Kierkegaard might put it, Descartes has found his reader. Indeed, when, on the 18th, he sends his reply to the Fourth Objections (except for the theological portion, which will go off on the 31st), he requests that Mersenne make a number of corrections in the text of the *Meditations*. He writes:

> I send you at last my reply to the objections of M. Arnauld, and I beg you to change the following things in my Metaphysics, in order that one may know from this that I have deferred to his judgment, and thus that others, seeing how ready I am to take advice, may express more frankly the arguments they have against me, if they have any, and behave in a less opinionated manner in wanting to contradict me without reason (*AT*, iii, p. 334).

A previous correction to the reply to Caterus (*AT*, iii, p. 330) seems also to have been motivated by Arnauld's questions. And in the Replies themselves, addressed to Mersenne, Descartes writes:

> I could not choose a more perspicacious nor a more obliging critic of my writings than I find him to be whose reflections you have sent me: for he treats me with such humanity, that I easily perceive that he favours me and my cause; and nevertheless what he opposes he has examined so accurately and has looked through so closely, that I dare hope nothing in the remainder has escaped his eye; and besides, he urges so keenly those things that he finds less worthy of approval, that I do not fear he could be thought to have dissimulated for the sake of courtesy, and that is why I am not so much moved by those things he objects to, as I rejoice that he does not oppose me in more (*AT*, vii, pp. 218–19).

In short, from Arnauld he has at last received the kinds of objections that are really of assistance, and he responds accordingly. Thus from total non-communication *vis à vis* Hobbes, and corresponding irritation with Gassendi, through polite and professional, if somewhat smug, disagreement with 'scholastic' objectors, we move to Descartes's eager reception of the one reader who has truly understood—and who, indeed, will spend the rest of his long life (and forty-three volumes of published writings) on the one hand in theological controversy, and on the other in defence of Cartesian philosophy.

What accounts for this harmony? Who is Descartes's chosen reader; why does his manner of thought adapt itself so easily to Cartesianism, as Descartes himself at once seems to perceive? That is the question I shall venture to ask in this chapter—'venture' because I can barely paddle in the deep waters of seventeenth-century theology. Yet the question seems to me inescapable. Descartes's relation to 'the great Arnauld' and to the first generation of the Port Royal group raises, in my view, the culminating paradox of Cartesian interpretation, a paradox we must at least take note of, even if we cannot satisfactorily resolve it.

It must be admitted, incidentally, that I am taking Arnauld very much as a Port-Royalist, in the spirit of Sainte-Beuve's reading (Sainte-Beuve, 1952–5). More precise accounts of Jansenism and by implication of Port Royal would make distinctions where I am making none, as Marxists see distinctions among Marxists, and Darwinians among Darwinians (cf. e.g. Orcibal, 1949). From my generalising, extra-theological perspective, however, I find convincing the bracketing of a version of Jansenist theology, like Arnauld's, with the spiritual intensity and penitentialism of the Port Royal solitaries. *En bloc* they stand opposed, surely, to the more urbane Thomists and, in particular, to the Jesuits, in their attitude both to spirituality and to doctrine. Taking that very global view of Jansenism-Port Royal, then, I am asking about the relation of Descartes as philosopher to this theological *and* spiritual movement of his time.[1]

Descartes wanted to found a new physics. To do that, he needed a new metaphysics—but not in fact wholly new: much that he held from 'natural light' he derived in fact from scholastic sources. Moreover, he wanted approval from theologians, for he hoped ultimately to have his new method and doctrine taught, and so needed the leaders of current educational institutions on his side. And why not, since he considered their authority appropriate in matters of faith, on which matters of philosophy were bound to touch, or to appear to touch? There was no reason why he should offend them and every reason why he should not. That is why, he explains to Mersenne, he wanted his Metaphysics circulated and assessed. Now at last he had, explicitly and by name, comments from one theologian of the Sorbonne, and a theologian—a *Sorbonne* theologian!—who plainly understood, and in large part accepted, his arguments. What could be better?

But who was that Sorbonne theologian? Antoine Arnauld, 'the great Arnauld' as he came to be called, would indeed prove for more than half a century the defender of pure Cartesian doctrine as he read it. At the same time, however, he was the most controversial figure in Sorbonne, in French, perhaps in European, theology. True, in 1641 Descartes could not have foreseen this; but even at that time the seeds of the trouble had been planted. As early as 1632 Arnauld had placed himself under the close guidance of M. de Saint-Cyran, the first spiritual director of Port Royal; his theological studies had been closely directed by Saint-Cyran. And he himself belonged, of course, to the 'first family' of Port Royal, being the youngest brother of Mother Angélique herself, the first reformer of the famous convent. Moreover, Arnauld's explosive work *On Frequent Communion* was to be published in Descartes's lifetime, in 1643. Yet, so far as I have noticed, Descartes, careful though he was, never revoked his gratitude and respect for Arnauld. Somehow the most reactionary and the most suspect school of theology, itself quite innocent of any special interest in the new mechanics, proves most welcome to and most supportive of Descartes's methodological and metaphysical reform. Descartes, if you will, founded modern philosophy and hence the philosophy of modern science: he gave it its characteristic epistemological bent, he left it with (depending how you see it) the triumph, the problem, or the absurdity of mind-body dualism; but he made that turn to modernism with the sympathy and support of the most anti-modern, anti-scientific movement of his time. That is the paradox I want to think about a little in this chapter.

2

First, let me consider the Fourth Objections and Replies, before moving on to the more difficult, and more fundamental, question of Descartes's relation to Arnauld as representative of Port Royal.

Recognising that Descartes, though writing as a philosopher, wishes to bring his work before the bar of theology, Arnauld proposes to play two roles: first as philosopher (while completing his theological theses, he had been teaching philosophy at Le Mans) and then as theologian (he was not only a licentiate at the Sorbonne, but had sustained three of the four required theses; the fourth he was to defend in December 1641). Not that, in Arnauld's case, philosophy and theology are separate in the same way as they are for Descartes. If Descartes, as a loyal son of the Church, brings his philosophy to the bar of theology, the young theologian, immersed in *his* professional disputes, will pass judgment, even on philosophical issues, from his (superior) theological perspective. And this holds, *a fortiori*, of a young, and intense, Jansenist-Augustinian theologian! But in the text 'philosophical' and 'theological'—or 'theological-related'—comments are given separately, and we are looking here, superficially enough, at the text.[2]

The 'philosophical' objections are presented in two parts: of the nature of the human mind, and of God. As to the former, Arnauld first cites an Augustinian passage that apparently anticipates the *cogito*, a citation Descartes briefly acknowledges. He must have been well used to such references by now: after the *Discourse*, both Mersenne and (as it appears) a Protestant minister named Colvius had brought this precedent to his attention. Descartes, in reply, had clearly distinguished his own use of this formulation from Augustine's (*AT*, i, p. 376; ii, p. 438; iii, p.261, and especially iii, p. 247; cf. Gouhier 1978b, ch. 1, secs 1 and 2).

Next, Arnauld considers whether, or how, from the *cogito* as starting point, one can prove the real distinction of mind and body. Indeed, this is the one criticism he formulates in any detail in this part of his Objections, and it does raise an interesting question. In effect, really, there is the same problem Gassendi will propose: of the paralogism involved in passing from what I *know* of mind at the *cogito* stage to what mind (or body) is in reality. But Arnauld puts it differently: in terms of adequate ideas on the one hand and, and on the other, ideas obtained through an act of abstraction by the human mind. Referring back to the *Discourse*, he believes Descartes has distinguished between complete, or adequate, ideas, from which indeed something further can be inferred about the entity in question, and ideas not so complete, from which no such inference could be drawn. With respect to the real distinction, the problem that results will be as follows: we want to know for sure whether mind and body are really separate, or whether, on the contrary, some bodies can think, or whether thought, when it occurs, is bodily. In terms of Meditation Six, in other words, we are asking whether God has in fact separated wholly what we know he *could* separate. There is no problem about bodies, since no one supposes they all think; therefore thought does not pertain to their essence. But what of mind? Might it not be the case that some bodies think and that therefore mind is a species of the genus body? And Arnauld proceeds to present a geometrical example illustrating a similar case. Descartes's answer has two parts. First, we must distinguish three kinds of ideas: those that are complete or truly adequate, such as only God possesses, those that we form of complete entities, not, indeed, totally adequate, like God's, but good enough to produce knowledge, and those we are aware of obtaining by an abstraction. This suggests that in Meditation Two we are abstracting from our full awareness of mind as thinking *substance* in order to put intellection in its proper, primary, place, before we turn to God, and only then to body as (divinely guaranteed) *object* of intellection. In the interim, body has to be held in abeyance lest we revert to the common-sensical misjudgments of our premeditative days. But, really, we always knew the difference. And this interpretation is confirmed by the second part of Descates's answer: in the geometrical case, Arnauld was dealing with a *thing*, a right triangle, and a *property* of it, the relation between the squares of the base and the sides. In the case of mind and body, it is a matter of two different substances: it seems to be assumed that we have always known this, even if, in the order of reasons, we dare not say so till later. So we cannot have here, as Arnauld has suggested, a case of the genus body and the species mind: of two different substances, with different attributes, one cannot be the species of the other as genus. Here, it seems, Descartes will accept relatively 'scholastic', that is, professional-philosophical, arguments—questioning the minor premise of his syllogism (in Meditation Six: from possibility to actuality of the real distinction), worrying about genus and species—where in other cases he has been more negative. Why? I suppose because in his discussion of ideas, Arnauld is in effect accepting the valid passage from ideas to things, as other critics from Caterus on have been unable to do. Although he is questioning that passage in cases where ideas are produced by abstraction, such a *direction* of thought does not seem to him intrinsically absurd, as it has to Descartes's other critics, and will do, for instance, to Gassendi. Descartes is happy in this context to elaborate on and refine the argument of the Sixth Meditation; and the geometrical objection, easily refutable, is a congenial one.

Arnauld's three further objections about mind are much more briefly put, and as easily answered. There is the problem of the minds of infants and of the mad: asleep in the former and destroyed in the latter. This suggests the dependence of mind on bodily organs 'as the impious murderers of mind suggest' (*AT*, vii, p. 204), Arnauld remarks—for Descartes, a happy phrase! Descartes replies that on the one hand the minds of madmen are perturbed, not destroyed, and in general, from the fact that we often find the mind impeded by bodily organs, 'it follows in no way that it is produced by them—nor can this be proved by any argument whatsoever' (*AT*, vii, p. 228). Yet it does, he admits, take profound meditation to understand this. Next, Arnauld comes to the problem of immortality. He had been on the verge of attempting to prove this from the author's principles, he says, when he received the Synopsis—and there it was, just the argument he had thought of! Felicitations on both sides (*AT*, vii, pp. 203, 229). Then Arnauld raises the question of the souls of beasts: Descartes, he concedes, has given his answer elsewhere (i.e. in the *Discourse*), but will people really be persuaded, he wonders, that it is only the reflection in its eyes, and not fear, that sends the sheep running from the wolf? (*AT*, vii, pp. 204–5). Descartes replies, elaborating a little on the nature of the body-machine, and restricts the effect of mind on body (in our allegedly unique case) to influence on the course of the spirits. But even in our case, he reminds his correspondent, the body does many things without consulting reason; so, in the case of the sheep, why not everything? Again, we have to rid ourselves of a mistaken opinion held since childhood (*AT*, vii, pp. 229–31). Finally, Arnauld congratulates Descartes on his distinction between imagination and thought, once more quoting St Augustine in his support. There is no need for an answer. Approval reigns.

The second part of Arnauld's 'philosophical' objections concerns the proofs of God, objections which, Descartes remarks, he will parry rather than answer directly as he has the first group of remarks. Arnauld has only one problem about the first proof, he says, and that has to do with the concept of material falsity. If falsity is found, strictly speaking, only in judgments, how can an idea be 'materially false'? Arnauld plays some neat tricks with Descartes's example of the idea of cold: if it is a privation, it's true, since cold is in fact a privation; if it is something positive, then it is not the idea of cold, and so on. The passage, in effect, calls for a further explication of the grading of ideas by their objective reality. The way in which Descartes supplies this in his reply is puzzling. It seems to me, again, as I noted in passing in the first chapter, that 'material falsity' is a notion first introduced rather lamely as a kind of side explication of objective reality. (Here Descartes concludes the discussion by confessing that he doesn't read the books of philosophers much, but has happened on the same usage in Suarez.) But it doesn't make very good Cartesian sense—or else it does so in more than one sense (cf. Kenny, 1968, pp. 117–21). Here, in response to Arnauld's remark that he is supposed to be restricting (truth and) falsity to judgments, he explains material falsity as 'giving material for false judgments'. But at the same time he distinguishes ideas taken *formally*, as *representative* (corresponding to the first enumeration of Meditation Three) from ideas taken *materially*, as modes of mind (as he does also in the Preface to the *Meditations*, *AT*, vii, p. 8)—but then 'they would relate in no way to the truth or falsity of objects': so, materially, ideas seem to be exempted from *any* relation to truth, while formally, that is in their proper being, they are related 'to the truth of objects' (*AT*, vii, p. 232.) In these terms, however, 'material falsity' seems a close to contradictory notion, and a 'material truth' of ideas pretty well inconceivable. It is *formally* that ideas are 'true' or at least bear on truth.

Note, incidentally, that, try as he may, Descartes is unable to stick to the Aristotelian thesis that things, or the concepts that represent them, have nothing to do with truth. The atom of evidence, which is ideational, is the unit by which we come to truth, even though it is in propositions that truths, once seen, will be asserted and stored away in the body of Cartesian science. And Arnauld, too, despite his obeisance to the 'truth in judgment' conception, speaks of the *truth* of our idea of God. In this part of the Objections and Replies, therefore, it seems clear, if anything is clear about it, that it is the way of ideas, in Meditation Three *via* objective reality, that Arnauld is struggling with and Descartes seeking to elaborate. That impression is confirmed by the way in which Descartes comes down, in his reply, on the obscurity of ideas of sense, which are responsible for most of our judgments. Here heat and cold, indeed, are on a par: though modes of mind, and so, when taken 'materially', as good as any other ideas, even the most clear and distinct, they are, unlike the latter, *formally* suspect, that is (according to the present text) containing little objective reality. Indeed, if we recall the *Principles*, they are best taken as mere subjective feelings, or here 'a feeling (*sensus*) which has no being outside the intellect' (*AT*, vii, p. 233). On the other hand, such positive being as these obscure ideas have, they derive from me 'insofar as I am a true thing'. An unAristotelian turn of phrase, surely, which Descartes is free to use in conversation with this first, and best, disciple. On the other hand, the use of 'formal' and 'material' here seems strangely at odds with the use of 'formal' (or 'eminent') v. 'objective' in the first proof itself: for here formal is identified with objective, and there contrasted with it. The formal reality of an idea in the proof is just what the material reality is here. This confirms my suspicion (in which I believe I am following Gueroult's example) that Descartes often plays fast and loose with scholastic usage, employing whatever apparatus he finds ready to hand in order to mediate his own, thoroughly anti-scholastic, method of discovery. I shall return to this point below.

Arnauld's first question is tangential to the proof from which he extracts it; the proof itself, clearly, he happily accepts. The second proof, however, from my existence, having the idea of God, to God as first cause, and especially Descartes's reply to Caterus's criticism of it, gives him more trouble. In particular—and it is clear both from Descartes's reply and from the correspondence (*AT*, iii, p. 337) that he was himself deeply concerned about the exact formulation—Arnauld was troubled by the thesis that God is *causa sui*, on the analogue of the efficient cause. Descartes, he points out, has distinguished two characteristics of the cause-effect relation insofar as it concerns efficient causes: cause and effect are distinct from one another, and are, respectively, prior and posterior in time. The latter, Descartes has remarked, is not manifest to natural light; indeed, the cause-effect relation may well be instantaneous. So far as that criterion goes, then, God, who is clearly omnitemporal, and thus coexistent with Himself, might be self-causing. But Descartes says nothing in this context, Arnauld points out, about the criterion of the *difference* between cause and effect. Perhaps he has not denied that this aspect of the cause-effect relation is manifest to natural light, just because it *is* so manifest, and so the cause-effect relation cannot hold for God, who clearly cannot differ from Himself. Descartes really must consider these matters carefully, Arnauld adjures him, since 'there is scarcely a theologian to be found, who would not be offended by that proposition, that God is from Himself, positively, and as it were by a cause' (*AT*, vii, p. 214).[3] Descartes replies scrupulously in this delicate matter, pointing out, for example, that by calling God a cause of Himself, he is not in any sense calling God an effect (*AT*, vii, p. 242). It is in this context also that he asks Mersenne to make some amendments both in his own text and in Arnauld's quotations from it. Again, it is a question of getting matters right, and the Objector in this case knows very well where the argument tends: in essence he agrees with it. This is all very satisfactory.

It should be noted here, in passing, by the way, that on the question of God as *causa sui*, Descartes claims to be speaking of cause analogically, so that he accepts the analogy of being, it seems, just at the point where Thomism rejects it. An odd dislocation of scholastic reasoning, rather as, we have seen, in the confrontation with Caterus, the move from thought to reality is radically rearranged. But as Descartes himself claims, his 'reply' here consists in using whatever moves are available to evade his critic's argument, not to reply directly. And this is, precisely, a clever evasion. As I followed Gouhier in arguing earlier (Ch. 4), Descartes's own idea of God is basically non-analogical, or, if you like, inversely analogical.

Arnauld's next point is our old friend, or enemy, the circle. His presentation of it is succinct and straightforward; Descartes in his reply refers back to his remarks in the second responses. Far be it from me to add another jot to the great flow of literature on this question.

Finally, Arnauld recalls that he has omitted from the questions about mind the problem of thoughts of which the thinker is not conscious. There's an easy answer to that one, Descartes replies: from the moment the infant's body is infused with mind, it thinks all right, but does not necessarily remember. Moreover, we need not be aware of our mental powers when not actually exercising them.

As to Arnauld's warning of 'things that can give pause to theologians' (*AT*, vii, p. 214), here, far from refuting or parrying, Descartes is happily submissive, or so he claims. In any case, two of the three points Arnauld raises are easily dealt with. First, on the method of doubt: true, it is a dangerous tool, but that is why Descartes reserved it for a Latin text, which lies beyond accessibility to fools (or females) (*AT*, vii, p. 247; cf. *AT*. i, p. 560). And incidentally, Arnauld warns him to clean up the language of Meditation Six and say 'when I pretended not to know the author of my being'—and he did alter the text accordingly (*AT*, vii, p. 77). Second, Arnauld wants him to distinguish clearly between the treatment of error in matters intellectual and questions of good and evil (Meditation Four); again, he brings to his (and Descartes's) support an Augustinian text on the distinction between faith, knowledge (*scientia*) and opinion. Descartes in reply points out that he has argued explicitly in the Fourth Meditation only about truth and error, and that he has made this restriction explicit both in his reply to the Second Objections and in his Synopsis (*AT*, vii, pp. 247–8). This he remarks in order to show 'how much he defers to the judgment' of his distinguished critic and 'how acceptable his advice is to him' (*AT*, vii, p. 248).

There remains, of course, the vexed question of Descartes's interpretation of the Eucharist. He defends it here, against Arnauld's questions, respectfully but firmly, as he does also in two letters to his ill-fated Jesuit supporter, Father Mesland (*AT*, iii, p. 387, iv, p. 163). As a total outsider to this debate, I cannot, I fear, see the inferiority of the Cartesian explanation, the rock on which in fact Catholic Cartesianism was to founder.

But although the whole question of Descartes's relation to Arnauld has, like any problem connected with Port Royal, a religious and hence theological cast, I can only bracket this particular question as too exclusively theological to be of concern in this essay. In any event, it was a question unresolved in Descartes's lifetime, and it is Descartes and his contemporaries, not his successors, that I am concerned with here.

3

So much, then, for the Fourth Objections and Descartes's enthusiastic reception of them. But Descartes's relation to Arnauld, and therefore by implication to Port Royal, and by a further implication to Jansenism and to seventeenth-century Augustinianism in general raises, as I have indicated, further and knottier problems. How is the affinity between Descartes and Arnauld, and beyond Arnauld between Descartes and the peculiar theology of Port Royal, to be explained? As with Gassendi and Descartes, there are several possible lines of explanation; in this case, however, some are questionable, and some, perhaps the most likely, remain, it seems to me, irredeemably odd. Before enumerating these, however, let me look at Arnauld himself and place him, with his fundamental interests, alongside the Descartes we know, or seem to know, by now.

Where Descartes was a good Catholic layman, who, while deferring for the most part to theological opinion, directed his chief inquiries to secular subjects, Arnauld was deeply involved from the very beginning and throughout his long life with religious, clerical and theological problems. He was, as we have seen, the youngest child of the Arnauld family; six of his sisters had taken vows, and of his three surviving brothers, the eldest, 'M. d'Andilly', was also closely tied to Port Royal, the second, the Abbé of St. Nicholas, was to become a bishop; only the third led a life wholly 'in the world', and was killed in combat in 1639. The family as a whole, in other words, was deeply involved in the religious life, and especially in that of the two convents of Port Royal. His mother, who died in 1641, had been for the previous twelve years Sister Cathérine de Ste Félicité at Port Royal. When she was dying, her son was not allowed to participate in administering the last rites, since 'that would be to give too much to nature', but some days later she conveyed to him, as her dying words, 'that he should never relax in the pursuit of truth' (Sainte-Beuve, 1952, I, p. 517). And when he came at last to meet M. de Saint-Cyran, still imprisoned at Vincennes, as he had been since 1638, he too adjured the young Arnauld that 'one must go where God leads and do nothing fearfully'. 'I am very glad,' Arnauld wrote to him thereafter,

> that you have strengthened me in the sense I have of my mother's last words, and, in the moment when I write this, there comes to me the thought of invoking them if I ever find myself in actual persecution. She has, it seems to me, left large enough signs of her felicity to hold her in the rank of the Chosen of God; and, as for miracles, I seek no greater than those that I feel in my heart. . .being no less the son of her tears than St Augustine of St Monica's (Sainte-Beuve, 1952, I, pp. 517–18 n.).

Such passages, of course, are legion in the literature of Port Royal. Arnauld himself, for example, appealed to Saint-Cyran for guidance in December 1638. It seemed he had been hastening too thoughtlessly forward in the hierarchy of clerical advancement, and after referring to the 'perpetual lethargy' in which he had lived till now, 'seeing the good and not doing it, contenting myself with having the thoughts of the children of God, while performing the actions of the children of the world' (Sainte-Beuve, 1952, I, pp. 510–11), he wrote: 'Finally, my father, for about three weeks God has cried to my heart, and has at the same time given me ears to hear'. Saint-Cyran replied: 'the doctoral dignity has deceived you as beauty deceived the two elders' (Sainte-Beuve, 1952, I, p. 511). Arnauld accordingly modified his schedule, and his conduct, submitting to the penance imposed on him; and it was Saint-Cyran, too, who, through his own struggles, directed Arnauld to the path that led to his involvement with the defence of Jansenism and to his book *On Frequent Communion* and the furore it brought with it. If one looks through the contents of his forty-three published volumes, one finds the majority of his works professionally theological: in particular there are his lengthy controversies with the Jesuits. And of course, he was to be expelled from the Sorbonne after a long and heated hearing: an event that gave the immediate occasion for the composition of Pascal's *Provincial Letters*. Indeed, the Arnauld case seems almost to have been to seventeenth-century France what the Dreyfus case was to be to the early twentieth: *the* scandal of the time.

4

What matters to us here, however, is not so much the future course of Arnauld's career and its largely theological context, as the spirit of the 'First Port Royal', as Sainte-Beuve calls it: the ultra-religiosity, the ultra-penitentialism of Port Royal during this time, and also its relation to Jansenius's *Augustinus* and its fate. Let me give one more example of the former, and set down the pure chronology of the latter, before returning to our Cartesian question.

Take for example the case of M. Le Maitre, one of the first 'solitaries' and great penitents of Port Royal, an 'elder nephew' of Antoine Arnauld. In an undated 'Declaration' to the nuns of Port Royal he writes:

> Although I am only a miserable sinner, covered by the crimes of my present life, I have nevertheless received too many proofs of the sovereign and ineffable mercy of *Jesus Christ* my saviour, not to hope for my conversion from his goodness and the prayers of his faithful servants. That is why although I am unworthy of speaking even to the least of the Religious of this house, and although the Mother Abbess knows that I ought to seek *a cave in the earth* to hide there and weep my sins and my penitence itself, which has been so false and so deplorable...(Sainte-Beuve, 1952, p.691).

and so on and so on and on. This is scarcely Cartesian discourse. But it does exemplify the spirit of Port Royal, and, by implication, of a Port Royal theologian like Arnauld, as well, one can only suppose, as of the 'little schools'—so different from La Flèche—through which the influence of Jansenism took root. If Descartes found it difficult to agree with his mechanistic critics, so close to him, it seems, in their fundamental aims, we shall have to ask, why did he find the best understanding of his work in Arnauld, the leading representative in his generation of what seems so extravagant a form of religiosity, or at any rate of one version of the theology associated with it?

Not that Descartes bore any direct relation to Jansenius and his work; the two thinkers, or their works, coincide in time, but without mutual influence. Although Mersenne had mentioned Jansenius's book to Descartes, there is no evidence that Descartes in fact procured, or read, it (*AT*, iii, pp. 386–7). Moreover, the *Discourse* was published in 1637; Jansenius died in 1638 and presumably had not seen it. His own work, *Augustinus*, which was to fan so vigorous a controversy, especially between Jansenists and Jesuits, was published in 1640. Its author had spent six years in his youth in the home of Saint-Cyran, before the latter became officially affiliated with Port Royal. They were clearly very close in their beliefs, and in particular in their profound Augustinianism and in their radical view of grace. The *Meditations* appeared the year after Jansenius's *magnum opus*, and, three years later, influenced by Saint-Cyran, Arnauld published his work *On Frequent Communion*. From 1641 on, at the same time, Arnauld was, in philosophy, an enthusiastic Cartesian, and, indeed, Cartesianism became, we are told, up to a point the official doctrine of Port Royal. It was Arnauld, for example, who was to sponsor the young Nicole and from their cooperation would spring the *Port Royal Logic* and the *Port Royal Grammar*, those immensely popular quasi-Cartesian texts of the late seventeenth century. So the Fourth Objections, our text for these reflections, do mark the existence of some kind of close kinship. What kind? I shall suggest several elements for an answer, some of them interconnected.

5

First, there is a suggestion of Leibniz that Descartes disliked Fermat, Hobbes and Gassendi because they were rivals, but did not mind Arnauld because he was not (Leibniz, 1880, IV, p. 321). And in a way, of course, that marches with his irritation *vis-à-vis* Hobbes and Gassendi. Yet even if we take a common interest in the new physics as reason for enmity, can we really take a total lack of such common interest as reason for mutual understanding? Surely not. There is something to the former point; that is clear also from Descartes's comments on Galileo. He does not like people who do his kind of thing, but not in his way. In fact, his scattered comments on Fermat are especially irritated, and irritating (e.g. *AT*, i, p. 484, and numerous passages in *AT*, ii). But his positive reception of Arnauld's comments and Arnauld's life-long loyalty to Cartesian philosophy can scarcely be explained on so negative a ground.

More simply and straightforwardly, we may say, as in fact we have found in reading the Fourth Objections and Replies, that Descartes welcomed the comments of a reader who, at long last, *understood* his arguments and so in large part accepted them. He accepted, therefore, it seems, the turn away from the senses, and the turn to clear and distinct ideas, and, associated with these reforming moves, the passage, on principle, from ideas to reality. If he raised objections to the use of scepticism or to the real distinction or to the possible circle in Meditation Three or to the account of God's causality, these questions were plainly voiced in aid of the argument, not against it. As against those hide-bound professionals who persist in starting with sense-perception, and therefore finishing with obscurity, and who want proofs and syllogisms where there is meditation and discovery, or that silly and probably malicious Englishman with his bad physics and geometry, who doesn't know thought from imagination and who even denies that there is an idea of God: at last Descartes now has a reader who has meditated with him, who is willing to have his mind led away from sense, and who, when so led, comes in effect to proper Cartesian conclusions. And Arnauld, being so led, and so convinced, happily accepts the philosophical upshot of the process, which he finds, in principle, consonant with his own theological, and especially, Augustinian bent.

So far, so good. But if Descartes finds himself so much more in sympathy with his one Augustinian than with his presumably more Thomistic, or Aristotelian, critics, let alone those with what we might call a more empiricist perspective, is it because he is himself an Augustinian thinker?

As we noticed in passing in ch. 4, he has often been so considered (see Gouhier, 1978b). Let us look at the evidence. First, there is his connection with the Oratory, a highly respectable Augustinian group, whose head, Cardinal de Bérulle, first encouraged Descartes to pursue his philosophical projects. And of course Malebranche, the most influential late-century Cartesian, was a member of the Oratory. Second, there are the references to Augustinian texts that Descartes's correspondents, Arnauld, Colvius, Mersenne, Mesland, repeatedly produce as showing that Descartes is following in St Augustine's path. Third, there is the reliance on the metaphor of light in Cartesian epistemology. Fourth, and allied to the light metaphor, there is the emphasis on mathematics as the model for knowledge. Order and proportion are prior to the concrete presentations of sense: this, too, may seem an Augustinian theme. Certainly, fifth, the consequent unity rather than the plurality of science is a Platonic, and thus an Augustinian, rather than an Aristotelian and hence Thomistic theme. Seventh, there is the manner in which for Descartes all knowledge depends, relatively directly, on God's veracity. Thus, while accepting the Thomistic separation-and-harmony of faith and reason, Descartes derives even reason insofar as it gives access to reality, and hence to knowledge, from God's truthfulness and incapacity for deception (if God can have an incapacity).

Nevertheless, while all these points do indeed suggest some kind of interlacing of Cartesian and Augustinian themes, they by no means prove Descartes to be an Augustinian philosopher in anything like the sense in which Arnauld or the author of the *Augustinus* were Augustinians.

First, as to the connection with the Oratory: Marion argues that Cardinal de Bérulle served only as a spiritual counsellor to the young Descartes, without specifically influencing the content of his philosophical undertakings (Marion, 1981, pp. 140–60). That may well be, or not be; the case is not a clear one, it seems, one way or another. And of course Malebranche, coming later, is a Cartesian with a twist, and one who, Arnauld argued, pretty thoroughly misunderstood the master. That, too, may or may not be (though it seems obvious to me that it is); in any case, how a new generation understands a philosopher tells little of what the philosopher himself, or his work, intended. Second, Descartes certainly had not, either directly or *via* Jansenius, *studied* Augustine, or derived his arguments from that source. Indeed, he insisted that his *cogito* clearly differed from the parallel in Saint Augustine (*AT*, i, p. 376; iii, pp. 247–8). Moreover, as Gouhier argues convincingly, when he does himself quote the great Church Father, he takes the passage in question in a thoroughly non-Augustinian sense. Thus, in a letter to Mesland in 1644 (*AT*, iv, p. 119), relative to the creation of the eternal truths, Descartes quotes from the final prayer of the *Confessions*: *Quia vides ea, sunt*: 'since you see them, they are', and comments that for God seeing and willing are identical. But the passage that follows in the original text (and which Descartes does not quote) in fact suggests a very different emphasis. Augustine continues: '*Et nos foris videmus, quia sunt, et intus, quia bona sunt; tu autem ibi vidisti facta, ubi vidisti facienda.*' 'And we see externally, that they are [that is, the things made in the six days of creation] and internally, that they are good; but you saw them made, there where you saw that they ought to be made.' But of course for Descartes there is no such 'ought'. As Gouhier comments, for Augustine creation is 'conceived with a priority in reason (*ratione*) of vision over action' (Gouhier, 1978a, pp. 239 and 239 n.).

But to return to Descartes: in general, he seems to be resigned to having his friends tell him he has been anticipated by St Augustine: for the sake of respectability, it's no harm (e.g. *AT*, ii, p.435; iii, pp.247–8; iv, pp.113 ff.) Yet, as the further points in question here will show, this is a rather superficial connection. Thus, third, Descartes's 'light' is natural, not divine: a difference, as we have seen, that Gassendi makes much of. True, this 'error' did not offend his Augustinian allies: because, one supposes, they could easily translate his 'natural' into their 'divine' illumination. If they did not do so, it would indeed seem heterodox to declare creation and concurrence knowable by natural rather than supernatural sources. But they seem instead to put his doctrine comfortably into their (theocentric) context, even though for Descartes the context was supposed to be a distinct one. Fourth, again, Descartes's use of mathematics entails *our* reading of a code that we hope is also nature's and hence God's; but it is not, as for Augustine, a revelation of order as God made it, as the Son illumines it and as the Holy Spirit guides us to live by it. Granted, so far as one can tell, the Cartesian cut between mind, nature and their Maker was invisible to Arnauld and the first generation of Port Royal Cartesians. (*See* for instance Arnauld's reference to Augustine on the distinction between science, faith and opinion.) For him, as a good Augustinian, faith must come first, science follow from it, and opinion of course is to be avoided. Descartes, too, obviously, admits the priority of faith, but it is a priority, not a primacy. Once more, he is a good product of the Jesuit fathers; science flows from *natural* reason, faith runs in harmony beside it, but is not directly its source. Philosophy ought not indeed to offend theology: hence his anxiety to find good theological critics for his Metaphysics. But it does not flow from it, is not its handmaid, as it was for Arnauld. It will take Pascal to see clearly, as Descartes himself as well as the Arnauld circle failed to do, that the geometrical spirit of Descartes is in fact anti-Augustinian, radically opposed to the life of faith.[4]

Fifth, admittedly, the unity of science would be an Augustinian-Platonic rather than an Aristotelian-Thomistic view; but surely not every unity of science programme is very closely or deeply Augustinian. There is no cause for disagreement here, but no very close meeting of minds either. Sixth, the acceptance of the ontological argument, and more generally of the passage from idea to reality, is indeed, as we have seen, a point at which Arnauld, alone among Descartes's objectors, does in fact grasp, and accept, the basic tenor of Descartes's argument. There is a true meeting of minds here. But what results is at best a kind of lay Augustinianism. What use it is that Descartes, as distinct from Arnauld, makes of this common emphasis is another matter, which we shall consider shortly. Seventh and finally, as I have already suggested in connection with the Cartesian geometrisation of nature, the way in which knowledge flows from the Divine source is much less direct, or much more tenuous, for Descartes than for his more profoundly Augustinian friends. All knowledge for Augustine is Christ the teacher teaching within; not so, surely, for Descartes. God is needed to found his physics, and eventually his morals and his medicine; but Christology is for theologians, not for him. In short, he is not in anything like the same sense as Arnauld and the Port Royal group a truly Augustinian thinker.

But perhaps we must yet reconsider this conclusion, or at least take another look at it. I conceded earlier, following Gouhier, that Descartes may be taken to be (almost?) as much a Christian apologist as a pioneer in the methodology of mathematical physics. And the argument of the *Meditations* does indeed run to God as the high point of its movement. Is this then after all another path of the mind to God, in the spirit of Bonaventura? There are two obvious reasons to give a negative answer. First, as I noted earlier (ch. 4), the movement of the *Meditations* is to God and *from* God. All of Descartes's physics, he boasts, is contained in that document; and although God is the fulcrum of the argument, the establishment of science is its aim. Foundations are needed for a building; in themselves, however, they are but the support of the architect's structure, not the structure itself. To start on Cartesian science, one must meditate; but, he warns, one mustn't make a habit of it (*AT*, iii, p. 695)! Meditation is not a Cartesian way of life. Second, the Cartesian idea of God, as we have seen, is a new one. Indeed, that may have been what Arnauld suspected when he questioned the *causa sui* formulation—although, once reassured, he could insert the Cartesian deity back into a more traditional context. But the problems of metaphysics, including God's existence, were questions, for Descartes, to be faced, as he said, by every man once in his lifetime: then one should go on to other matters. The God of the Augustinians, once found, however, is never to be so neglected; Port Royal in particular seems saturated daily with thought of sin and redemption, and even its theologians must, one supposes, be influenced in their doctrines by this emphasis on a penitential-spiritual way of life. Descartes's God, maker of eternal truths, deviser of nature's code, though of course possessing the traditional attributes: all good and all wise as well as all powerful, and of course, as faith reveals Him to us, identical with the Trinity: Descartes's God in his right place in the order of reasons seems scarcely fit to play this penitentially or theologically and philosophically all-pervasive role.

6

What, then, shall we say, in conclusion, about the relation of Descartes to the early Port Royal group and to the Augustinianism of his day? To understand this, we need, I believe, to consider briefly once more Descartes's relation to the philosophical tradition of his time. Educated by the Jesuits, he was equipped with the scholastic apparatus appropriate to philosophical investigation. He intended to reform radically the approach to the knowledge of nature, in order to permit the liberated mathematical mind to disclose in due order the secrets of nature, including eventually human 'nature', morality, and medicine. But in the course of the 'analysis' by which he moves to that reform, he uses the tools, or better, the building materials, his training has made available. Everything he says he knows by 'natural light'—including the concept of natural light itself—everything he employs to assist himself, and his co-meditating reader, on that path, he has in fact derived from his scholastic education. We have noted, for example, how he picks up the pincers 'formal' and 'material', applying them in his reply to Arnauld differently from the way he had used them in the Third Meditation, and indeed employing 'material' in at least two ways at once. The point he wants to make is clear; and once you see what a clear and distinct idea really is, and how it bears on its intended target, what does it matter *how* you made that point? But the chief move he *must* make against scholastic methodology is the move *against* the primacy of sense-perception and *to* the liberation of geometrising mind for the exploration of nature's code. Now in the case of God, one does indeed move in Augustinian philosophy explicitly from the idea of God to His existence. Thus the acceptance of the ontological argument, and of arguments akin to it, as against the Thomistic *a posteriori* style of argumentation, is an obvious characteristic of an Augustinian perspective. So far, Descartes and his Port Royal admirers are on common ground. Further, Descartes's chief move, to lead the mind away from the senses, is also convergent, up to a point, with a more Augustinian style of philosophising. One does play down the senses, and even common sense, in favour of an inner message: *verbum cordis*. True, that is not in fact what a Cartesian clear and distinct idea amounts to; far from it. Again, *verbum cordis* is thought imbued with religiosity, with the spirit of prayerful humility and the hope of (unmerited) grace. Nevertheless, the Cartesian perspective does entail a stress on inner thought rather than on outer sensing, and, like Augustinian philosophy, it demands the admission of the principle that, rightly used, inference from idea to being may be valid. So there is a genuine convergence of philosophical views, so far, between Descartes and his Augustinian adherents. They can then adjust, it seems, Descartes's philosophising, so much more secular in intent than theirs, into the pattern of their thought (at least until the radicalism of Pascal breaks them apart).

Nevertheless, Descartes is no Augustinian; we have yet to pin down *his* use of this branch of the tradition. He is willing, if sometimes reluctantly, to accept allusions to Augustine on his behalf; but he certainly did not study the saint and live on him as Jansenists did. What he did do, I believe, was, as in the case of more Thomistic scholastic terms and turns of thought, to use whatever means he found available to implement his argument in order to move, step by proper step, along the road of analysis; and sometimes the concepts he found suitable were in fact concepts belonging to the Augustinian rather than the Aristotelian thread in the fabric of contemporary thought. In particular, the light metaphor—though, as Gassendi saw, an illicit transformation of divine into natural illumination—served his purpose well. So did the denigration of sensation: not as a denigration of 'life in the world', but for an intellectual purpose. And so, correspondingly, in a bowdlerised way, did the emphasis on inner truth. For once more, it must be stressed, at the close as at the beginning of my argument, Descartes was initiating a new way of ideas, in which it was the unit of clear and distinct thought, not some scholastically well-formed propositions in some special figure of the syllogism, that was to take us, one step at a time, with uninterrupted certainty, along the path to truth. When we arrive at our goal, of course, we will store up our science in the form of true judgments, but to get there we need to rely on the objective reality—the tendency to truth—of our clear and distinct ideas. And that kind of talk sounds more Augustinian than Thomistic. In short, Descartes selects from the store of available philosophical concepts those most suitable for his reforming purpose; and they turn out, in important cases, to be concepts which only the most Augustinian of his readers understand and accept.

Finally, there is a more negative but nonetheless significant way in which Descartes and his Port Royal adherents seem, if not to concur, nevertheless to develop their positions, in their divergent fashions, from a point of congruence. Descartes's chief aim is to understand 'nature', in the sense of geometrically intelligible extended matter; Port Royal's chief aim is to live in Christ, in the hope of grace. What aims, what existences, could be more different? Yet they have in common a fateful bond: the denial of nature in the traditional, Aristotelian-common-sensical sense. As we have seen, the alienation of mind from nature is its Cartesian liberation. And the alienation of the inner life from nature is, just as fundamentally, the necessary starting point for the asceticism and penitentialism of Port Royal. The geometer's mind, turning against the 'natural impulses' of common sense, which had filled the world, obscurely and deceptively, with sights and sounds, bright colours and alluring songs and tempting fragrances, the geometer's mind 'knows' instea..., conquers, a dead expanse of machine-like matter above which it stands in what Merleau-Ponty was to call a position of 'survol' (Merleau-Ponty, 1964). On the other side, the solitary soul, filled with the sense of himself as miserable sinner, or the theologian, like Arnauld, who develops doctrines in harmony with that penitential attitude, equally rejects the temptations of 'nature' and in particular of his own nature, to revile himself before his Redeemer, seeking (for himself alone; Descartes at least was seeking something accessible to all mankind!) an eternal blessedness wholly, if unintelligibly, sundered from the sense-based life the rest of us are condemned to lead. No wonder Port Royal accepted enthusiastically the doctrine of the bête-machine: nothing lives truly except the souls of those who might be saved.

Somewhere in Kierkegaard's *Journals* there is a note reminiscent of this fateful juncture in our intellectual history. To his path (the path of the ironic individual, even more solitary than were the solitaries of Port Royal), to the path of subjectivity as truth, he opposes a fearsome alternative. If we do not choose the tormented, Christian, inner way, he says, we are faced with only one alternative, in which everything amounts to: sense-data plus tautology. True, that is not (yet) the way of Descartes. But it is the issue of the Cartesian way of ideas in twentieth-century positivism: an issue we can now see as foredoomed, once nature—the 'nature' of our lives and of scholastic tradition—is denied, whether in favour of breast-beating inwardness or of machine-adoring scientism. Admittedly, this is the Cartesian alternative at its absurd extreme; but perhaps that is how we need to see it if we are, at long last, to find a way beyond it.

Notes

1. Nor am I inquiring about the later relation(s) of Cartesianism and Augustinianism. *See* Gouhier, 1978b, a text I regret to say I had overlooked when writing this chapter, or indeed, this book. I am grateful to Dr J.P. Pittion for calling my (belated) attention to it, as to much else in this context.
2. Again, I am grateful to Dr Pittion for pointing out to me the theological

orientation of the *whole* of Arnauld's objections, and also for calling my attention to the remarkable way in which the order of the points Arnauld raises corresponds to the conventions of (late) seventeenth-century theses (and courses) of (or for) theological students of philosophy. Unfortunately, I can only look at the Objections as a series of philosophical questions oriented to the text of the *Meditations*; the subtleties of seventeenth-century theological rhetoric lie quite beyond my competence (J.P. Pittion, personal communication).

3. Arnauld here quite explicitly ties even his 'philosophical' objections to the sensibility of theologians.
4. Not that even the later Port-Royalists necessarily rejected the pursuit of Cartesian physics; rather, they put it in its proper place in relation to the ultimate aims of the good (Christian) life.

Epilogue

8 *Toward a Counter-Cartesian Beginning, or The Powers of Perception Vindicated*

1

As I began, in my first chapter, with an interpretation of a particular passage in the *Meditations* as a guide to reading Descartes, so I want to close here with a reading of another passage that will, I hope, in our gloss on it, help to take us beyond our crippling Cartesian heritage to the possible beginning of a more fruitful style of philosophical thought.

Revolutions in philosophy seem to be slow and difficult. The one we ought, in my view, to be in the middle, if not the far side, of has taken most of this century and may be still lagging in the next. The trouble—or one trouble—is that every computer-carried triumph sets it back so much the further. But I am not going to try to tackle that problem, which could be almost all-embracing. What I want to broach here, as an epilogue to our Cartesian reflections, is one particular philosophical question, one, however, that is, I believe, fundamental to our conception of knowledge as well as of the relation of mind to body: that is, the problem of sense perception. Granted, the major context within which I have been considering our relation to Descartes is the all-too-standard one of dualism and the divided cosmos, or pseudo-cosmos, of thinking mind and extended matter. But an important aspect of Descartes's would-be reform, as we have seen, was the turn against sense perception as the starting-point of knowledge. Ancillary to this move, and as fateful for our conception of the way we make contact with the world around us, was the impoverishment of the concept of sense-perception itself, through the alleged distinction of (full) perception from (mere) sensation. That distinction, I believe, together with the interpretation of perceptions as hypotheses or 'unconscious inferences' has misled philosophers (and *a fortiori* psychologists) persistently for the past three centuries and recurrently for much longer. Perception was not only denied its proper place as the starting point of knowledge, but it was distorted in such a way that when, in the empiricist branch of the tradition, we *were* told to rely on sense-perception, it was to the pure subjectivistic 'sensations' of the *Principles* that we were referred. And this misinterpretation of perception, in turn, has guided our reflections about mind and about knowledge into dead ends from which egress seems difficult if not impossible. At this juncture, therefore, a psychological theory of perception that has truly turned its back on the dominant but mistaken view may help us think our own way out of our Cartesian impasse. I have in mind here J.J. Gibson's theory of perception, developed over thirty years and given its most elaborate expression in his last book, *The Ecological Approach to Visual Perception* (1979; cf. Reed and Jones (1982)). Like any really revolutionary view, however, Gibson's theory is far from easy to assimilate. I believe we might advance our understanding of it, and at the same time find, or glimpse at least, a fruitful starting point for philosophising beyond the Cartesian tradition—by now the Cartesian impasse—if we applied Gibson's theory to a familiar example, Descartes's piece of wax. For the story of the wax, together with the reference to hats and cloaks that might conceal automata (to which I shall refer very briefly at the close of my remarks) constitutes a *locus classicus* for the sensation/perception/judgment distinction, and it may help us overcome our prejudices if we see how smoothly it fits into a radically novel conceptual frame.

2

So let us look at the second part of Descartes's argument in the Second Meditation, recalling the incident of the wax, then looking at it in some detail from what seems to be a common-sensical, but will turn out to be a Gibsonian, point of view and finally contrasting Descartes's interpretation of what has happened with Gibson's very different approach (*AT*, vii, pp. 29–32).

Descartes, you will recall, once more seated by the fire, has discovered that he knows with certainty his own existence as a thinking thing. Yet the restriction of thought to itself and the suspension of belief in body are difficult to maintain. So he will give free rein to his roving mind, in order the better to restrain it bye and bye. That is the juncture in the *Meditations* that we are considering now. Meticulous though Descartes's rhetoric is, one finds, when one looks at them closely, grave difficulties even in the paragraphs preceding the wax example. In what sense, for instance, is sensing 'precisely understood' thinking, as Descartes declares it to be? It would take all Descartes's mechanistic reasoning plus the pineal gland, to explain that—or (depending on one's bent) to exhibit its absurdity. What does it mean, for example, to say that 'images of bodies are formed by thought'? Surely, according to the chief Cartesian view, images are shapes and therefore corporeal beings, which can be somehow inspected by the (non-spatial) soul so precariously (and unintelligibly) located in mid-brain. Images are *formed* by the animal spirits, not by thought. And so on. But let us put such puzzles aside for the moment and embark, with Descartes, on the inspection of a particular body.

Strictly, we ought to do this really, ourselves, in the flesh. Descartes has reminded his readers a number of times that they should meditate with him, and he often excuses himself from commenting on Mersenne's reports of experiments by insisting that he can take seriously only experiments he does himself. So we shall have to pretend that we have a piece of fresh beeswax, either a bit dropped in the hive, or a piece of honeyless comb molded into a roundish shape. Moreover, we must not imagine the wax, but pretend (or imagine) we are *perceiving* it—a difficult task for those of us for whom it is, to say the least, an unfamiliar object. But this is an important distinction. Descartes is talking about perceiving, not imagining. His reduction of sense-perception to a series of imaginings, or their alleged equivalent, brain movements, plus thought, is the very move he is making, not the situation from which he begins, or wants his readers to begin. He wants to take every perceiving and reduce it to motion and thought.

So let us try to follow him in this project. 'Let us consider,' he says, 'those things which are commonly thought to be grasped most distinctly of all, that is, the bodies that we touch, that we see.' But he will not consider, he goes on, bodies in general, 'since these general conceptions (*perceptiones*) are usually much more confused' (*AT*, vii, p. 30). No, he will consider one body in particular. Here is an oddity at the very beginning of our experiment. In the sequence of doubts in the First Meditation, you will recall, particulars go first: distant and unreliable particulars, then near-at-hand particulars, my body, clad in my winter dressing-gown, seated here by the fire, and so on. And what remains, surviving the dream argument, is 'generals', heads, hands, bodies as such. Then the more generals survive the next round, and the most universal 'things', extension, figure, number, are the most resistant of all. It takes the possibility that an omnipotent God has deceived us to call them in question. Why the reversal of order here?

Two reasons come to mind. First, we are talking here about common opinion, what is vulgarly considered to be the case. But at this level the general is, Descartes would hold, 'more confused' than the particular. The popularly accepted general concept of any body, like wax in general, rose in general, human face in general, is confused insofar as it includes such sensible properties as colour, texture, smell and so on. Wax is whitish or yellow, roses are coloured (pink, red, white and so on) and (usually) fragrant, faces, when not infantile or deprived, are crowned with hair—and so on. Although all these properties can, Descartes would argue, be reduced to terms of motion and hence extension, they are not popularly so reduced. Usually, we mingle properties that Descartes would consider purely 'subjective', like colour and smell, with what he thought was really there, namely shapes. So the popular general is confused. The particular, on the other hand, when stripped of any existential claim, can be found to have (as the previous paragraphs have argued) its pure subjective clarity. Even though I may be dreaming and so not 'really' see the light, hear the noise, feel the heat, yet 'certainly I seem to see, to hear, to grow warm'. On that Descartes and the vulgar can agree, even though not on the general concept of wax, rose or human face.

Secondly, the confusion inherent in everyday general concepts of kinds of bodies will be stressed in the Fifth and Sixth Meditations, when we come to understand that our clear and distinct ideas of the essence of bodies, and therefore even our judgments that they exist, when guaranteeable by God's veracity, must be restricted to their extended nature, to the properties accessible to the minds of geometricians. As I have already noted, the ordinary concepts we are talking about here, while our minds are given a looser rein, include those of what Locke will call secondary qualities: the distinctive scent and the colour of roses, what used to be called the crowning glory of a female human face, according to TV commercials, soft to touch, fragrant to smell, glowing to see. Concepts of this full-bodied sort, however, are the intrinsically confused ideas in virtue of which, as minds-times-bodies, we find our way around in everyday contexts, reliant on God's goodness, but straying necessarily beyond the restricted range his veracity and our intellect allow. Such concepts are useful in particular situations, but as we have seen, unreliable for science, and such generals are therefore more confused than the particulars we deal with, recurrently, under their practical but less than perspicuous guidance.

This situation will be reversed, however (*AT*, vii, p. 30), once we understand that this very wax is 'perceived', i.e. apprehended, 'by the mind alone'. Then Descartes can say: 'I am speaking of this [wax] in particular; for of wax in general it is clearer'—clearer, that is, that its existence is grasped by the mind alone. For now, however, we must eliminate our everyday, confused generals, and focus on the particular, in order to find thought—and hence *clear* general concepts—even in our awareness of it.

Well, then, let us look at what under the everyday conditions of life is supposed to be 'most distinctly grasped': one body in particular, of a fixed shape (Descartes does not say precisely, but one gathers when he describes its changing shape, in some sense round), whiteish (this is not specified here either, though he refers later to 'this whiteness'), hard to the touch, cold, sounding when struck with the knuckle, still redolent of flowers, tasting of honey. At this moment, here preserved for posterity, Descartes records these givens of sense. He moves the piece of wax toward the fire, waits, we suppose, a few moments ('while I am speaking', he says) and reports again. All has changed: 'the remains of taste are removed, the fragrance dies, the colour changes, the shape is destroyed, the size increases: it becomes fluid, it becomes hot, it can scarcely be touched, nor if you strike it does it emit a sound' (*AT*, vii, p. 30). Yet it is still the same piece of wax. Why? Because I *understand* it to be so. Each percept has changed; nor, as the next paragraph argues, could we get from one set to the other by imagining, since that would entail an infinite series of images. Understanding alone can do the job. We are presented with two stills, in the second of which each item has altered. We receive each instantaneously, or at any rate, in a briefly enduring moment,[1] also, one assumes, passively: they are 'givens'. We can bring them together only by an act of intellect, by imposing on them the concepts of 'something extended, flexible, mutable'.

3

Is that really what has happened? Let us go back and reflect a little on our story. That each list of properties is presented in a moment follows from the Cartesian view of time (to be made explicit in Meditation Three). That sensory appearances are passive is less clear. Sensing, strictly speaking, we have just been told, is thought, and thought, the characteristic attribute of mind, seems to be an activity, in contrast to the inertness of extension, the essential attribute of bodies (should there prove to be any such).[2] Moreover, the contrast between the sense-carried way in which I seem to apprehend the wax, seeing it with my eyes, and the judgment performed by my mind, through which I really understand it: that contrast must run between what I seem to be receiving through sense and what I am really grasping actively by my mind. But there is also the passive *seeming*, a *passion* of the soul, which arises somehow when it turns its attention to its body. Descartes, I think, would have accepted the Chisholmian locution: I am being appeared to waxily, though of course waxily$_1$ and waxily$_2$, yet at both moments, he will assure us, I am understanding wax, judging this to be the same piece of wax as before. Only that pure intellectual act can unite stills one and two.

What a Pandora's box this opens! On the one hand, the *Meditations* is an infinitely subtle text. Descartes will not write again till Easter, he says to Mersenne in January 1639, because he is busy with a little piece on metaphysics, and then he writes again in February about the usual questions of physics (*AT*, vii, pp. 491–2). Yet what skill, what infinite ingenuity of thought, what weighing of every word, went into that 'little piece'! On the other hand, equally striking and contributing equally to the difficulty of interpreting our text is the profound incoherence of the dualism in which Descartes is engaging us and from which our thought still finds it so hard to escape. Sensing strictly speaking is thinking, yet sensory appearances come to us passively, through the perturbations of the spirits in the brain (or through nerve impulses—it makes no difference); and images are physical configurations, snapshots which would have to follow in an (impossibly) infinite sequence to effect, in our minds, the transfer from the first to the second waxy appearance. The more one looks into this reasoning, the less sense it makes. Only the incoherent coherence of the Cartesian trio: mechanistic nature (including the machinery of human bodies), the pineal gland, and the incorporeal, inextended yet mysteriously situated soul makes this episode an episode at all. Without the peculiar Cartesian apparatus to support us, how can *we* interpret the wax-inspecting interlude?

It *is* an episode: that's the first clue. The two snapshots are a pretence, moments abstracted from a process that takes time. 'Look,' says Descartes, 'while I am speaking (the wax) is moved to the fire, the remains of taste are removed. . .the odour dies. . .' (*AT*, vii, p.30) and so on. 'While I am speaking': no utterance is instantaneous. One sound has to succeed another, even in a minimal expression. Correspondingly, moreover, on the object side, so to speak, there is a continuous transition from being appeared to waxily$_1$ to being appeared to waxily$_2$. And each of the changes in perceptible properties recorded from stage$_1$, to stage$_2$ is an itemisable process: the remains of flavour 'are purged', the scent 'dies', the colour 'is changed', the shape 'is destroyed', the size 'grows', the wax 'becomes liquid and hot'. Only with respect to touch and sound are we given something that looks at first sight like the terminal image: it can scarcely be touched, and if you strike it it makes no sound. These also of course entail duration, since it takes time to reach out and touch the melted wax and to try to rap it with a knuckle. I shall return in a few moments to these two statements; meantime let us look a bit more at the other items. For, like Descartes in 1639, we need to train our minds to break their misleading habits, by now the habit of looking at perceiving with three centuries of Cartesian prejudice to misguide us (not to mention the Platonic and sceptical traditions!).

Again, Descartes is here setting down not, as he wants us to believe, a second list of brief appearances, but a bundle of processes, all of which together sum up to what I am sensing. Granted, we cannot in fact 'watch' the flavour being 'purged', for we cannot taste the wax at the same time that we are melting it. The gustatory system, we might say, is less elaborately structured than the visual. That is a bodily difference, of course, a fact which ought to put us on our guard against the dualistic solution to come. For the moment, that is by the way. The smell, however, we sense dying away, the colour gradually changing, the shape being annihilated, the size increasing. All these are sensible processes, not snapshot-like presentations. They would be better described as slow interchanges between organism and environment—in the manner of the *Theaetetus*—than in the snapshot-inference terms of the tradition established by Descartes in this very text.[3] Alternatively, we could redescribe this cluster of transitions in terms of Husserlian 'time-consciousness' as entailing retentions from the starting point and protensions toward the end of the process. On either model, the snapshot/inference account is shown to be a strange and strained abstraction from what plainly does go on. And as we have just seen, even Descartes's own account fails to adhere to the austere interpretation he is engaged in developing.

If you look at the wax episode in the context of the *Meditations* as a whole, moreover, the temporal context becomes even clearer. To write them, Descartes has had to wait until he was mature enough to embark on 'the overthrow of all (his) former opinions'. So there was a right time in his history for this particular incident. He might have seen beeswax before often enough, but it had not told him, as it had not told others, the story of sensed givens against concepts grasped by disembodiable intellect. *Both* his training by the Jesuits at La Flèche, as he kept assuring them, and his awakening to the new physics and to his own method necessarily precede this incident as its historical setting. A single perceptual event takes time: that's the first point in our first lesson. But every perceptual event also has its place, however routine, in the history of the perceiver. And some perceptual events, like this one of the wax, as Descartes is quite self-consciously using it, may mark turning points in a history, such that the perceiver's world will be in some ways never the same again. That is the second point: perceptions fit into a personal history.

Every personal history, however, forms a history not only as the record of this particular living being; but also, and just as fundamentally, as this particular expression of a complex network of cultural traditions, institutions, rituals. In the case of the wax, for example, the perceptual 'givens' Descartes is listing, though seen, heard, touched and so on, in short, sensory, would not have been available to him in that form had there not been a European apiculture, and had he not learned, presumably as a child, about beeswax and its source in the hive. What we see, hear and so on as persistent through change, depends, like so much of our perception, on what we have learned to notice in our cultural situation. It is not a question of multitudinous sheer givens tied by a concept, but of the kinds of objects and events our environment has brought to our attention and that we have learned to discriminate—to discriminate *perceptually*. Even what we actually see, it is by now, I should think, universally acknowledged, is in large part a function of individual interest and cultural training.

In short, perceiving the wax is an event spreading through a period, itself in turn forming an ordered part of a complex individual biological-social history.

If it takes time to watch the wax melting, secondly, it also takes attention. It is something Descartes is *doing*. In the everyday terms Descartes is letting himself indulge in at this juncture, perception is usually supposed to be passive. What my senses tell me, they tell me whether I will or no: so much is undeniable. I want a nice sunny day today, but there's the rain. In Descartes's own terms, on the other hand, there is a difficulty here. Sensing, we have already noticed, is, *strictly speaking*, thinking; indeed, that is what he is trying to show us in this passage. In that case, however, it would seem to be fundamentally active, yet also quite different from what we ordinarily call sense-perception, let alone from philosophers' or psychologists' 'sensations' or 'sensory stimuli', or even from the sense-engendering events Descartes himself 'describes'. For what the senses give me, in Cartesian terms, is purely a series of shapes, extended things moving, in particular, movements of the animal spirits in the brain. And what is 'sensory' about that? In the Cartesian reading, it seems, then, everyday perception will be analysed entirely away. In the present context, however, while Descartes is giving his wandering thoughts free rein, he starts from the ordinary opinion that he is seeing, hearing, feeling, smelling, tasting something, receiving 'adventitious' ideas, ideas that come to him through the senses from some external thing. And that kind of process, when one looks at it carefully, seems to be neither a pure 'mental act' nor a pure being acted on, but both at once. Seeing, the exercise of our preeminent sense, is not just being affected by visibles: it is *looking*. Being seen is not just being physically or physiologically within my 'visual field'; being seen is being looked at, inspected, not overlooked. My body—which, when able to be activated in certain ways, *is* my mind: as Aristotle puts it, the first actuality of an organised being potentially having life—my body reaches out, through my senses, to pick up what the environment affords it: parts of my own body, the typewriter under my hands, the hills in view through the window—you can fill it in from your own experience. What matters to us here is Descartes's experiment insofar as we can reenact it. There he is, seated by the fire, feeling the warmth, pen in hand. What care he takes in noticing each property! He not only looks at the wax, he strikes it with a knuckle, tastes it—by breaking off a bit, or how? And then of course he has to move the wax to the fire and note its altering and, finally, altered state. Again, he watches the changing colour and shape, tries to touch it, taps it, obtaining no sound, sniffs for the fragrance he can no longer find—and so on. Surely, this is neither a pure thinking nor a pure sequence of local movements, but an event in the life of an active embodied being. Open out the context further, as we did with the place of this incident in Descartes's history, and reflect how much care and attention it has entailed: can you think of another example where the dicta of all five senses would change so dramatically, thus allowing Descartes so dramatically to make his point? And then, although one assumes he only gave orders, somebody had to procure the wax for him. Further, it is not an ordinary 'natural' object that might just turn up in view, but the product of a craft, an excellent illustration of Heidegger's counter-Cartesian thesis that things are ready-to-hand (*zuhanden*) more fundamentally than they are just there (*vorhanden*), indifferently spread out in space. It is within the confines of a human world that pieces of wax turn up and tell us, if we pay attention, what they have to tell. This little history of Descartes and the wax is a unified piece of behaviour, an action, like that of a cat at a mouse hole. Sniff, wait, pounce: sensing and bodily attitude are much too intimately intertwined to be divided. Such is every act of perceiving, and most especially this, philosophically so fateful, incident.

Words have misled us, Descartes says when he comes to his resolution of the problem. Let us listen carefully once again to his own words (or rather to an English rendering of them) and see just how we have been misled:

> Yet I marvel meantime how prone my mind is to errors, for although I am considering these matters by myself silently and without speaking, I nevertheless stick in the words themselves, and I am nearly deceived by the very use of language: for we say that we see the wax itself when it is present, not that we judge it to be there from its colour or shape. Whence I would at once infer that I know the wax by the vision of my eye, not by the inspection of the mind alone, were it not that I now happened to recall men passing on the street outside the window, whom I say I see just as habitually as I say I see the wax. Yet what do I see besides hats and cloaks, under which automata might be hiding, although I judge that they are men: and so what I thought I saw with my eyes, I comprehend by the sole faculty of judging, which is in my mind (*AT*, vii, pp. 31–2).

Consider yet again that last clause: 'and so what I thought I saw with my eyes, I comprehend by the sole faculty of judging, which is in my mind'. *Those* are the misleading words from whose reverberations we and our philosophical forebears have been suffering ever since that winter day three and nearly a half centuries ago. To say that I see the wax with my eyes is not *so* bad: I do indeed receive the evidence of its presence, its shape and colour, its distance from me, by means of my visual system. To say, on the contrary, that I grasp it solely by the power of judgment that is in my mind is to bait an intellectual trap from which we are still seeking an escape.

4

Such an escape, I believe, J.J. Gibson's theory of perception affords us. For our case, the starting point is simple. Descartes has been sitting there watching the wax all the time. He admits, we all admit, it is the same wax. Why? Not because he imposes (we impose) some sort of conceptual overview upon underlying bits of motion (or of sensation). No one has brought him (or us) separate data cards that he (or we) must somehow unite with a conceptual formula. No, it is perception, *sense* perception, that unifies the process from beginning to end: here's this wax, now watch it melt, smell its scent fading, see its shape change, and so on. True, some of our behaviours, like testing it with a knuckle, can only be tried discretely, from time to time. But as we have seen, the whole incident nevertheless forms one continuous process, in which, as we must now stress, we are engaged *with our senses* from first to last. We, sense-endowed living beings, have been taking a powerful sight of notice of the fate of a particular object in our natural, and at the same time, our cultural, environment. The optical array afforded us here, by daylight and firelight, has been changing in certain noticeable ordered ways: surfaces, contours, edges have been flowing. And our sight of all these features has been reinforced, too, by our other, supporting, perceptual systems. We have been sniffing, tasting, touching, listening as well as looking, and what surrounds us, bodily, is what we have been subjecting to all these tests. In other words, this is not only an incident in an individual history, taking time while taking place (taking time *because* taking place), entailing behavioural as well as sensory events, doing as well as being done to. Like every incident in every individual history, this is also and equally fundamentally an *ecological* incident. It is a segment from the story of a living being, developing, as all living beings, including human beings, do, as one expression of a complex network of organism-environment interactions.

Up to now, I believe, we have been deflected from understanding what is going on here by our ingrained conviction that the senses—if they are anything more than motions: nerve-impulses, the modern analogue of Descartes's turbulent animal spirits—present to us only images: the snapshot-like glimpses Descartes enumerates. With Locke as well as Descartes, we believe that a piece of wax neither hard nor molten, neither cold nor hot, neither fragrant nor odourless, because it cannot be imaged, cannot be sensed, and so must be grasped, if at all, by some wholly non-sensory power. A contrariety of pictures cannot give us the awareness of this wax as the *same* entity. The *sameness* must be added somehow, non-sensibly. Hobbes would say we do this by convention, Descartes says by thought, by the superposition of the concepts extension, flexibility, mutability.

It is this fundamental, mistaken equation of sensation with a bundle of images that leads us astray, and that is what Gibson's theory can help us overcome. Do we really see little flashes of sensory bits, or do we see things and events around us, as living beings taking up clues from our environment? When we looked closely at the incident of the wax, we found that it was a unified process, taking place over an interval of time and involving the active attention, which in turn entails the bodily presence, of a living being caught up in a particular historical situation. To take this description seriously we need to make a very fundamental shift in the way we interpret our sensory experience. Modern epistemology and philosophy of mind as well as the major traditions of experimental psychology have built their reflections, and experimental programmes, about sense-perception on the very foundation established by Descartes in the passage we have been examining: the reduction of the full-bodied perceptible world to locomotion, inspected by thought. Perception, if it can be discovered to survive at all in this improverished universe, can get by only at the meeting point of motion and mind, as fleeting, atomising, meaningless sensations, which must then be reconstructed into an analogue of itself, whether intellectualised in quasi-Kantian or physicalised in quasi-Hobbesian fashion. But there is an alternative, and that is what Gibson in his psychological theory has been trying to develop. Let me quote a brief passage that puts the contrast well:

> Instead of assuming that stimuli can give rise only to meager sensations, let us now consider the opposite assumption: that the environment is rich in varied and complex potential stimulus information, capable of giving rise to diverse, meaningful complex perceptions. Let us suppose that there is information in stimuli, to be picked up by a sensitive, exploring organism (E.J. Gibson, 1969, p. 75).

The psychological-technical term 'stimuli' in this passage gives some misgivings, since the concept stimulus itself is a product of the Cartesian approach we are trying to reverse. We could just omit its second and third occurrences and say:

> Let us now consider the opposite assumption: that the environment is rich in varied and complex potential information, capable of giving rise to

> diverse, meaningful, complex, perceptions. Let us suppose that there is information to be picked up by a sensitive, exploring organism.

Although this statement in fact occurs in Eleanor J. Gibson's *Principles of Perceptual Learning and Development*, published in 1969, it seems to me, when so amended, to summarise well the theory J.J. Gibson was to elaborate in his last book, published ten years later. By then, Gibson had in general dropped 'stimulus' language, and, even in this earlier text, Eleanor Gibson too noted that 'stimuli' in fact probably do not exist at all (E.J. Gibson, 1969, p. 102). The point, here, however, is that by 1979 J.J. Gibson had come to speak instead of what the environment *affords* a perceiving organism, or, for short, of *affordances*. So, he suggests, for instance, a rabbit affords a hunter the opportunity of eating, while a tiger affords the danger of being eaten. Köhler published many years ago a book called *The Place of Values in a World of Facts* (Köhler, 1938). Gibson, on the contrary, is starting from the premise that there is no world of mere facts, that it is not our pure intellects, let alone our Sartrean wills, that make 'values'. Instead there are 'sensitive, exploring organisms' picking up, for their own purposes, information from the environment that surrounds, supports, threatens, in multifarious ways *interests* them. This is of course a radical denial of just the turn in thinking about sense perception, and in general about knowledge, that Descartes was trying to effect. Thus, in the final paragraph of the wax passage he delivers what seems to him the knockout blow to the 'common-sense' or scholastic view. What was distinct, he asks, in his first 'perception' (i.e. in what he held, following the language of the vulgar, that he saw by external sense or by the power of imagining)? What was there in it, he goes on, that 'could not, as it seems, be possessed by some animal?' (*AT*, vii, p. 32). And to be 'possessed by some animal' means for Descartes precisely to be purely mechanical, a sequence of motions and nothing more, without sentience, without meaning, without any bearing on action or understanding.

What Gibson is doing in psychology, by contrast, like what Merleau-Ponty was doing in philosophy, is to restore our primary means of making contact with the realities around us to an organic place in the living world, that is, to put our intellectual activities back into their place in our natures as living things, and thereby also to put meaning back into the natural world. Note, however, that although Gibson's ecological approach makes excellent evolutionary sense, this is not the biologism of doctrinaire Darwinian evolutionists. It is if you like ecologism: talk about communities of interacting living things (interacting also, of course, with the non-living features of their environment). It is a question, not of genes or gene pools mechanically generated by mutation, isolation, natural selection, but rather of a world where, though in a complicated and often messy way, things make sense.

Now this is a very difficult position to present, partly because the appropriate technical vocabulary is not yet current. I have already mentioned one central term of Gibson's: *affordance*. As we have already seen, the theory of affordances is an ecological theory: as such it interprets environment and sense-mediated information, in Gibson's words, as 'properties of things taken with reference to an observer, but not properties of the experiences of the observer' (J.J. Gibson, 1979, p. 137). And clearly this entails a very radical shift in philosophical as well as psychological thinking.

Yet there must be more to it than just that. *What* affordances do objects, events, surfaces in the world offer us? What we pick up to guide us in our explorations, Gibson explains, is *invariants* specified most clearly through environmental change, though also, sometimes, in unchanging contexts. The detailed study of invariants, however, was only beginning when Gibson died. It is still in large part difficult, if not impossible, to specify exactly what they are. Gibson lists a number of them, but does not define the term, and I certainly shall not try to do so. In our case, I think, it is pretty clear what is going on: that is why I thought of the wax as an example. Extension (that is, being a spread-out thing), flexibility and mutability are functioning here, not, or not primarily, as intellectual concepts imposed from outside on two sets of contradictory sensed bits, but as invariants perceived, grasped through our bodily perceptual systems, and thus maintaining our awareness of the wax as *this same thing.* A child understands what an object is before it grasps reflectively the concept of something extended: it knows pick-upables and droppables; and of course it knows squashiness—flexibility—and changeability, prereflectively, if you like, tacitly, Gibson would say. Here, in the *perception* of identifiable objects, and the events through which they persist or alter, we find in fact the tacit foundation of *all* knowledge, which is also always at bottom knowing one's way around. As I have put it elsewhere, all knowledge is orientation (Grene, ed., 1969, p. xi; cf. Grene, 1983a).

It should be added, perhaps, that Gibson counts melting as a form of going out of existence; but since the object in question here could be let cool and reconstituted, we may perhaps count its melting as change rather than cessation. In any case, invariants of course also underlie what Aristotle would call substantial as well as less drastic forms of change. In short, information about the identity of events and objects in our environment is afforded us by the underlying invariants that enable us to see, and hear, and so on, *what* is changing.

Perhaps I should try to say a little more about what invariants are (or may be) in general, and then I want to go back, finally and very briefly, to Descartes and make two final points about the advantages offered us by the Gibsonian reform.

Well, then, invariants. It may help to specify more closely what they are not. First, they are not forms—at least they need not be and often are not. Some people think they are, but it is easy to show by counter-example that this is wrong. Michotte's tunnel experiment, for instance, presents a perception of permanence to which no image, and hence no shape, corresponds (Michotte, 1963). So do the experiments exhibiting the perception of ratios or proportions that go back to Köhler's hens who learn to peck on a darker gray square even when the same colour that was darker in the first presentation is now lighter (Köhler, 1947).

Nor, I believe, are invariants abstractions in the way that concepts are sometimes thought to be. Here let me follow the authority of Gibson himself (in a handwritten note, and this time, against that of his wife). In a note called 'Formless and wordless invariants' he writes:

> The interchangeability of depth and width gets noticed by children; gets *seen* in that respect
> the interchangeable nature of *projected* and *unprojected* surfaces
> the interchange of interior and exterior surfaces
> the interchange of *seen-from-the-side*, front, back, top, bottom
> This *interchange* is an *invariant* (E.g., how the child *sees* a kitten (How it *sees* a human *head*))
> *It sees an *invariant* kitten. Not an *abstract* kitten!

I.e. not 'catness', as I first suggested in discussing this question (Cornell Archives).

Watching a year old child with cats and pictures of cats, I think this is probably true, and it also fits Eleanor Gibson's account of perceptual discrimination. For instance, in the recognition of phonemes and graphemes, what is noticed is a persistence of *differences* in sound or shape; this is not the imposition of an abstraction, but something that is *seen* to be the same. Concepts are built on such foundations, not used to construct them out of the shifting sands of sensory atoms.

Sometimes, as in the case of the dark-light relations, invariants are ratios. How often they are ultimately as precise as that it is so far hard to say, but I trust that as work goes on among Gibson's students and collaborators more will be discovered. At worst, it will turn out to be a case for Merleau-Pontyan radical reflection, nothing very precise will be said, even though some progress may be made toward a more reasonable approach to perception and to knowledge. That remains to be seen.[4]

5

Finally, however, let me add, as I threatened to do, two further brief reflections about Descartes v. Gibson on the senses. I mentioned hats and cloaks at the beginning, and later in passing, I quoted that sentence: Descartes has recalled that he says he sees men passing outside the window. 'But,' he asks, 'what do I see besides hats and cloaks, under which automata might be hiding, although I judge that they are men...' Now I used to think this was just another sensation/judgment remark, not carried as far as it might have been to: coloured patches, judged to be hats and cloaks judged to be worn by men. But in reading Descartes's correspondence I came to see why the formulation was just like this: 'hats and cloaks might conceal *automata,* but I judge that what they conceal are men'. This is the beginning of that identical, disastrous, science-fiction philosophising in which so many of our colleagues and our students are still so gleefully entangled. There is motion, and machinery, which is clockwork motion, and inside some machines, according to

Descartes we judge that there are mathematising minds. For Descartes, be it noted, these are far from being ghosts, while for many of us nowadays they are less than ghosts, ephemeral epiphenomena, or nothing. We are 'persons without minds' as Richard Rorty puts it. Do let us return for our reflections to a more reasonable beginning. Gibson can help us, I believe, in this badly needed conceptual shift.

Second and finally, there is another important reason for abandoning the Cartesian perspective on sense-perception in favour of Gibson's— of both Gibsons', I should say, since it is E.J. Gibson who has specialised in the study of perceptual development. Descartes has told us that the linguistic usage of the vulgar has misled us. Behind that usage, too, there lies, in his view, a more basic, because tacit and unnoticed (alleged) deception to which he often alludes. As infants, as children, we believed we had access to real things through our senses. We were quite wrong, Descartes insists; so now we must learn undeception. Indeed, we must meditate, with Descartes, meditate long and hard, precisely in order to recover from those mistaken, childish beliefs. Now admittedly, children do hold some strange beliefs: they believe in Santa Claus, sometimes, in angels, in God? A four year old once assured me the moon must come up from the earth at night and return there in the morning. It couldn't just hang there in the sky. But these are strange beliefs floating on the surface of language. Tacitly, perceptually, infants, as they mature, learn their way around in organised ways in an organised nature: in a world, again, that makes sense. Why go on accepting a philosophical mythology that undercuts that obvious insight? Again, the Gibsons' psychological account of children's being-in-the-world may help us think more concretely and more fruitfully about perception, about knowledge, about what it means to be human, than the still dominant Cartesian, anti-realistic, anti-developmental style of thought permits.

Notes

1. Although J.M. Beyssade (1979) argues firmly against the instantaneity of the Cartesian moment, Descartes's use of the concept of concurrence unequivocally demands the independence of each such temporal unit,

however 'long' it may 'last'. There may well be a problem about the difference between Cartesian space and Cartesian time with respect to continuity, but that does not, I believe, affect my argument here. For a recent analysis of Deacartes's theory of perception, based largely on the *Dioptrics*, *see* Arbini (1983).

2. *See* Chapter 2 above, also with respect to references to the 'activity' of mind throughout this chapter.
3. Descartes is of course not without predecessors in making this distinction. For the history of the doctrine of the 'sensory core', *see* Hatfield and Epstein, (1979).
4. The best philosophical analysis of Gibson's theory of perception I have seen so far is that of David Blinder (Blinder, 1985); he compares clearly and effectively Gibson's principles with those of the, alas, still Cartesian establishment in what is called 'cognitive science'. Edward Reed and Gary Hatfield are also working in this area (Reed, 1983).

References

Up to 1956, the literature on Descartes is fully documented by G. Sebba in his *Bibliographia Cartesiana* (Nijhoff, The Hague, 1964). Willis Doney and Vere Chapell are engaged in completing the sequel to this classic volume. Since I could not hope to emulate them, I have listed here only such books and papers as are in fact referred to in my own essay. As I noted in the Preface, the works and correspondence of Descartes are referred to by the Adam and Tannery volume and pages (C. Adam and P. Tannery, eds, *Oeuvres de Descartes,* new edition, Vrin, Paris, 1973–6) as e.g. *AT* i, p. 211. Where I have quoted (with permission; see preface) Kenny's version of the letters (Anthony Kenny, ed. and trans., *Descartes: Philosophical Letters,* Oxford University Press, Oxford, 1970), this is referred to as *K*, while Gassendi's *Disquisitio Metaphysica* (ed. and trans. B. Rochot, Vrin, Paris, 1962) is abbreviated as *DM*. What follows here is a list of all other literature cited, or alluded to, in my text.

Alquié, F. (1956) *Descartes,* Hatier, Paris.

(1960) *La Découverte métaphysique de l'homme chez Descartes,* 2nd ed. (1st ed., 1950), Presses Universitaires de France, Paris.

Alquié, F., (ed.) (1967) *Oeuvres philosophiques de Descartes,* Garnier, Paris, 3 vols, 1963–73; 2nd vol., 1967.

Arbini, R. (1983) 'Did Descartes have a philosophical theory of sense perception?', *Jl. Hist. Phil, 21,* pp. 317–37.

Beck, L.J. (1965) *The Metaphysics of Descartes: A Study of the Meditations,* Oxford University Press, Oxford.

Berr, Henri (1960) *Du scepticisme de Gassendi*, A. Michel, Paris.

Beyssade, J.M. (1979) *La philosophie prémière de Descartes,* Flammarion, Paris.

Blinder, David (1985) 'Revolution and Counterrevolution in Psychology', paper delivered at Pacific Division, Amer. Phil. Assoc.

Bloch, O.R. (1971) *La philosophie de Gassendi: nominalisme, matérialisme et métaphysique,* Nijhoff, The Hague.

Brockliss, L.W.B. (1981a) 'Aristotle, Descartes and the new science: natural philosophy at the University of Paris 1600–1740', *Annals of Science, 38,* pp. 33–69.

(1981b) 'Continuity and change in early modern universities', in *History of Universities* (Avebury, Aversham, Bucks.), pp. 131–67.

Cassirer, E. (1953) *Substance and Function,* Dover Publications, New York.

Caton, H. (1973) *The Origin of Subjectivity: An Essay on Descartes,* Yale University Press, New Haven, Conn.

(1981) 'Analytic history of philosophy: the case of Descartes', *Phil. Forum, 12,* pp. 273–94.

Clarke, D. (1976) 'The ambiguous role of experience in Cartesian science', *PSA 1976, 1,* pp. 151–64.

(1982) *Descartes's Philosophy of Science,* Manchester University Press, Manchester.

Cook, J.W. (1969) 'Human beings' in P. Winch (ed.), *Philosophy of Wittgenstein* (Routledge, London), pp. 147–78.

Costa, M.J. (1983) 'What Cartesian ideas are not', *Jl. Hist. Phil., 21,* pp. 537–49.

Curley, E.M. (1978) *Descartes against the Sceptics,* Harvard University Press, Cambridge, Mass.

Frankfurt, H. (1970) *Demons, Dreamers and Madmen, The Defense of Reason in Descartes's Meditations,* Bobbs-Merrill, Indianapolis, Ind.

(1971) 'Freedom of the Will and the Concept of a Person', *Jl. Phil., 68,* pp. 5–20.

(1977) 'Descartes on the creation of the eternal truths', *Phil Rev., 68,* pp. 288–96.

Gabbey, A. (1980) 'Force and inertia in the seventeenth century: Descartes and Newton', in Gaukroger (ed.) (1980) pp. 230–300.

(1984) 'Problems of mechanism' in J. Pitt, (ed.), *Change and Progress in Modern Science* (Reidel, Dordrecht), pp. 9–84.

Galilei, Galileo (1965) *Il Saggiatore, Opere,* Edizione

Nazionale, Florence, vol. VI.
Gaukroger, S. (1980) 'Descartes's project for a mathematical physics', in Gaukroger (ed.) (1980) pp. 97–140.
Gaukroger, S., (ed.) (1980) *Descartes: Philosophy, Mathematics and Physics,* Harvester Press, Brighton, Sussex; Barnes & Noble Books, Totowa, N.J.
Gibson, E.J. (1969) *Principles of Perceptual Learning and Development,* Prentice-Hall, Englewood Cliffs, N.J.
Gibson, J.J. (1979) *The Ecological Approach to Visual Perception,* Houghton Mifflin, New York.
Gilson, E. (1913) *La Liberté chez Descartes et la Théologie,* Alcan, Paris.
(1975) *Etudes sur le Rôle de la Pensée Médiévale dans la Formation du Système Cartésian,* 4th ed. (1st ed., 1930), Vrin, Paris.
Gilson, E., (ed.) (1967) *Descartes. Discours de la Méthode. Textes et Commentaires,* Vrin, Paris.
Gouhier, H. (1972) *La Pensée Religieuse de Descartes,* 2nd ed. (1st ed., 1924), Vrin, Paris.
(1978a) *La Pensée Metaphysique de Descartes* 3rd ed. (1st ed., 1962), Vrin, Paris.
(1978b) *Cartésianisme et Augustinisme au XVIIe Siécle,* Vrin, Paris.
Grene, M. (1976) *Philosophy in and out of Europe,* University of California Press, Berkeley and Los Angeles.
(1983a) *The Knower and the Known,* University Press of America, Washington, D.C. (1st ed., Faber, London, (1966).
(1983b) *Sartre,* University Press of America, Washington, D.C. (1st ed., Franklin Watts, New York, 1973).
(1985) Perception, interpretation and the sciences: towards a new philosophy of science' in D. Depew and B. Weber (eds), *Evolution at a Crossroads,* Bradford Books, MIT Press, Cambridge, Mass.
Grene, M. (ed.) (1969) *M. Polanyi; Knowing and Being,* University of Chicago Press, Chicago.
Gueroult, M. (1968) *Descartes selon l'Ordre des Raisons,* 2nd ed. (1st ed., 1953), 2 vols, Aubier-Montaigne, Paris.
(1980) 'The metaphysics and physics of force in Descartes' in Gaukroger (ed.) (1980), pp. 196–229.
Hacking, I. (1975) *The Emergence of Probability,* Cambridge

University Press, Cambridge.
(1980) 'Proof and eternal truths: Descartes and Leibniz', in Gaukroger (ed.) 1980, pp. 169–80.
Hatfield, G.C. (1979) 'Force (God) in Descartes's physics', *Stud. Hist. Phil. Sci., 10,* pp. 113–40.
(1985) 'The Senses and the fleshless eye: the *Meditations* as Cognitive Exercises', in A. Rorty (ed.), *Essays on Descartes's Meditations,* University of California Press, Berkeley and Los Angeles.
Hatfield, G.C. and Epstein, W. (1979) 'The Sensory Core and the Medieval Foundations of Early Modern Perceptual Theory', *Isis. 70,* pp. 363–84.
Hooker, M. (ed.) (1978) *Descartes: Critical and Interpretive Essays,* Johns Hopkins University Press, Baltimore, MD.
Hull, D. (1980) 'Individuality and selection' *Ann. Rev. Ecol. Syst., 11,* pp. 311–32.
Jones, H. (1981) *Pierre Gassendi 1592–1655: An Intellectual Biography,* B. de Graaf, Nieuwkoop.
Joy, L.S. (1983) *Gassendi the Atomist: Advocate of History in an Age of Science,* Unpubl. diss.
Kennington, R. (1971) 'The finitude of Descartes's evil genius', *Jl.Hist.Id., 32,* pp. 441–46.
Kenny, A. (1968) *Descartes: A Study of his Philosophy,* Random House, New York.
Köhler, W. (1938) *The Place of Values in a World of Facts,* Liveright, New York.
(1947) *Gestalt Psychology, Liveright, New York.*
Kosman, A. (1984) 'Substance, Being and *Energeia,* in J. Annas (ed.), *Oxford Studies in Greek Philosophy, 2,* Oxford University Press, Oxford.
Kraus, P.E. (1983) 'From universal mathematics to universal method. Descartes's 'turn' in Rule IV of the *Regulae*', *Jl. Hist.Phil., 21,* pp. 159–74.
Lachterman, D.R. (1983) 'Descartes and the philosophy of history', *Indep.Jl.Phil., 4,* pp. 31–46.
(1984) *Mathematics, Method and Metaphysics: Essays toward a Genealogy of Modern Thought,* Unpubl. diss.
(1985) '*Objectum purae matheseos:* mathematical construction and the passage from essence to existence', in A. Rorty (ed.), *Essays on Descartes's Meditations.* University of California Press.

Laudan, L. (1981) 'The clock metaphor and hypotheses: the impact of Descartes on English methodological thought: 1650–1670', in L. Laudan, *Science and Hypothesis* (Reidel, Dordrecht) pp. 27–58.

Leclerc, I. (1980) 'The ontology of Descartes', *Rev.Met., 34,* pp. 297–323.

Leibniz, G.W.V. (1880) C.J. Gerhardt (ed.), *Die philosophischen Schriften,* vol. IV., Weidmannsche Buchh., Berlin.

Lenoble, R. (1971) *Mersenne ou la naissance du mécanisme,* 2nd ed. (1st ed., 1942), Vrin, Paris.

Locke, J. (1975) *An Essay concerning Human Understanding,* Oxford University Press, Oxford.

Machamer, P. (1978) 'Causality and explanation in Descartes's natural philosophy', in P.K. Machamer and P.G. Turnbull (eds.) *Motion and Time, Space and Matter* (Ohio State University Press, Columbus, Ohio) pp. 169–99.

MacIntyre, A.C. (1981) *After Virtue,* University of Notre Dame Press, Notre Dame, Indiana, pp. 174–76.

Marion, J. -L. (1975) *Sur l'ontologie grise de Descartes,* Vrin, Paris.

(1981) *Sur la théologie blanche de Descartes,* Presses Universitaires de France, Paris.

Maull, N. (1980) 'Cartesian optics and the geometrisation of nature', in Gaukroger (ed.) (1980) pp. 23–40.

Merleau-Ponty, M. (1944) *La phénoménologie de la perception,* Gallimard, Paris.

(1964) *L'oeil et l'esprit,* Gallimard, Paris

Michotte, A. (1963) *The Perception of Causality,* Methuen, London; Basic Books, New York.

Olscamp, P.J. (1965) 'Introduction' to translation of *Descartes, Discourse on Method, Dioptrics, Geometry and Meteors,* Bobbs-Merrill, Indianapolis, Ind., pp. ix-xxxv.

Orcibal, J. (1949) *Louis XIV contre Innocent XI,* Vrin, Paris.

Pellegrin, P. (1982) *La classification des animaux chez Aristote,* Société des Editions, 'Les Belles Lettres', Paris.

Polanyi, M. (1958) *Personal Knowledge,* Routledge, London and University of Chicago Press, Chicago.

(1966) *The Tacit Dimension,* Doubleday, Garden City, New York.

Price, H.H. (1969) *Thinking and Experience,* Hutchinson University Library, London.

Reed, E.S. (1982) 'Descartes's Corporeal Ideas Hypothesis and the origin of Scientific Psychology', *Rev.Met., 35,* pp. 731–52.

(1983) 'Two theories of the intentionality of perceiving', *Synthese, 54,* pp. 85–94.

Reed, E. and Jones, R. (eds) (1982) *Reasons for Realism: Essays of J.J. Gibson,* Erlbaum, Hillsdale, N.J.

Richardson, R.C. (1982) 'The 'scandal' of Cartesian interactionism', *Mind, 91,* pp. 20–37.

Rochot, B. (ed. and trl.) (1962) Gassendi, *Disquisitio Metaphysica,* Vrin, Paris.

Rodis-Lewis, G. (1950) *L'Individualité chez Descartes,* Vrin, Paris.

(1971) *L'Oeuvre de Descartes,* 2 vols, Vrin, Paris.

Rodis-Lewis, G. (ed.) (1959) *Descartes, Lettres à Regius,* Vrin, Paris.

Ross, W.D. (ed.) (1936) *Aristotle's Physics,* Oxford University Press, Oxford.

Sainte-Beuve, C.A. (1952, 1954, 1955) *Port Royal* (Ed. Pléiade), M. Leroy (ed.), 3 vols., Gallimard, Paris.

Sakellariadis, S. (1982) 'Descartes's use of empirical data to test hypotheses', *Isis, 73,* pp. 68–76.

Schuster, J.A. (1980) 'Descartes' *Mathesis Universalis,* 1619–28', in Gaukroger (ed.) (1980), pp. 41–96.

Sober, E. (1984) 'Sets, Species and Evolution: Comments on Philip Kitcher's 'Species'. *Phil.Sci., 51,* pp. 334–41.

Turbayne, C. (1962) *The Myth of Metaphor,* Yale University Press, New Haven CT.

Waterlow, S. (1982) *Nature, Change and Agency in Aristotle's Physics,* Oxford University Press, Oxford.

Wiggins, D. (1980) *Sameness and Substance,* Harvard University Press, Cambridge, MA.

Williams, B. (1978) *Descartes: The Project of Pure Enquiry,* Penguin, Harmondsworth and Harvester, Brighton, Sussex.

Wilson, M.D. (1978) *Descartes,* Routledge, London and Boston.

Indexes

1. Descartes's Writings

2. Index of Proper Names

3. Index of Topics

FM discussion groups

Prof Jones (chair) & Christine ~~Roost~~ Geddes

(chair) [Summer Edn, Research & Dev?]
Philip Boden & (young chair or younger staff 'child' with
from Ferme???

Richard Kinder (chair) &

Brian McQueen (chair) &
[1st group?]

[Geologist] Graham Park (chairman) & ~~Ian~~ John Whittow
(scientists)

[chairman] Ian Miller & *

of Les (economist)
(New Ams) & Dundee (biologist)
['treats nuclear food']

showcased

Prof Charlton [Chair]

Colin Martin (chemist)

Fellow Interviewers – Kate Muir
Ron Pinder
Philip (economist) Gay
Arthur Todd
Frank Dornberg
Andy Dobson
Prof Mark Harrison
John Kelly

Marjorie Grene

Williams
Heidegger
Polanyi
(Secondo)
Aristotle
MP

Tapping wasps
stick 74

will 29

commonsense 15

self cp 48
135 – Pollock
175

MS 145 (6, 7, 8)
149 (9, 152)

mysticism 160

mog 199
200
202 f

Essence / Existence 161
Parmenides